Knowledge in Medieval Philosophy

The Philosophy of Knowledge: A History

General Editor, Stephen Hetherington

'*The Philosophy of Knowledge* is a truly remarkable work. In addition to its vast breadth, the set is commendable for the expertise of the contributors and the clarity and rigor of their essays. The set has three chief virtues: it provides a clear understanding of Western epistemology; each individual volume makes for an ideal resource for courses focusing on that period; and the individual essays themselves are perfect complements to primary works of the philosopher(s) addressed. Summing Up: Highly recommended. Lower-division undergraduates through faculty; general readers.' *CHOICE*

'*The Philosophy of Knowledge: A History* is a tremendous achievement. Its four volumes cover the entire scope of Western epistemology, from the ancient world through the medieval and modern periods to the contemporary scene, with essays on the most influential figures in each of these periods. The result is a splendid overview on how fundamental questions about knowledge have been thought about over the millennia. These volumes will be the standard resource for all those interested in the history epistemology for decades to come.'

Richard Foley, Professor of Philosophy, New York University, USA

'This series of four volumes gives a reader the opportunity to take a fascinating voyage through the history of epistemology with an emphasis on the evolution of various theories of knowledge. The authors who contribute to the volumes are experts in their fields and the chapters in each volume are uniformly excellent.'

Richard Fumerton, F. Wendell Miller Professor of Philosophy,
University of Iowa, USA

The Philosophy of Knowledge: A History presents the history of one of Western philosophy's greatest challenges: understanding the nature of knowledge. Divided chronologically, these four volumes follow conceptions of knowledge that have been proposed, defended, replaced, and proposed anew by ancient, medieval, modern, and contemporary philosophers.

Each volume is centred around two key questions. What conceptions of knowledge have been offered? Which ones have shaped epistemology in particular and philosophy in general? Together, these volumes trace the historical development of knowledge for the first time.

Volume I *Knowledge in Ancient Philosophy*, edited by Nicholas D. Smith

Volume II *Knowledge in Medieval Philosophy*, edited by Henrik Lagerlund

Volume III *Knowledge in Modern Philosophy*, edited by Stephen Gaukroger

Volume IV *Knowledge in Contemporary Philosophy*, edited by
Stephen Hetherington and Markos Valaris

The Philosophy of Knowledge: A History

Volume II

Knowledge in Medieval Philosophy

Edited by Henrik Lagerlund

BLOOMSBURY ACADEMIC

LONDON • NEW YORK • OXFORD • NEW DELHI • SYDNEY

BLOOMSBURY ACADEMIC
Bloomsbury Publishing Plc
50 Bedford Square, London, WC1B 3DP, UK
1385 Broadway, New York, NY 10018, USA
29 Earlsfort Terrace, Dublin 2, Ireland

BLOOMSBURY, BLOOMSBURY ACADEMIC and the Diana logo
are trademarks of Bloomsbury Publishing Plc

First published in Great Britain 2019
Paperback edition published 2024

A catalogue record for this book is available from the British Library.

A catalog record for this book is available from the Library of Congress.

ISBN: PB: 978-1-3504-4661-8

Typeset by Jones Ltd, London
Printed and bound in Great Britain

To find out more about our authors and books visit www.bloomsbury.com
and sign up for our newsletters.

Contents

Contributors

Deborah L. Black (University of Toronto, Canada)

Richard Cross (University of Notre Dame, USA)

Christophe Grellard (University of Paris 1 Panthéon-Sorbonne, France)

Alexander Hall (Clayton State University, USA)

Benjamin Hill (University of Western Ontario, Canada)

Gyula Klima (Fordham University, USA)

Henrik Lagerlund (Stockholm University, Sweden)

John Longeway (University of Wisconsin, Parkside, USA)

Rafael Nájera (University of Cologne, Germany)

Jennifer Pelletier (University of Louven, Belgium)

Richard Taylor (Marquette University, USA)

Volume Editor's Preface

Some readers are perhaps surprised that there is a whole volume devoted to epistemology and treatments of knowledge in the Middle Ages. Many still, despite what have by now been decades of serious scholarly research on medieval philosophy, think that medieval philosophers did not develop epistemologies or theories of knowledge. These people maintain that it is only after the resurgence of scepticism in the sixteenth century, and with Descartes, that epistemology enters the Western philosophical tradition. As can be seen in this volume, epistemology and even scepticism is part of philosophy from the late thirteenth century onwards, and knowledge was of great philosophical concern throughout the Middle Ages. I am very happy to be able to present this volume as part of a set of volumes on knowledge from ancient to contemporary philosophy. It puts the medieval discussion in a nice context, and will contribute to further illuminating it, as well as to making it relevant for contemporary epistemologists.

I would like to thank my wife, Eliza, for her patience and love. She is my inspiration.

Henrik Lagerlund
London, Ontario, 6 September 2017

General Editor's Preface

Stephen Hetherington

The Philosophy of Knowledge: Introduction to a History

Welcome to philosophy – to part of it, at any rate. A powerful and pivotal part of it, though: *epistemology*. Welcome to this survey – a tour, across four volumes – of a significant segment of epistemology's history. Western philosophy began in ancient Greece, before travelling far afield, still prospering. And whatever it is now is at least partly a consequence of whatever it has been. Within these four volumes, we meet much of whatever epistemology has been and is.

Why is this form of historical engagement philosophically important? Why is it important *now* to have some understanding of what epistemology has *been*? One reason is the possibility of current epistemology's being more similar to some or all of its former selves than it might at first seem to be, in productive and destructive ways. We should not merely be reinventing the epistemological wheel; nor should we repeat past epistemological mistakes – design flaws in earlier epistemological conveyances. To know epistemology's history is to know better what contemporary epistemology could be and perhaps should be – and what it need not be and perhaps ought not to be.

Epistemology is usually said to be the philosophy of knowledge and of kindred phenomena. But what makes it *the* philosophy of such matters? Well, epistemology has long been a collective endeavour – a gathering of individual efforts, by a plethora of epistemologists over oh-so-many years – to understand the nature of knowledge and those kindred phenomena. (Some of those efforts even ask whether there *is* a phenomenon of knowledge in the first place.)

How does that collective endeavour take shape? A first – a partial – answer is that epistemology is ineliminably *theoretical*. It is one theory, another theory, yet more theories, and so on. And so it is theories linking with, and departing from, other theories. It is theories living, developing, dying, reproducing, influencing, succeeding, failing. It is new themes replacing old ones. It is old themes replacing new ones.

And these four volumes will introduce you to such theories – competing conceptions of knowledge and those kindred phenomena, conceptions from across the ages. Volume I introduces us to theories from parts of the ancient world, the fount of all Western epistemology. Volumes II and III trace theories of knowledge as these arose over the following two millennia, late into the nineteenth century. Volume IV then tells a tale of the past century or so – while gesturing also at how epistemology might continue into at least the near future, taking us there from here. Not all of epistemology's past or present theorists and theories appear in these pages; but many do. The result is a grand story of sweeping intellectual vistas with striking conceptual foundations and ramifications. It is living philosophy. It is here, with you right now.

Introduction

Henrik Lagerlund

It is often said that epistemology, as we know it, was born in the seventeenth century. Anyone reading this volume can plainly see that this is false. Knowledge and other epistemic attitudes like belief, opinion, testimony, and so on were widely discussed in the Latin and the Arabic philosophical traditions that we commonly call 'medieval'. Perhaps it was emphasized more during certain times, and at other times it was underbuilt by metaphysics and played a less important role, but analysis of knowledge has always been present in philosophy. Through the influence of Aristotle, the framework of his *Posterior Analytics* became very important for medieval treatments of knowledge, but there were substantial changes made to this framework in the beginning of the fourteenth century.

The Greek word for knowledge, ἐπιστήμη (*epistêmê*), was translated into Latin by '*scientia*'. Through Aristotle and the enormous influence that he exerted on the development of early medieval philosophy, it came to be associated with scientific knowledge, since this was the kind of knowledge that one obtained from demonstrations. It retained its connection to science throughout the Middle Ages, and it is obviously no coincidence that it came to be the basis for the English word 'science'. *Scientia*, or scientific knowledge, is the result of the scientific process as it was understood in the Aristotelian tradition.

The word for knowledge in Arabic is علم (*ʿilm*), but, through Fārābī, certain knowledge in the Aristotelian sense came to be referred to as *ʿilm yaqīnīy*, which incorporated both knowledge of principles and the conclusions of demonstrations. Avicenna takes his starting point from Fārābī, and builds his own epistemology around Aristotle's account of *epistêmê* in the *Posterior Analytics*. He, however, introduces several novel ideas that came to have great influence on both the Arabic tradition and the Latin Western tradition through translations of his various works into Latin.

One of these is the distinction that he draws between conceptualization and assent. It cannot be found in Aristotle, but came to play a central role later in the Latin tradition. A conceptualization for Avicenna is the mind's basic capacity to conceive of the quiddity of something, while the notion of assent presupposes an act of conceptualization and involves the forming of a judgement that something is true or false. There can be acts of conceptualization without assent, but the main form of conceptualization, as far as knowledge is concerned, is definition, which is also assented to and judged to be true or false. Avicenna also thinks that conceptual knowledge contains potentially assentive knowledge, as Deborah Black points out in Chapter 1, since we cannot seek what is completely unknown to us. Some knowledge is always presupposed. Does this mean that we must presuppose some innate knowledge? Avicenna does think that all conceptualization has its roots in some basic concepts like 'existence', or 'thing', which are presupposed when we conceive of anything. He never says how such concepts are acquired, but, as Black points out in her chapter, Avicenna uses the idea of self-awareness as a kind of knowledge of one's own existence. It is possible that these basic concepts are acquired in such a way, which would make them innate. Avicenna is here very close to Descartes.

Drawing on the *kalâm* tradition, Avicenna introduces another novel distinction. He draws a threefold distinction between levels of assent – namely, between certitude, near-certitude, and probable opinion. Demonstrations are certain, he claims, as are some other necessary principles, but he also includes empirical propositions among those that can be certain. Interestingly, however, he does not think that certainty implies infallibility, since some empirical knowledge can be certain, he seems to think, but is nevertheless fallible. As we will see later, in the Latin tradition this kind of distinction will play a very important role in response to scepticism; but, for Avicenna, it was not related to epistemological scepticism, which was something that never worried him. In this respect, he was very much an Aristotelian.

Through Avicenna and other non-Aristotelian sources, there was knowledge of Aristotelian epistemology, and the concept of *scientia*, before Aristotle's *Posterior Analytics* was translated. There was a translation into Latin as early as 1150, although the first Latin commentary is by Robert Grosseteste from the early thirteenth century. The discussion of *scientia* before the translation had strong Platonic overtones, and gave *scientia* the status of a higher level of cognition with a very special status – a status that it was to keep until the beginning of the fourteenth century. Influenced by Augustine, it is primarily Hugh of St. Victor who lays down the dominant interpretation of *scientia* before the translation of the *Posterior Analytics*, as explained by Rafael Nájera in Chapter 2.

One of the most contentious parts of Aristotle's account of knowledge is how he explains the acquisition of first principles. In the beginning of the *Posterior Analytics*, he notes that there must be principles that are not demonstrated, but are acquired in some other way and are better known than the conclusion of a demonstration. In II.19 – the final chapter of the book – he goes on to explain how this is supposed to work. It is a notoriously difficult chapter to understand, at least in its details. In the later Greek and Arabic traditions, it was explicated by reading it together with another infamous chapter from his *De anima* – namely, III.5 – about abstraction and the passive and active intellects. One of the most important contributors in this tradition was Ibn Rushd (Averroes). In Chapter 3, Richard Taylor shows how Averroes developed his interpretation, and explains the influence it had on the Latin tradition, particularly on Aquinas.

The first full Latin commentary on Aristotle's *Posterior Analytics* was written by Robert Grosseteste between 1220 and 1230. It naturally presents a notion of knowledge (*scientia*) closer to Aristotle's own text. According to Grosseteste, as Longeway shows in Chapter 4, Aristotle holds that, strictly speaking, only demonstrations lead to knowledge. However, there is a wider sense of knowledge that includes the first principles, but these principles are then known through their terms and are as a result necessary, or analytical, as we would now perhaps put it. As such, then, the view laid out in the *Posterior Analytics* is primarily set out for mathematics. Knowledge based on sense perception will always involve contingent propositions, but, to be truly known, it must be necessary and about the natures or essences behind the things perceived. We can come to know these, Grosseteste thinks, but we cannot be absolutely certain unless we have received a proper illumination from God. There is an Augustinian element to knowledge through the senses, as this idea is present in Grosseteste.

No doubt, the most influential account of knowledge in the thirteenth century in the Latin tradition was formulated by Thomas Aquinas. It also draws heavily on Aristotle (as well as Averroes), and is based on the account found in the *Posterior Analytics*. Aquinas contrasts his and Aristotle's projects with Plato's, and understands these as attempting to ground certain knowledge without transcendental forms and the theory of recollection. Aquinas does not subscribe to the theory of divine illumination; instead, he puts the emphasis on induction, to ground certain knowledge based on sense perception. Unlike much other medieval discussion of knowledge, Aquinas' account has been studied a lot and has received a variety of interpretations. Alex Hall outlines several of them in Chapter 5. He also gives his own take on Aquinas' theory.

Aquinas presents a broad epistemology, which includes several of what we now would call *epistemic attitudes*, among which *scientia* is the strictest – what could be called 'certain knowledge'. As far as scientific or certain knowledge is concerned, Aquinas' theory is foundational and based on a few principles that are all per se, or necessary. Hence, a conclusion of a demonstration must also always be per se. Hall lays out the account to demonstration that is found in Aquinas' commentary on the *Posterior Analytics*. Aquinas thinks that, since the premises of a demonstration are isomorphic with reality (he sets up his theory of cognition to guarantee this), the premises can be thought of as giving the causes or explanations of the conclusion. The principles, hence, are a metaphysical foundation as well as an epistemological one.

The strong metaphysical underpinning of knowledge was rejected after Aquinas, and greater emphasis was put on explaining cognition and how humans acquire knowledge. As a result, problems that have become familiar in more modern philosophy became real concerns – that is, epistemological scepticism and the problem of intentionality. In the early fourteenth century, the problem of intentionality is foremost a problem about how the mind can acquire content, and hence is related to scepticism. As can be seen in Chapter 6, by Richard Cross, on John Duns Scotus on knowledge and cognition, it is cognition of things external to us that is the starting point of all knowledge. As can also be seen from Cross' chapter, Scotus reemphasizes the distinction found in Avicenna between assent and conceptualization. Knowing something is ultimately assenting to a mental proposition or some mental content. Cross outlines three stages – namely, the cognition of simples, the composition and analysis of content acquired, and the forming of arguments (i.e. syllogisms).

Perhaps the most important contribution by Scotus to the medieval discussion of knowledge is the introduction of the distinction between intuitive and abstractive cognition. For Scotus, these are intellectual acts of cognition. An intuitive cognition is about something present to the intellect through sense cognition. What is cognized are individuals through their common natures, which means that, for Scotus, humans do not actually have intuitive cognitions about individuals per se. Their intuitive cognitions are only about the common features present in individuals. An abstractive cognition is also about a common nature, but it does not have to be present to the intellect during this cognition. These two kinds of cognition are what ground knowledge and are that upon which it is based. Scotus also draws a distinction between two kinds of definition – nominal definition and real definition. The aim of the scientific process is the formulation of real definitions. Scotus also thinks that these cognitive processes are reliable and as such can be trusted to produce knowledge.

The account of knowledge laid down by Scotus was developed by William Ockham. For him, knowledge is ultimately an assent to a true mental proposition, but he presents analyses of several epistemic attitudes in terms of cognition and assent. He introduces the notion of evidence, to distinguish knowledge from belief. Knowledge is an assent to a true proposition with evidence or evidentness, while belief lacks evidence. The proposition known can be either necessary or contingent. If it is contingent, it is based on a direct intuitive cognition like 'the paper is white' when I presently cognize the whiteness of the paper. Such a cognition then provides the evidentness of the assent. Ockham's analysis of knowledge was very influential, and we see it throughout the fourteenth century and well into the sixteenth century as well.

An important aspect of epistemology, one that has huge importance for our everyday life, is the notion of testimony. Avicenna, as well as Scotus, deals explicitly with this kind of knowledge, or rather with knowledge based on testimony; but in Jennifer Pelletier's Chapter 7 we find a special treatment of it in relation to Ockham's epistemology. To have knowledge based on testimony means to know something because someone else (another speaker or an authority of some kind) states it. This is important, since most medieval epistemologists would like to claim that religious authorities and scripture provide knowledge and true testimony. According to Ockham, a subject can be said to know that p if (i) p is true and (ii) she firmly adheres to p because (iii) some speaker says that p. A lot hangs on what kind of speaker or authority expresses p. It must be an authority that holds p to be true, and the authority in question is by definition non-deceivable, unable to err, and unable to be disproved – namely, an infallible religious authority, such as Sacred Scripture. Ockham by no means spends a lot of time on testimonial knowledge, since he is, like everyone else, mostly interested in *scientia*.

In the beginning Chapter 8, Christophe Grellard writes: 'Fourteenth century epistemology is characterized by the attempt to give an account of the fallibility of our knowledge. Such an attempt leads to questioning an epistemology grounded in the certitude, elaborated in the thirteenth century, from Robert Grossesteste onwards, and to paying a greater attention to the contingency of the world and to the diversity of the cognitive methods.' Basically, all treatments of knowledge in the medieval tradition up to the time of Ockham assume that certain knowledge is infallible and that anything fallible is merely probable and not really knowledge. This all changed after Ockham, starting with Nicholas of

Autrecourt; but it was put in place by a new account of knowledge developed by John Buridan – Autrecourt's contemporary and, for a short time, his colleague at Paris University.

As Grellard puts it, Autrecourt and Buridan chose two different paths to change the notion of certainty and, with it, science. Grellard explains that Autrecourt weakens science, so that it does not necessarily cover or include certain knowledge anymore. Only some sciences – like mathematics, logic, or anything reducible to the principle of non-contradiction – can be said to be certain, on his account. Natural science only deals with what is probable, and not with knowledge, strictly speaking. Buridan, however, makes knowledge itself fallible. He introduces levels of certainty, and hence relativizes it. Different sciences correspond to different levels of certain knowledge: mathematics and logic have one level of certainty, natural science another, and moral science a third. Gyula Klima, in Chapter 9, describes this new account of knowledge that takes shape in Buridan's different works. It is a genuinely new and revolutionary account of knowledge.

Part of the reason why the traditional account of knowledge changed with Autrecourt and Buridan was the introduction of a new form of scepticism in the early fourteenth century. Because of a new account of God's omnipotence, medieval philosophers started to worry about the possibility that God is a deceiver. Buridan (1964: II, q. 1, fol. 8rb-va) puts it succinctly, in his commentary on Aristotle's *Metaphysics*:

> As is commonly said, the senses can be deluded, and it is certain that the species of sensible things can be preserved in the organs of sense in the absence of sensibles, as is mentioned in *De somno et vigilia*. And then we judge about what does not exist as if it existed, and so we err through the senses. And the difficulty is greatly augmented by the fact that we believe on faith that God can form sensible species in our senses without the sensible things themselves, and preserve them for a long time. In that case, we judge as if there were sensible things present. Furthermore, since God can do this and greater things, you do not know whether God intends to do this, and so you have no certitude and evidentness [regarding the question] whether there are men before you while you are awake or while you are asleep, since in your sleep God could make a sensible species as clear as – indeed, a hundred times clearer than – what sensible objects could produce. And so, you would then judge formally that there are sensible objects before you, just as you do now. Therefore, since you know nothing about the will of God, you cannot be certain about anything.

Given the possibility of divine deception or external world scepticism, the context of the discussion of knowledge has radically changed, and Autrecourt and Buridan are the first to see this and to adapt to it. As mentioned, they do it in different ways, but it is ultimately Buridan's account that wins out, becoming influential well into the sixteenth century.

As can be seen in Chapter 10, by Henrik Lagerlund, the definition of knowledge found in Ockham is accepted by Buridan and his followers – Albert of Saxony in the late fourteenth century and John Mair in the early sixteenth century. Knowledge, for them, is firm assent with evidentness to true propositions. By varying the notion of evidence or evidentness, they are able to allow for different levels of knowledge. Buridan, as well as Albert and Mair, gives three levels – namely, absolute, natural, and moral evidentness. Hence, they accept the conclusion that something can be knowledge even though it can be defeated or given a counter-instance: that is, for them, knowledge is no longer infallible, but is fallible.

Even though knowledge and epistemological scepticism were discussed well into the sixteenth century by the followers of Buridan, there seems to have been a slight change to this later in the sixteenth century. One reason for this might, of course, be the renewed interest in Sextus Empiricus' Pyrrhonian style of scepticism, which had very little influence in the Latin Middle Ages, even though medieval thinkers were well aware of the Academic style of scepticism from Cicero and Augustine, at least after the late thirteenth century (Lagerlund 2010). However, aspects of Aristotelian epistemology remained front and centre in the philosophical discussions of later-sixteenth-century thought. One such aspect was the *Regressus* theory, which developed out of *Posterior Analytics* II.19. It was developed by philosophers like Augustino Nifo and Giacomo Zabarella, as a way of explaining or spelling out Aristotelian *epagôgê* or induction. For Zabarella, the first stage of the regressus involves the apprehension of a causal principle based on sense experience. The second involves a 'mental examination' of the cause, and this is where we come to have knowledge, properly speaking, of the causal principle. The third stage is the reformulation of the principle to serve as a premise in a scientific demonstration. Zabarella develops several examples of how this is supposed to work, but the idea is similar to Aristotle's, although much more detailed, and progresses from sense perception to a principle that can be used in a demonstration.

In Chapter 11, Benjamin Hill highlights three aspects of later-sixteenth-century epistemology that play a role in forming attitudes to knowledge. These are, first, the *Regressus* theory, which becomes very influential and is taken up by Thomas Hobbes, for example. Second, he mentions the reinvigorated debate over scepticism, particularly through the new Latin translation of Sextus' *Outlines of Pyrrhonism* from 1562. It became important, foremost through Montaigne who used it to establish his own form of fideism; but, as had happened in the early fourteenth century, scepticism served to emphasise the mere fallibility of knowledge in the late sixteenth and early seventeenth centuries. A third aspect of epistemology from this time was the role played by educational reform. Through humanist and Jesuit efforts, large changes were made to education. If this is taken together with the introduction of the printing press that had occurred in the late fifteenth century, a whole new era for education and the spread of knowledge was opened up.

References

Buridan, J. (1964 [1518]), *Quaestiones in Aristotelis Metaphysicam: Kommentar zur Aristotelischen Metaphysik*, Frankfurt am Main: Minerva.
Lagerlund, H. (ed.) (2010), *Rethinking the History of Skepticism: The Missing Medieval Background*, Brill: Leiden.

1

Avicenna on Knowledge

Deborah L. Black

1. Introduction

Avicenna's epistemology is primarily framed around the theory of knowledge or science put forward in Aristotle's *Posterior Analytics*. But Avicenna also introduced a number of novel elements into his epistemology, some of which were the result of earlier developments within the Islamic world, while others reflect his personal philosophical commitments and concerns. The most significant developments among his predecessors can be traced back along two main lines. The first leads to the founder of Islamic Aristotelianism, the so-called second teacher, Al-Fārābī (870–950), who established what became the paradigm for understanding the nature of philosophy and its relation to religion along largely epistemological lines. Taking his cue from certain peculiarities in the Arabic translation of the *Posterior Analytics*, Fārābī identified philosophy as the path to *certain* knowledge (*ʿilm yaqīnī*), contrasting philosophical certitude with the lesser epistemic states produced by various other sources and methods, including those employed by religion, law, and theology. Following him, Avicenna, too, focused his epistemological discussions on the topic of certitude and its relation to lesser epistemic states. The second line of influence on Avicenna comes, somewhat ironically, from the main intellectual rivals of the Islamic philosophers, the rational theologians or *mutakallimūn*. A characteristic feature of the theologians' method was to begin their treatises with a discussion of the nature and principles of knowledge. While Avicenna often criticized the details of this *kalām* epistemology, he nonetheless incorporated some of its epistemological categories into his own treatises on demonstration. As a result of this critical appropriation of his rivals' views, Avicenna developed new lines of epistemological enquiry that were largely foreign to the Aristotelian tradition itself, such as his account of testimony as a legitimate source of knowledge, and his recognition of the epistemic value of introspection.

2. Two types of knowledge: conceptualization and assent

Like most philosophers within the Aristotelian tradition, Avicenna (1952: 16–17) pursued most of his epistemological theorizing within his logical works, since logic was generally viewed as an instrumental science whose ultimate goal was to produce knowledge of the unknown:

> Since the perfection of human beings, insofar as they are humans possessed of an intellect … consists in their knowing the truth for its own sake, and the good for the sake of doing it and acquiring it; and [since] the first and inborn nature (*al-fiṭrah al-ūlā wa-al-badīhah*) of human beings on its own is of little help in this, because most of the knowledge that is attained by them only comes through acquisition (*bi-al-iktisāb*); and [since] what causes the unknown to be acquired is what is known – it is necessary that human beings first begin to know how they can acquire the unknown from the known.[1]

In this account of the epistemological function of logic, Avicenna appeals to a distinction drawn from his theological rivals, between natural or innate knowledge (*ʿilm badīh*) on the one hand – which the *mutakallimūn* also describe as 'necessary' (*ḍarūrīy*) – and acquired knowledge (*ʿilm muktasab*) on the other.[2] Avicenna uses this distinction to set up another important dichotomy in his theory of knowledge, between conceptualization or concept-formation (*taṣawwur*) and assent (*taṣdīq*).[3] Conceptualization and assent are the two basic kinds of knowledge that are available to human knowers: each type of knowledge is reducible to a set of basic principles, and the principles of assent can themselves be analyzed into concepts. The distinction between conceptualization and assent is not Aristotelian, but from al-Fārābī onwards it becomes the standard framework for discussions of knowledge and the logical tools that produce knowledge.[4]

Conceptualization is the basic capacity of the mind to conceive the nature or quiddity (*māhiyyah*) of something, such as that of 'humanity' or 'triangularity' (Avicenna 1985: 43; trans. Ahmed 2011: 3, §1). One can conceive of such a quiddity without any corresponding act of assent: I can think about a triangle without affirming or denying that triangles exist, or that they have certain properties. Assent, however, presupposes the prior act of conceiving that to which one assents. The key characteristic of assent is that it involves a judgement that some proposition, *p*, is either true or false. Avicenna sometimes frames this as a judgement regarding the correspondence between what the proposition asserts and the way things exist outside the mind: 'Assent causes the relation (*nisbah*) of [the conceived] form to the things themselves which correspond to it to arise in the mind. And falsification does the reverse of this.' For this reason, not everything that is complex or propositional in form involves assent; rather, all mental acts that do not involve a judgement of truth or falsity are classified as acts of conceptualization by default. For example, the mental act that corresponds to a command such as 'Do this!' counts as conceptualization on Avicenna's (1952: 17) account; and even a statement such as 'Every white is an accident' can be merely conceptualized if, for example, one doubts whether it is true or false (cf. 1985: 97).[5] From an epistemological perspective, however, Avicenna's main interest is in the conceptualization of quiddities, since these form the building blocks out of which assent may be constructed. The main logical tool that is used to produce new acts of conceptualization on the basis of previously known concepts is the definition; to acquire new acts of assent, one employs various inferential methods, in particular – as one might expect from an Aristotelian – syllogisms.

3. Meno's paradox and the principles of knowledge

Avicenna holds that complex acts of both conceptualization and assent can ultimately be reduced to simpler acts which we grasp immediately. These are the 'known' things from which the search begins for what is unknown. Avicenna links this foundationalist structure of knowledge to the resolution of the paradox of inquiry, once again following the lead of his predecessor Fārābī. This famous paradox, raised by Meno in Plato's eponymous dialogue, asks how it is possible to learn anything anew – to arrive at what is unknown from what is known.[6] If we don't know the thing that we are seeking, then we won't recognize it when we find it; if we are able to recognize it, then it seems that it was not really unknown to us. Avicenna illustrates what is at stake in this paradox with an example drawn from the paraphrase of the *Posterior Analytics* by the Greek commentator Themistius (c. 317–88): 'This is akin to one who seeks a runaway slave he does not know. If he finds him, he would not recognize him' (Avicenna 1956: 74; trans. Marmura 2009: 55).[7] Avicenna resolves the paradox by appealing to the distinction between conceptualization and assent. He admits that if something is totally unknown to us, we are not in a position to seek it. But there are many different kinds of unknown things: some are unknown conceptually, whereas others we may have conceived, without having yet assented to any claims about them. Using the example of the runaway slave, Avicenna points out that we might know his escape route and have a description of some identifying mark that will allow us to recognize him when we find him. These items of knowledge will be akin to prior conceptual knowledge; by the same token, as we embark on our search, we will also pick up additional clues through observation and inference that will aid us in apprehending him. For Avicenna, then, the answer to Meno's paradox is to recognize that conceptual knowledge already contains potentially the assentive knowledge that is built upon it; so long as we are not without prior concepts, we will be able to escape the dilemma as posed by Meno.

Since Avicenna does admit that we cannot seek what is entirely unknown to us, the adequacy of his solution depends upon rejecting the possibility that we could ever be completely lacking in conceptual knowledge. Plato had posited the theory of recollection as a way to account for the soul's latent possession of pre-existent knowledge, but Avicenna argues that this is a defeatist position which 'acquiesces to the doubt' posed by Meno by pushing the act of acquisition into a previous existence of the soul. The correct solution is instead to recognize the existence of primary items of both assentive and conceptual knowledge that arise naturally, without our ever being aware of our ignorance of them (Avicenna 1956: 75–6; Marmura 2009: 57–9). As Avicenna remarks in *The Deliverance*, the syllogisms that produce assent and the definitions that produce concepts are divisible into parts which are in turn assented to (the premises) or conceived (the terms). But since 'this cannot go on to infinity, so that knowledge of these parts is only attained through the acquisition of other parts, whose nature is to proceed to infinity', Avicenna (1985: 97) argues that all knowledge must 'terminate in something which is assented to and conceived without any intermediary' (cf. Ahmed 2011: 87–8).

4. Primary concepts

In his logical works, Avicenna generally focuses his attention on the primary propositions that are the foundational acts of assent. For an account of the primary concepts we must look instead to the *Metaphysics of the Healing*, Book 1, chapter 5. There, Avicenna (2005: Bk. 1, c. 5, 23, §4) reprises his argument against an infinite regress on the conceptual level: 'If every conception were to require that [another] conception should precede it, then [such a] state of affairs would lead either to an infinite regress or to circularity.' Avicenna identifies a small number of primary concepts, of which the two most important are that of 'the existent' (*al-mawjūd*) and 'the thing' (*al-shay*'), the latter of which he identifies with essence or quiddity. To these, Avicenna adds the modal concept of 'the necessary' (*al-ḍarūrīy*), and the concept of 'the one' (*al-wāḥid*). These concepts, he says, are 'impressed in the soul in a primary way': that is, they are the most basic concepts we have, and they cannot be analysed into any simpler, prior notions upon which they depend for their comprehension. They are instead 'conceived in themselves', and thus serve as the 'principles' (*mabādi*') for all other concepts. By this, Avicenna seems to mean that these concepts are implicitly presupposed whenever we entertain more complex concepts: we cannot understand any other concepts at all unless we implicitly understand them as the concepts of existent things, that is, beings possessing some determinate essence or nature. For example, as soon as I acquire the concept 'cat', I implicitly conceive an existent thing, that is, a being with a feline essence. That does not mean, of course, that I explicitly formulate the abstract metaphysical concepts of essence and existence; it means that to conceive a cat is already to have the concepts of 'existent' and 'thing'.[8] This entails that the primary concepts cannot be defined, since they have no parts; moreover, we should not need to define them, since, as primary, they are naturally known to all human beings who have any concepts whatsoever. Still, that knowledge may be merely implicit and unconscious, or confused. In such cases, one's only recourse is to alert the person to the fact that he presupposes these concepts whenever he thinks about anything at all (Avicenna 2005: 22–4).

One question that arises from Avicenna's account of the primary concepts is that of how they are acquired. Are they innate or a priori in some way, or do they arise from sensory experience, like other concepts? This question is not one that Avicenna himself shows any great interest in addressing, at least not in this form. As we will see, his distinctive account of self-awareness may offer such an alternative route for acquiring these primary concepts, but for the most part Avicenna adheres to the standard Aristotelian view that the human intellect has no innate concepts, and the concepts that it does acquire presuppose some prior acts of sensation in order to arise.

5. The hierarchy of assent

On Avicenna's view the various types of assent, and the corresponding syllogistic arguments that produce them, form an epistemic hierarchy whose apex is certain knowledge. Developing an approach already present in Fārābī, Avicenna (1956: 51) appeals to a second-order act of assent, an act of 'knowing that we know' (what we would now call a KK-condition), to differentiate certitude from less secure forms of belief: 'Certain [assent] is when one believes at the same time [*ma'a-hu*] a second belief, either actually or in proximate potency to actuality, that what one has assented to cannot be otherwise than it is, since it is not possible for this belief concerning it to cease.'[9] If I have certain knowledge of *p*, then that knowledge generates a simultaneous belief to the effect that *p* cannot be otherwise, and thus that my belief in *p* can never become false. Less-than-certain forms of assent fail to live up to these conditions in some way. A dialectical belief which is 'certain-like' (*shabīh al-yaqīnī*) either lacks any actual second-order belief about *p*, or it is accompanied by a second-order belief that leaves the original proposition intact (*mutaqarrar*), despite an awareness that *p* might cease to be true, or that one's confidence in its truth might at some point become less stable (ibid.).[10] For example, if I have a dialectical belief that it will rain this weekend, and someone asks me if I'm sure, I might affirm my belief, while admitting that the forecast might change later during the week. Rhetorical assent, the lowest type of belief, produces a merely persuasive opinion (*iqnā' ẓannīy*). As with certain assent, there is a second-order belief involved here, but in this case it involves an awareness that the opposite of one's belief, not-*p*, might be true, although, in giving one's assent to *p*, 'the mind does not attend' to this possibility, and so the believer accepts the truth of the proposition instead of doubting it (51–2).

Avicenna's acceptance of the foregoing epistemic hierarchy within the order of assent has two important consequences. The first is that it allows him to uphold the traditional strict account of knowledge – now rebranded as 'certitude' – which applies only to necessary, unchanging, and universal truths, while at the same time admitting that there is *justification* for believing probable opinions which confer various less secure levels of certitude. The second is that it provides the structure for Avicenna's detailed and nuanced account of the principles of assent. Together, these two features of his epistemology provide Avicenna with a framework for considering the precise epistemic status and justification of many different types of knowledge that were on the periphery of traditional peripatetic discussions of knowledge.

6. The principles of certitude

Avicenna opens most of his discussions of the nature of demonstration with an extensive classification of the types of basic propositions that are able to serve as principles of arguments that attain each of these levels of assent – certitude, near-certitude, and probable opinion. It is in these texts that his debt to his *kalām* rivals is also evident. For while this extensive classification of the principles of knowledge has no real precedent in the peripatetic tradition, it seems to be loosely modelled on the theologians' enumeration of the varieties of necessary or natural knowledge (*'ilm ḍarūrīy/badīhīy*), which formed part of their account of the difference between necessary and acquired knowledge, which, as we saw above, Avicenna also incorporates into his account of the epistemic goals of logic.[11]

The principles of demonstration as a whole are characterized as propositions that are 'necessary of acceptance' by the intellect (Avicenna 1892: 58; trans. Inati 1984: 119; Avicenna 1956: Bk. 1, c. 4, 63). Avicenna's (1956: 63–4) main criterion for differentiating among these propositions is that of whether the necessity of assent derives from something internal to the intellect in some way, or whether it requires additional evidence provided by other psychological faculties:

> And that which is by way of necessity is either such that its necessity is external (*ḍarūrah-hu ẓāhirīyah*) – and this is either through sensation (*bi-al-ḥiss*) or experience (*al-tajribah*) or unbroken testimony (*al-tawātur*) – or its necessity is internal (*bāṭinīyah*). And internal necessity is either from the intellect or external to the intellect, belonging to another, non-intellectual power. As for that which is from the intellect, it is either from the pure intellect, or from the intellect supported in it by something.

This passage is rather obscure and requires some unpacking. The fundamental point is that only the intellect, on Avicenna's view, is able to assent to propositions; when he appeals to other faculties here as externally necessitating the intellect's assent, he is recognizing their contribution in providing *evidence* to the intellect, but the intellect remains the source of the judgement itself. Moreover, Avicenna recognizes distinct layers within this basic division between external and internal necessity. This is because he wishes to incorporate into his account of the principles of knowledge propositions that are not immediate in the standard Aristotelian sense: that is, their logical structure requires a middle term conjoining the subject and predicate, although psychologically they do not depend on an explicit inferential process to cause assent.

Avicenna's point becomes clearer when we examine the categories of propositions whose assent is wholly a function of the intellect unaided by any other powers. Principal among these is the standard category of 'primary propositions' (*al-awwalīyāt*), which in the *Healing* Avicenna identifies as being necessitated by 'the bare intellect' ('*an mujarradi al-'aqli*), that is, the intellect operating on its own. These are immediate and self-evident propositions, and Avicenna gives the standard example: 'The whole is greater than the part.' These propositions are such that the predicate term is either identical with the subject term or expresses a part of its essence. Thus, as soon as both terms are understood and the predicate is asserted of the subject, the mind necessarily assents to the truth of the composition (Avicenna 1892: 56)[12]; there is no need to seek a further cause or middle term linking the predicate to the subject (ibid.; trans. Inati 1984: 119). In addition to such primary propositions, however, Avicenna also recognizes another variety of propositions whose acceptance is necessitated by the intellect alone, but that lack the immediacy of the primaries. At first glance, this seems odd. As Avicenna himself notes, if the propositions in question are not natural or innate (*lā gharīzīy*) to the intellect in the sense that it doesn't assent to them as soon as it understands their terms, then assent to them would seem, in the language of the theologians, 'to occur through an acquisition (*bi-kasbin*)', and in that case they would not be principles at all, but instead propositions known inferentially, that is, as the conclusions of syllogisms (Avicenna 1956: 64). In these cases, however, Avicenna argues that, while the intellect requires some aid in addition to the simple grasp of the terms of the proposition, the 'helper' (*mu'īn*) – that is, the middle term – 'is innate, that is, present (*ḥāḍiran*), in the intellect', and so there is no need for any active seeking to acquire it. As soon as the extreme terms have been conceived, the mind immediately conceives the middle term 'by natural disposition (*bi-al-fiṭrah*)':

> For whenever the thing being sought (*al-maṭlūb*), which is composed from two terms, a major and a minor, is present, the middle which is between them is represented in the intellect without any need for its acquisition. And this occurs, for example, in our saying, 'Every four is even.' For whoever understands 'four' and understands 'even', that 'Four is even', is represented for him, for it is immediately represented that it is 'divisible into two equal [parts]'. And in the same way, whenever four is represented in the mind, and two is represented, that [four] is double [two] is represented immediately. But if, in place of these [terms], it is six and thirty, or other numbers, the mind needs to seek the middle. (Ibid.)[13]

Avicenna's claim, then, is that these propositions are like the primaries, and distinct from premises that have been offered explicit syllogistic proof, because there is no need to carry out an actual investigation to discover the middle term. That middle term, while logically and conceptually distinct from the extremes, nonetheless naturally occurs to the mind in conjunction with the extremes. Since there is an intermediary here, these propositions differ from what we would now call analytic truths. They add something over and above our knowledge of the extreme terms themselves, even though we 'learn' that new knowledge and perform the calculation that produces it automatically.[14]

Avicenna always gives as examples of these types of propositions basic arithmetic truths, but he does not explicitly state that such propositions are limited to the realm of mathematics. Nor does he say whether these propositions vary from person to person, but, given that he admits that the truth of even some primary propositions may not be recognized by those who do not comprehend their terms, it seems likely that he holds that a similar situation will be true of these propositions.[15] Simple arithmetical calculations become automatic for most people from an early age; others may, or may not, be automatic, depending on one's ability or training. Nonetheless, the mind must be doing some sort of inference or calculation, since the logical structure of the proposition demands it. If I do not assent to this sort of proposition by way of the middle term that explains the connection between its extremes, then I will not be certain of its truth and my belief in it will be nothing more than a product of rote memorization.

Avicenna's inclusion of this variety of mediated proposition among the principles of knowledge exemplifies a general feature of his epistemology – namely, a willingness to incorporate psychological as well as formal logical criteria into his account of certitude. What makes a proposition basic in his view is not just its immediacy, but also whether the knower is able to achieve certain assent without the effort of any further investigation or conscious calculation or ratiocination. This feature becomes especially important in Avicenna's account of many of the empirically grounded propositions that he admits as principles of certitude.

7. Empirical knowledge

Avicenna includes, among the principles of certain knowledge, propositions whose assent requires the aid of another faculty, usually a sensory one.[16] This allows him to incorporate empirical knowledge into his account of the principles of demonstration.[17] He recognizes several distinct categories of what we would broadly consider empirical knowledge: sensible propositions (*al-maḥsūsāt*), experientials (*al-mujarrabāt*), and testimonials (*al-mutawātirāt*). In his later work, the *Remarks*, Avicenna adds the umbrella category of observational propositions (*al-mushāhadāt*), under which the sensibles are subsumed, along with 'reflexive' propositions (*al-i'tibārīyāt*); and intuited propositions (*al-ḥadsīyāt*), which are treated as a subset of experientials.[18]

Standard sensible propositions are those to which sensation (*al-ḥiss*) causes assent to occur. Avicenna gives as examples our judgements that 'the sun exists', 'the sun is luminous', and 'snow is white'.[19] He does not present these propositions as statements about occurrent sensations, such as my sensory awareness that today the sun is shining (whereas yesterday, a rainy day, it was not). Nor do they seem to be claims about particular sensible objects, such as the snow bank in front of my house. They are general intellectual judgements about the properties of sensible bodies that we learn immediately through sensory observation: the intellect requires nothing over and above the sensory evidence to recognize their necessity; nor do the observations need to be repeated to necessitate the intellect's assent.

By contrast, repetition is one of the foundations for Avicenna's account of experiential knowledge, *tajribah*.[20] In describing experiential propositions (*al-mujarrabāt*), he often gives a medical example, that 'scammony [a plant] purges bile'.[21] He identifies two bases for the certitude that these propositions elicit: (1) the repeated and remembered sensory experience of two things – such as scammony and the purgation of bile – concurring; and (2) a hidden syllogism 'connected with the memory' (*qiyās iqtarana bi-al-dhikri*) (1985: 98; trans. Ahmed 2011: 88 (modified)). But what, exactly, is this hidden syllogism, and why is it needed to produce experience? The answer to this lies in Avicenna's views on the limitations of our sensory faculties for revealing causal powers.

In the *Metaphysics of the Healing*, he notes that 'sensation leads only to concomitance (*al-muwāfah*)': that is, our senses can only tell us that, whenever some object, C, is present, another object, E, accompanies it. Avicenna (2005: 1.1, §16, 5–6; trans. modified) then acknowledges that 'if two things are concomitants, it is not necessary that one of them is the cause of the other'. The scammony plant does not, of itself, present any sensible features that indicate its purgative effect on humans who consume it. Nor does the simple repetition of observing purgation in those who ingest scammony reveal any *necessary* connection between the two. Beliefs based on repetition alone are the products of mere induction (*istiqrā'*), and, according to Avicenna (1956: 98), induction is not the same as experience, since it fails to 'necessitate a universal either conditionally or unconditionally' yielding only a 'probable opinion' (*ẓann ghālib*).[22] By this, Avicenna means that it offers something like a summation of all the individual observed particulars, without thereby reaching the belief that the observations are indications of an innate causal property in the subject.

This is what the hidden syllogism provides. Through it, the mind subconsciously subsumes its repeated memories under the general principle (which becomes the major premise of the hidden syllogism) that 'if this matter (*al-amr*) … were something arbitrary and accidental (*ittifāqīyan ʿaraḍīyan*), and not due to some requirement of nature, then it would not occur consistently in most cases' (1985: 98; trans. Ahmed 2011: 88).[23] The mind thereby recognizes, without performing any overt inferential operation, that the connection between the two objects – scammony and purgation – is indicative of an intrinsic causal power in the very nature of scammony (*min shaʾni-hā*).[24] Avicenna doesn't say much about the mechanism by which this latent syllogizing occurs. He assumes that it is a reliable one that produces certitude, but he claims that it's not the job of the logician to provide the explanation of why that is the case (1892: 57; Inati 1984: 120). This is not to say that such an explanation is not possible, but only to recognize that it depends on theoretical investigations in psychology regarding the cognitive mechanisms that explain how we acquire universals of any kind. Our certitude itself does not explicitly invoke these theoretical justifications, even if we happen to be aware of them; rather, when the mechanism of the hidden syllogism 'kicks in', so to speak, we assent to the proposition immediately.[25]

Nonetheless, experience does not provide complete or perfect knowledge of the connection between the subject and predicate. Avicenna makes it clear that what experience involves is simply the recognition *that* there is a causal power in the subject that necessitates our assent to experientials. But experience does not tell us *what* that power is. His admission of this point sounds, at first reading, like a classic case of the position famously derided by Molière's example of the allegedly vacuous 'dormitive power' of the Scholastics: 'So by this type of evidence it is verified that there is in scammony by nature, or with it, a cause (*ʿillah*) which is purgative of bile. And if the power by which it is purgative of bile (*al-quwwah al-muhsil*) is sound, and there is a patient ready, the action and the passion occur' (1956: 95; cf. McGinnis and Reisman 2007: 149, §11).

Since the role of experience is not to explain *why* causal connections hold, but simply to affirm them, the purgative power verified by experience can be viewed as a sort of placeholder that expresses that the believer has recognized a necessary connection between two things that she did not see before. For a medical doctor, discovering that such powers are 'necessary accidents' of certain drugs, even without understanding why that is so, has a non-trivial bearing on his medical practice. Recognizing that scammony has a purgative power, whereas opium has a dormitive one indicates which drug he should give to his constipated patient, and which one he should prescribe to an insomniac. For this reason, experiential propositions are in no way epistemically vacuous when they assert the mere existence, though not the nature, of hitherto unnoticed causal powers.[26]

Avicenna does admit that experiential propositions may be fallible under some conditions, despite their classification as certain principles. While he affirms that the intellect can reliably recognize when the connection between two things is essential and not coincidental, this does not prevent the believer from being mistaken about the conditions under which that necessary connection holds. To address the concerns that such an admission seems to raise, Avicenna imagines a sceptical objector who provides the following counterexample to his account of experience as a source of certitude. Suppose that there is someone from the Sudan who has never met anyone from outside her own country; she will naturally form the false empirical belief, 'All human beings beget black offspring.'[27] Experience, then, seems as likely to generate erroneous beliefs as to produce true, let alone certain, ones, if this example is any indicator.

Avicenna's response to this challenge is to differentiate between absolute and conditional universal knowledge, and to restrict experience to the latter, since, as we've seen, experience alone does not grasp the nature of the causal connection itself, but only that such a connection is present. The problem, then, is not that the Sudanese person has erroneous experiential knowledge, but that she has not formulated the proposition expressing her experience to reflect the limited conditions under which it is certain. While it is false, taken absolutely and universally, that '[h]uman beings produce black offspring', it is nonetheless true that 'Sudanese human beings produce black offspring'. By the same token, the proper formulation of the physician's experiential proposition is not that 'scammony purges bile', but rather that 'the scammony in our country always purges bile, when it is sound'. Just as there might be other races of humans of whom we are not aware, so too there might be subspecies of scammony that are lacking the purgative power, whether naturally, or because something in their cultivation has gone awry and rendered *this* crop ineffective. Avicenna adds an interesting analogy here. He points out that the ability of any cognitive process to produce certainty is not in itself a guarantee against error – 'How could it', he asks, 'when not even the syllogism does that?' Just as we can make mistakes in our formal reasoning, so too we can be overconfident about the scope of our empirical data. Certitude, then, does not imply infallibility: 'For there are beliefs that seem to be certain but are not certain' (1956: 97; trans. McGinnis and Reisman 2007: 151, §17).

We may wonder, however, whether Avicenna's fallibilism regarding *tajribah* is compatible with his claim that experience is a source of epistemic principles rather than the result of a painstaking investigative process. To address this concern, Avicenna differentiates between the hidden syllogism that forms part of experience, and any additional theorizing that we undertake to ensure that we have not misinterpreted the scope of our empirical knowledge. Experience on its own does not provide unrestricted certitude 'unless it is accompanied by speculation (*naẓar*) and a syllogism other than the one which forms part of the experience' (McGinnis and Reisman 2007; §19). Once we have discerned through repeated observation that scammony is a purgative under the conditions in which we have actually observed it, we have the starting point that we need for testing whether its purgative power holds more broadly, and ultimately for discovering *why* it is that scammony has this causal force.

8. Testimony and authority: an inchoate social epistemology

Avicenna has no explicit concept of 'social epistemology'. But following in the footsteps of both his philosophical predecessors and his theological rivals in the Islamic tradition, he gave considerable attention to the epistemic status of testimony and of other types of belief formed on the basis of authority. Avicenna's fellow philosophers classified most socially derived beliefs as dialectical or rhetorical, since these were viewed as falling short of certitude in varying degrees. Avicenna's predecessor, al-Fārābī, identifies 'testimony' (*al-shahādah*) as the common source for all forms of dialectical and rhetorical assent (1987: 20–1; trans. McGinnis and Reisman 2007: 64–5, §§5–6). While Avicenna generally accepts this framework, he departs from the philosophical tradition on one important point: he allows that one particular variety of testimony, *tawātur*, is capable of producing certain knowledge. *Tawātur* is a technical term within Islamic law, where it is used to determine which sayings attributed to the Prophet Muḥammad form a legitimate part of the prophetic tradition or *ḥadīth*.[28] It applies to historical reports that have been transmitted by an unbroken and unanimous chain of testimony.

Avicenna, however, generalizes the concept to cover our knowledge of all types of geographical and historical facts that we have not experienced ourselves. He puts forward this view of *tawātur* by including *mutawātirāt* – which I will simply call 'testimonial propositions' – among the sources of certitude. He describes these propositions as deriving from 'the necessity of our assenting to the existence of actual (*al-mawjūdah*) cities and towns even if we have not observed them', citing Mecca as an example. Testimonials also include our belief in the existence of historical figures, such as Euclid and Galen.[29] In the *Remarks* Avicenna treats testimonials as akin to experientials, and he offers a somewhat elliptical explanation of why that is the case. The most obvious similarity between testimony and experience is that the ultimate basis for testimony is also repeated sensory observation – we know that Galen existed because we have numerous reports attesting to that fact, from contemporaries who were directly acquainted with him.[30] By the same token, we also need something like a hidden syllogism that warrants our confidence in the veracity and dependability of those witnesses. At some point, our minds simply recognize that the number of witnesses and the nature of their corroborating reports cannot be the result of conspiracy or some other ulterior motive.[31] Instead of unconsciously inferring that what happens frequently cannot be merely coincidental, as in experience, we automatically infer that these many people could not be colluding or delusional. Avicenna acknowledges that testimony is nonetheless concerned with matters about which doubt remains possible, so testimony, like experience, is fallible. But he resists the theologians' tactic of trying to mitigate this fallibility by establishing quotas on the number of witnesses, on the grounds that such arbitrary external criteria will not produce certitude in someone who is not otherwise convinced. Instead, Avicenna insists that the only criterion for determining whether a testimonial proposition is certain is whether the reliable mechanism that naturally removes doubt has in fact been triggered: 'It is certainty, therefore, that determines the sufficiency of the testimonies (*al-shahādāt*), and not their number' (1892: 57; Inati 1984: 121, modified).

Not all testimony is created equal, however, and Avicenna's remarks regarding propositions based on *tawātur*-style testimony cannot be extended beyond the historical and geographical sorts of knowledge that his examples evoke. Testimony of this sort is limited to knowledge that we would normally acquire through our own direct observation, but to which we have no direct access because of the limitations imposed by temporal and spatial distance. Testimony may, however, contribute additional evidence to supplement our limited sensible observations of causal relations. Since experience depends upon our acquisition of a sufficient number of observations to trigger the hidden syllogism, our empirical knowledge will be severely hampered if we cannot draw on the knowledge of previous philosophers and scientists. For Avicenna to utilize the medical observations of Galen and other ancient physicians, for example, he will need to be certain that Galen was a real person, and that reports of Galen's medical practice are trustworthy and accurate.

Nonetheless, it is clear that testimony itself cannot, on Avicenna's view, lead directly to certain knowledge of any *universal* medical truths that Galen has discovered. To be certain that scammony purges bile, or that the Pythagorean theorem is true, a physician or mathematician must verify the proposition in question on her own. Testimony is not authoritative on the level of the universal, and authority in general is, on Avicenna's view, a source of the merely probable sort of belief that is characteristic of rhetorical assent. One needs testimonial evidence from other people because the object known is a sensible particular; the Pythagorean theorem, by contrast, is knowable in itself, via mathematical demonstration, to anyone with the requisite intelligence.

Avicenna calls beliefs based on the sort of authoritative testimony that yields probable rather than certain knowledge, 'received' (*al-maqbūlāt*). While such beliefs can never be certain, they may be justified for people who lack the ability to acquire demonstrative knowledge of them. Avicenna characterizes received beliefs as those that are accepted as true simply because the believer trusts in the person who propounds them. In the *Healing* he describes them as depending on 'obedience' (*ṭā'ifah*) to one or more authority figures, whether they be political or religious leaders, or experts in some science (1956: 66; cf. Inati 1984: 125 (§I.2.A)). In the *Deliverance*, Avicenna gives the example of 'our believing things which we received from the Imams of the Laws', but, he adds, '*before* we had verified them through demonstration or what is similar to it' (1985: 98, emphasis added; cf. Ahmed 2011: 89).[32] This suggests that received premises may serve as the starting point for more secure knowledge: we begin by believing true propositions on the basis of authority – perhaps that of a teacher – and then, as we deepen our knowledge, some of us are able to raise them to the level of certain knowledge.

When Avicenna discusses received propositions, he is primarily thinking about cases where assent is given on a less stable basis than the propositions themselves allow. In such cases, the social dimension of knowledge is required to make up for deficiencies in the *believer's* cognitive abilities. But Avicenna does not think that all socially derived assent is inherently capable of transformation into certain knowledge. By their very nature, ethical beliefs in particular have an intractable social component. This is reflected in his assessment of the category of propositions under which ethical beliefs fall – namely, the 'commonly accepted' or 'popular beliefs' (*al-mashhūrat*).[33] Examples are the belief that 'lying is bad' or that 'stealing is vile'. Despite the widespread consensus as to their truth, Avicenna rejects any claim that this elevates these propositions to the level of primary, self-evident principles. To support this view, he puts forward a thought-experiment designed to show his audience that their ethical beliefs are 'conventional' (*iṣtlāḥīyah*) and thus fall short of being necessary of acceptance and certain (1959: Bk. 1, c. 5, 45–6).[34] Avicenna asks us to imagine ourselves 'created at once with a complete intellect', but without having been taught the moral lessons of our culture, and then to consider whether, under these circumstances, we would affirm that such propositions are true. He thinks it is obvious that we would not be able to form any decisive beliefs about such matters under these conditions, either through our intellect itself, or through any sensory faculty. What, then, are the grounds for our acceptance of these propositions? Avicenna suggests that, in addition to being habituated to them from earliest childhood, they might also have emotional appeal to us[35]; or they might be the residue of ancient traditions that have never been questioned. But he also acknowledges that we might come to believe them through inductive judgements to the effect that they hold true in most cases, by which he seems to mean that most societies have discovered that lying, stealing, and so on are generally not conducive to human flourishing or social harmony.[36]

What exactly is Avicenna's point here, regarding the limits of social consensus for conferring certain knowledge? His immediate target is the Muʿtazilite school of theologians, which upheld an objectivist ethical theory according to which moral beliefs are intrinsically and universally necessary, and their necessity can be rationally intuited by any human of normal intelligence. One standard argument that they put forward in support of their view was that, all other things being equal (i.e. there being no reward or punishment or any other external consequences attached to the action), a human being will always choose to tell the truth, for example, rather than to lie.[37] So what Avicenna is rejecting, against the Muʿtazilites, is the idea that ethical beliefs are exceptionless truths whose application does not depend upon the individual circumstances of the agent: there may be times when lying or stealing is warranted. Epistemologically, Avicenna's view also seems to depend on the nature of the concepts from which ethical propositions are composed. Such concepts depend in part upon an understanding of social institutions which, while rooted in humanity's nature as a political animal, in themselves are conventional, not natural. The very definitions of lying and stealing will depend upon the conventions and practices to which humans have agreed in their societies and laws. Avicenna admits that some of these concepts and the judgements concerning them will be almost universal – that is the basis for his reference to 'induction' as grounding some widely accepted propositions. But it is induction, not experience, that Avicenna invokes here, and this indicates that particular circumstances will always be relevant to determining their truth or falsity in any given situation.

One final point in Avicenna's account of the principles of knowledge will help to illustrate the nuances of his views on social consensus as a source of knowledge. He makes it clear that we can be mistaken in a non-trivial way about popular beliefs when he differentiates them from the propositions that he calls mere 'opinions' or 'suppositions' (*maẓnūnāt*). These beliefs are characterized as ones that mimic widely accepted beliefs and that thereby lead people to false ethical judgements. Avicenna's standard example is the maxim 'Help your brother, whether he be the wrongdoer or the victim.' Many people will unreflectively accept this as an obvious truth, since they correctly believe that it is virtuous to help your kin. But the proposition is a false widely accepted proposition, since one's duty to one's kin is superseded in most cases by the duty to seek justice for the victims of wrongdoing (1956: 66, 1892: 61; trans. Inati 1984: 125). Ethical propositions, then, are not subjective; they are determinately true or false, and one can be mistaken about them, not only with respect to their application in specific circumstances, but also insofar as they express general ethical rules.

9. Introspection as an epistemological principle

One of the best-known aspects of Avicenna's philosophical system is his appeal to a thought experiment, often called the 'Flying' or 'Floating Man', to show that human beings have a primitive, innate awareness of themselves and their existence.[38] While Avicenna himself usually invokes the Flying Man to support some version of dualism – that the human soul has an existence that is distinct from that of the body – it also has epistemological implications, since it establishes introspection as a legitimate source of knowledge, and thereby opens up the possibility of at least one source of innate, a priori knowledge. Avicenna himself does not fully spell out his own views on the broader epistemological role of self-awareness, however, leaving this aspect of his philosophy open to various interpretations.

In the Flying Man experiment, Avicenna asks his interlocutor to imagine herself in a state much like the one we saw above in the account of ethical propositions – born all at once, but with fully formed intellectual capabilities – so as to discount any learned knowledge or acquired memories. To this scenario,

Avicenna adds that we should also imagine ourselves suspended in a void with our limbs not touching one another (i.e. as if floating or flying), so that we are deprived of any occurrent sensory awareness both of our own bodies and of any external objects. He then asks us whether we would be aware of ourselves even in that state of deprivation, a rhetorical question to which he thinks that the answer is resoundingly affirmative.

Avicenna thinks that the sort of self-awareness revealed in the Flying Man is always present to us, but that it is something beneath the level of consciousness and thus easily overlooked. We can bring it to the surface, however, through the sort of alerting that is available through introspection, which the Flying Man experiment is meant to trigger. In later texts, Avicenna (2013) makes it clear that the primitive self-awareness involved in the Flying Man is innate in the human soul and ever-present from the very first moment of its existence. He even says that self-awareness *is* the soul's very existence, and he likens it to the sort of knowledge that we have of the primary concepts and propositions, in the sense that it is presupposed by our knowledge of all other things (211, 480–2, 484).[39]

Avicenna's recognition of a primitive level of self-awareness that is independent of, and prior to, our reflexive knowledge of ourselves through our knowledge of other things sets him apart from most other philosophers in the Aristotelian tradition. It also reveals a certain kinship between Avicenna and later continental rationalists like Descartes and Leibniz, for whom self-awareness provides the psychological foundation for all other knowledge.[40] But what role does Avicenna himself assign to self-awareness in his discussion of epistemological issues?

In his latest enumeration of the principles of knowledge in the *Remarks*, Avicenna adds a category of necessary propositions that he calls 'reflexive' (*i'tibārīyah*). They are presented as a subclass of 'observational' premises (*al-mushāhadāt*), another new category posited to encompass these reflexive propositions, along with the sensibles. Avicenna describes reflexive propositions as resting on the observations of 'the non-sensible faculties' (*al-qūwā ghayr al-ḥiss*), in contrast to those of the senses themselves.[41] His examples once again do much of the work of filling this description. Avicenna (1892: 56) mentions 'our knowledge (*ma'rifah*) that we have (*la-nā*) thinking, fear, and anger'; 'our knowledge that we are aware of ourselves (*shu'ūr bi-al-dhāt*)'; and our knowledge 'that we are aware of the acts of ourselves'.

Avicenna seems to be affirming here that primitive self-awareness is certain, and that its certainty extends to our knowledge of our own acts.[42] Because of its immediacy, it is assimilated to sensory awareness of other objects. Moreover, by including reflexive knowledge among the principles of knowledge that are necessary of acceptance, he seems to be suggesting that introspective knowledge can form the basis of scientific demonstrations, and that appeals to introspection are legitimate starting points in philosophy. That certainly reflects aspects of Avicenna's own philosophical method, but we must be careful to specify the nature of the information provided by reflexive propositions. Since Avicenna seems to indicate that reflexive propositions function analogously to sensible propositions, the foundational knowledge they provide cannot simply consist in appeals to our subjective awareness of ourselves, just as sensible propositions do not simply refer to our subjective awareness of our occurrent sensations (e.g. that we are seeing red or feeling heat). Avicenna seems to be affirming here that introspection can reveal to us the *sorts* of psychological states that human beings experience, and that these do not require independent verification and research to be used in our sciences, just as we do not need to verify our sensory evidence that the sun shines or that fire is hot. Introspection and sensation are both reliable sources on the basis of which the intellect can construct certain propositions.

But does the soul's primitive self-awareness play any more direct role in Avicenna's epistemology? As the sole item of purely innate knowledge that he clearly endorses, is it able to provide any additional a priori knowledge in his epistemology? The most promising possibility in this regard comes from the direction of the primary concepts, which we examined in Section 4. According to Avicenna, these concepts – in particular, 'thing' and 'existent' – are absolutely basic and prior to all other concepts. We cannot conceptualize anything unless we implicitly recognize it as a thing with an essence of its own, and as an existent. If this is the case, then it would seem that, as soon as we are aware of ourselves, at the very first moment of our existence, we must concomitantly be aware of ourselves as existents and things. Indeed, Avicenna often speaks of the Flying Man affirming his *existence* (*mawjūdah*), and, as we have seen, he even identifies self-awareness as the soul's very existence. So, primitive self-awareness seems ideally suited to providing the first occasion for awakening our knowledge of the primary concepts.

While this seems to be a plausible and promising way to read Avicenna's texts on self-awareness and the primary concepts in the light of one another, Avicenna himself does not make such a connection explicit. One possible reason for this is that he struggles to classify the type of knowledge given in self-awareness: while it is intellectual rather than sensory (since its object, the human soul, is immaterial), it is also not conceptual and universal, and so perhaps is not immediately suited to provide a source for the primary concepts as universals.[43]

It is more likely, however, that Avicenna's very different aims in the texts where he discusses the primary concepts and self-awareness, respectively, simply did not lend themselves to forging a connection between the two themes. In the *Metaphysics* his main interest is in establishing the epistemic primacy of the concepts that form the subject-matter of the science of metaphysics, whereas in his discussions of self-knowledge the concern is not with the broader contribution of self-awareness to human knowledge, but only with its ability to alert us to the true nature of our rational souls.

Overall, Avicenna's way of framing epistemological problems does not lend itself naturally to a focus on the question of whether human beings are able to have innate knowledge in the way that we now understand innateness. For Avicenna, affirming the reality of innate knowledge would be tantamount to accepting the Platonic theory of reminiscence, which he emphatically rejects. And, as an Aristotelian, Avicenna remains committed to the idea that the human intellect is a potential one, a faculty of the soul whose main function is to acquire knowledge of *other* things, and that therefore requires some form of sensory preparation in order to think of any objects other than itself. For Avicenna, then, the possibility of innate knowledge simply does not resonate as a central concern for an epistemology focused squarely on the conditions by which certain, demonstrative knowledge can be acquired.[44]

Notes

1 Unless otherwise indicated, translations are my own.
2 See Abrahamov (1993) for this concept in the theologians.
3 *Taṣdīq* literally means 'believing to be true' and is sometimes paired disjunctively with *takdhīb*, 'believing to be false'; more often *taṣdīq* is used to cover both affirmation and denial. See Wolfson (1943) for the classic study of this couplet.
4 The distinction is evocative of Aristotle's distinction between simple 'thoughts' (*noēmata*), that are neither true nor false, and composed and divided thoughts, that is, sentences or propositions, which do have a truth value. See *De interpretatione*, c. 1, 16a10-18.
5 Trans. Ahmed (2011: 87, §102), where the example is that of conceiving but not assenting to the proposition 'The vacuum exists'.
6 See Plato, *Meno* 80d-86c. For a recent examination of the paradox in Plato and his ancient successors, see Fine (2014). Fārābī's appeals to the paradox are discussed in Black (2008b); Avicenna's account in the *Burhān* (*Demonstration*) of the *Healing* is translated with commentary in Marmura (2009).

7   For the original example, see Themistius (1900: 4.20); the Arabic version is not extant.

8   Medieval Latin authors often cited this Avicennian thesis, but their formulations suggest that these concepts are somehow the first ones explicitly formulated by children. For example, Thomas Aquinas, in the Prologue to *On Being and Essence* (*De ente et essentia*), writes: 'But being and essence are *what are first conceived* by the intellect (*sunt quae primo intellectu concipiuntur*), as Avicenna says in the beginning of his *Metaphysics*.'

9   See Black (2006) for Fārābī's appeal to the KK-condition, along with other criteria for certitude that Avicenna adopts.

10 Avicenna says that, in the first scenario, if the believer were to have her attention drawn to the possibility of a second-order belief, that is, if she were asked whether she is certain that *p*, it would weaken her conviction, though not to the point of causing her to doubt it or to withdraw assent.

11 See Avicenna (1952: 16–17). For an overview of the Mu'tazilite's epistemological discussions, see Dhanani (1994: 21–33). Standard examples of necessary/natural knowledge in *kalām* are perceptual knowledge, knowledge of oneself and one's inner mental states, and knowledge of logical laws such as the principle of non-contradiction.

12 Avicenna makes it explicit here that one needs both to conceive the terms and to 'discern their composition' (*wa-al-faṭānah li-l-tartībi*).

13 Avicenna sometimes focuses on the fact that such propositions have accompanying middle terms; in other cases he speaks of them as being accompanied automatically by an innate *syllogism* (*qiyāsātu-hā ma'a-hā; fiṭrīyah al-qiyās*), which is then explained by the presence of the middle term.

14 Elsewhere (see Black 2013: 127), I suggest that this is evocative of the Kantian notion of the synthetic a priori; in this, I disagree with Gutas (2012: 410 n41), who takes these propositions to be analytic. I don't see how this can be the case when a middle term is involved, since this precludes the identity or partial identity of the subject and predicate.

15 See the *Remarks* account of the primary propositions, where Avicenna (1892: 56; trans. Inati 1984: 119) admits that the necessity of assent will depend upon whether or not the meaning of the terms is evident to the believer. While some terms are evident to all people, others will require effort in order for the terms themselves to be conceptualized; once this occurs and the proposition is composed, assent is again automatic.

16 That is, an addition to the role of the senses in the acquisition of the concepts represented by the terms of any proposition.

17 I use 'empirical' here as a generic term for all the certain principles that depend in some way on sensory evidence to necessitate assent. As such, it has no exact

equivalent in Avicenna's own Arabic usage; it does, however, form a distinct
subcategory in Avicenna's enumeration of the principles in the *Healing*, where he
groups together sensation, experience, and testimony as principles whose source of
necessity is external to the intellect (*ḍarūrah-hu ẓāhirīyah*) (1956: 63). Gutas (2012),
uses 'empirical' and 'empiricism' in a similar way, although he uses 'experience' as
translation of Avicenna's *mushāhadah* (396), which I am rendering as 'observation'.
The closest equivalent to 'empirical' in Avicenna's Arabic is *tajribah*, the term that
translates the Greek *empereia*. I render it as 'experiential'.

18 I discuss these in Black (2013: 130–2). Intuited propositions are intended to
    invoke Avicenna's discussion of intuition or *ḥads*, the centerpiece of his cognitive
    psychology and his rationalist theory of prophecy. For discussion, see Marmura
    (1991) and Gutas (2001; 2014: 179–201).

19 Avicenna (1892: 56; trans. Inati 1984: 120) and Avicenna (1985: 97; trans. Ahmed
    2011: 88, §103).

20 For discussions of *tajribah* in Avicenna, see McGinnis (2003), Janssens (2004),
    Gutas (2012), and Black (2013: 127–30). For Avicenna's most detailed account of
    experience and its distinction from induction, see Avicenna (1956: 1.9, 93–105;
    trans. McGinnis and Reisman 2007: 147–56).

21 In the *Remarks* the example is 'hitting with wood is painful'; the *Deliverance* adds
    'the observed movements (*al-marṣūdah*) of the heavenly bodies'. See Avicenna
    (1892: 57; trans. Inati 1984: 120) and Avicenna (1985: 97–8; trans. Ahmed
    (2011: 88, §104).

22 Thus induction is merely dialectical or rhetorical. The distinction between
    induction and experience is already drawn by Fārābī in his *Book of Demonstration*
    (*Kitāb al-Burhān*), although Fārābī does not have any conception of a hidden
    syllogism. See Al-Fārābī (1987: 23–5; trans. McGinnis and Reisman 2007: 67, §4).

23 This major premise is essentially a negation of Aristotle's definition of chance
    in *Physics* 2.5, 196b10-13. On this, see Marmura (1965: 195; 1990: 13–15).
    I disagree with Gutas (2012: 400) regarding the nature of the hidden syllogism in
    experientials. Gutas reconstructs the syllogism as follows: '[Minor] Scammony
    has by nature the power to purge; [Major] whatever has by nature the power
    to purge causes purging when ingested; [Conclusion] therefore scammony by
    nature causes purging when ingested.' This reconstruction does not capture the
    fact that the hidden syllogism in experience isn't meant to add any content to the
    observed connections – it merely explains the grounds for our taking them as
    necessary. In all experiential propositions, then, the major premise should be the
    same: 'Whatever happens always or for the most part cannot be coincidental.'

24 In the *Demonstration of the Healing*, Avicenna (1956: 95) adds that this shows
    that the ability to purge bile is a necessary or inseparable accident (*'araḍ lāzim*)
    of scammony. In the *Remarks* he notes (1892: 57; Inati 1984: 120) that experience

may yield either a 'decisive' (*jazman*) judgement, that is, one that admits of no exceptions; or one that holds 'for the most part' (*akthariyan*).

25 This claim reflects Fārābī and Avicenna's recognition that ordinary people are able to recognize necessary causal connections without any theoretical knowledge of cognitive psychology. If certitude in experiential propositions required an understanding of the mechanism that causes the intellect to assent to them, then only philosophers or psychologists could have certain, experiential knowledge.

26 Avicenna's class of intuited propositions, added in the *Remarks*, seems designed to allow cases where someone recognizes not only that a cause and effect are essentially connected, but also *why*. On these, see note 18. The more likely scenario, however, is that the experiential premises provide the starting points for further investigation to discover the cause itself and construct properly scientific, *propter quid* demonstrations based on it.

27 This discussion is found in the chapter on *tajribah* and its distinction from induction in the *Demonstration of the Healing*. See Avicenna (1956: 95–8; trans. McGinnis and Reisman 2007: 149–52, §§12–21). Avicenna initially formulates the objection using the proposition, 'All human beings are black', as if it were a standard sensible proposition that predicates a non-essential property (skin colour) of a subject. Since this formulation makes no claim about a causal connection between two *distinct* things, it doesn't seem properly experiential; perhaps this is why Avicenna corrects the oversight in his response, changing it to the proposition, 'Humans beget black offspring', which does make a causal claim.

28 For a brief overview of *tawātur*, see Juynboll (2011): there is an excellent discussion of al-Ghazālī's account of *tawātur*, which borrows much from Avicenna, in Weiss (1985).

29 Avicenna (1985: 98; trans. Ahmed 2011: 89) and Avicenna (1892: 57–8; trans. Inati 1984: 121). Avicenna (1956: 67) lists testimonials as propositions that are 'necessary of acceptance', but it does not discuss them further.

30 Avicenna (1892: 57; trans. Inati 1984: 121) refers to doubt being removed because of 'multiple observations' (*li-kathrati al-mushāhadāt*). Since he has adopted the label of *tawātur*, we should add, in addition to the observations made by the original witnesses, the unbroken line of auditory and written evidence transmitting them to subsequent generations.

31 Avicenna (1892: 57): 'Doubt (*al-rības*) concerning the occurrence of this witnessing (*shahādah*) is eliminated by way of agreement and corroboration.'

32 Ahmed's translation is based on a different edition as well as additional manuscript evidence, and he leaves out the final disclaimer regarding later personal verification.

33 The alternative label 'widespread' (*dhāʾiʿāt*) is used in the *Deliverance*. See Avicenna (1985: 99–100; trans. Ahmed 2011: 92–3, §108).

34 For further discussion of how these propositions are formed by the practical intellect, see Avicenna (1959: Bk. 5, c. 1, 207–208).

35 Avicenna (1959: 46) mentions specifically human emotions, such as shame and mercy. In his psychology he identifies these emotions as the product of an interaction between the practical intellect and the sensory appetites.

36 See Avicenna (1892: 59; trans. Inati 1984: 122–3) and Avicenna (1985: 99–100; trans. Ahmed 2011: 92–3). The scenario with which the thought-experiment begins is, of course, evocative of Avicenna's more famous Flying Man experiment, discussed at note 38 below.

37 For this argument, see Marmura (1994).

38 For an overview of the Flying Man see Marmura (1986). The main occurrences of the experiment are in *The Healing: The Soul*, Bk 1, c. 1, and Bk 5, c. 7; and in the Remarks. See Avicenna (1959: 15–16, 255–56; 1892: 119; trans. Inati 2014: 94–5).

39 For discussions of Avicenna's views on self-knowledge and self-awareness, see Pines (1954), Black (2008a), and Kaukua (2015).

40 Gutas (2012) argues that Avicenna is an empiricist after the model of John Locke. While I do not disagree with many of the details of Gutas' account of empirical knowledge in Avicenna, I do not think that Avicenna's primitive self-awareness can simply be identified with Locke's reflexive knowledge. It is worth noting in this regard that reflexive knowledge is the wedge that Leibniz (1996: 'Preface' 51–3) uses in the *New Essays* to suggest that Locke must accept some sort of innate knowledge despite himself.

41 Inati (1984: 120 n8) takes the contrast to be between the external and internal senses, but there is no indication that Avicenna means to exclude the intellect here; he also includes emotional states as well as cognitive ones.

42 Avicenna may also be indebted to the theologians here, since they too included awareness of ourselves and our inner states among the necessary principles of knowledge, along with evidence from the senses. See note 11.

43 On Avicenna's wrestling with these points, see Black (2008a). It's not clear how far this objection goes, however, since many of the concepts that we acquire as children are no more articulated as explicit universals than is our concept of ourselves.

44 This research was supported by the Social Sciences and Humanities Research Council of Canada.

References

Primary texts

Al-Fārābī (1987), *Kitāb al-Burhān (Demonstration)*, vol. 4 of *Al-Manṭiq ʿinda al-Fārābī (Al-Fārābī's Logic)*, ed. R. Al-ʿAjam and M. Fakhry, Beirut: Dar el-Machreq.

Avicenna (1892), *Al-Ishārāt wa-al-Tanbīhāt (Remarks and Admonitions)*, ed. J. Forget, Leiden: Brill.
Avicenna (1952), *Al-Shifāʾ: Al-Madkhal (Healing: Isagoge)*, ed. G. Anawati, M. El-Khodeiri, F. al-Ahwani, and I. Madkour, Cairo: General Egyptian Book Organization.
Avicenna (1956), *Al-Shifāʾ: Al-Burhān (Healing: Demonstration)*, ed. A. E. Affifi and I. Madkour, Cairo: General Egyptian Book Organization.
Avicenna (1959), *Al-Shifāʾ: Al-Nafs (Healing: The Soul)*, ed. F. Rahman, *Avicenna's De anima, Being the Psychological Part of Kitāb al-Shifāʾ*, London: Clarendon Press.
Avicenna (1985), *Kitāb al-Najāh (Deliverance)*, ed. M. Fakhry, Beirut: Dar al-Afaq al-Jaddah.
Avicenna (2005), *The Metaphysics of the Healing*, ed. and trans. M. E. Marmura, Provo, Utah: Brigham Young University Press.
Avicenna (2013), *Al-Taʿlīqāt (Notes)*, ed. S. H. Mousavian, Tehran: Iranian Institute of Philosophy.
Leibniz, G. W. (1996), *New Essays on Human Understanding*, trans. P. Remnant and J. Bennett, Cambridge: Cambridge University Press.
Themistius (1900), *Analyticorm Posteriorum Paraphrasis (Paraphrase of the Posterior Analytics)*, ed. M. Wallies, *Commentaria in Aristotelem Graeca* V.1, Berlin: Reimer.

Studies and translations

Abrahamov, B. (1993), 'Necessary Knowledge in Islamic Theology', *British Journal of Middle Eastern Studies*, 20: 20–32.
Ahmed, A. Q. (trans.) (2011), *Avicenna's Deliverance: Logic*, Oxford: Oxford University Press.
Black, D. L. (2006), 'Knowledge (ʿilm) and Certitude (yaqīn) in al-Fārābī's Epistemology', *Arabic Sciences and Philosophy*, 16: 11–45.
Black, D. L. (2008a), 'Avicenna on Self-Awareness and Knowing that One Knows', in S. Rahman, T. Hassan, and T. Street (eds), *The Unity of Science in the Arabic Tradition*, Dordrecht: Springer Science.
Black, D. L. (2008b), 'Al-Farabi on Meno's Paradox', in P. Adamson (ed.), *In the Age of al-Fārābī: Arabic Philosophy in the Fourth/Tenth Century*, London: Warburg Institute.
Black, D. L. (2013), 'Certitude, Justification, and the Principles of Knowledge in Avicenna's Epistemology', in P. Adamson (ed.), *Interpreting Avicenna*, Cambridge: Cambridge University Press.
Dhanani, A. (1994), *The Physical Theory of Kalām*, Leiden: Brill.
Fine, G. (2014), *The Possibility of Inquiry: Meno's Paradox from Socrates to Sextus*, Oxford: Oxford University Press.
Gutas, D. (2001), 'Intuition and Thinking: The Evolving Structure of Avicenna's Epistemology', in R. Wisnovsky (ed.), *Aspects of Avicenna*, Princeton: Princeton University Press.

Gutas, D. (2012), 'The Empiricism of Avicenna', *Oriens*, 40: 391–436.

Gutas, D. (2014), *Avicenna and the Aristotelian Tradition*, 2nd edn, Leiden: Brill.

Inati, S. C. (trans.) (1984), *Remarks and Admonitions, Part One: Logic*, Toronto: Pontifical Institute of Mediaeval Studies.

Inati, S. C. (trans.) (2014), *Remarks and Admonitions: Physics and Metaphysics*, New York: Columbia University Press.

Janssens, J. (2004), '"Experience" (*tajriba*) in Classical Arabic Philosophy (al-Fārābī-Avicenna)', *Quaestio*, 4: 45–62.

Juynboll, G. H. A. (2011), 'Tawātur', in P. Bearman et al. (eds), *Encyclopaedia of Islam*, 2nd edn, Leiden: Brill Online.

Kaukua, J. (2015) *Self-Awareness in Islamic Philosophy: Avicenna and Beyond*, Cambridge University Press.

Marmura, M. E. (1965), 'Ghazali and Demonstrative Science', *Journal of the History of Philosophy*, 3: 183–204.

Marmura, M. E. (1986), 'Avicenna's "Flying Man" in Context', *The Monist*, 69: 383–95.

Marmura, M. E. (1990), 'The *Fortuna* of the Posterior Analytics in the Arabic Middle Ages', in S. Knuuttila et al. (eds), *Knowledge and the Sciences in Medieval Philosophy: Proceedings of the Eighth International Congress of Medieval Philosophy (S.I.E.P.M.)*, 3 vols, 1: 5–103, Helsinki: Acta Philosophica Fennica.

Marmura, M. E. (1991), 'Plotting the Course of Avicenna's Thought', *Journal of the American Oriental Society*, 111: 333–42.

Marmura, M. E. (1994), 'A Medieval Islamic Argument for the Intrinsic Value of the Moral Act', in E. Robbins and S. Sandahl (eds), *Corolla Torontonensis: Studies in Honour of Ronald Morton Smith*, Toronto: TSAR.

Marmura, M. E. (2009), 'Avicenna on Meno's Paradox: On "Apprehending" Unknown Things through Known Things', *Mediaeval Studies*, 71: 47–62.

McGinnis, J. (2003), 'Scientific Methodologies in Medieval Islam', *Journal of the History of Philosophy*, 41: 30–27.

McGinnis, J. and Reisman, D. (trans.) (2007), *Classical Arabic Philosophy: An Anthology of Sources*, Indianapolis: Hackett.

Pines, S. (1954), 'La Conception de la Conscience de soi chez Avicenne et chez Abū'l-Barakāt al-Baghdādī', *Archives d'histoire doctrinale et littéraire du moyen âge*, 29: 21–56.

Weiss, B. (1985), 'Knowledge of the Past: The Theory of *Tawātur* according to Ghazālī', *Studia Islamica*, 65: 81–105.

Wolfson, H. A. (1943), 'The Terms *Taṣawwur* and *Taṣdīq* in Arabic Philosophy and Their Greek, Latin and Hebrew Equivalents', *The Moslem World*, 33: 1–15.

2

Scientia in the Twelfth Century

Rafael Nájera

The Latin word '*scientia*' can be translated simply as 'knowledge', but doing so would be somewhat misleading when it comes to Latin medieval thought. Medieval thinkers talk about knowledge in terms that might sound strange to contemporary philosophers. In the thirteenth century '*scientia*' becomes the translation of the Greek '*epistēmē*' (sometimes translated as 'scientific knowledge'), which is the word that Aristotle uses in the *Posterior Analytics*[1] to refer to a special kind of knowledge that is the product of demonstrations. The *Posterior Analytics* was available in Latin as early as the 1150s, when John of Salisbury (c. 1115–80) provides a summary in his *Metalogicon*. There, John (1929: IV.9) says that the book is poorly translated and that demonstrations are hard to do, but he does not really engage with the text. We will have to wait until the early thirteenth century for the first full commentary (1981) on the work by Robert Grosseteste (c. 1170–1253). Later, Aquinas accepts this view of *epistēmē* as a special kind of knowledge and puts forth the idea of *scientia* as indeed a higher kind of intellectual activity in comparison with the simple cognition of extra-mental objects. How to explain the cognition of extra-mental objects is, however, the question that comes up more frequently in the writings of Aquinas, Scotus, Ockham, and other thirteenth- and early-fourteenth-century thinkers.

In the twelfth century we do not find the level of technical sophistication and argumentation of the thirteenth, but we find the seeds for the acceptance of *scientia* as higher level knowledge. In the Latin intellectual world, the twelfth century represents roughly, in its first half, a continuation of the development in logic and dialectics started in the eleventh, and, in its second, the discovery of the bulk of the Aristotelian corpus and Arabic sources. As we will see in this chapter, in prominent accounts *scientia* is understood mainly in Platonic terms as a higher level of cognition, one that is closer to the purely intellectual. Hugh of St. Victor (1096–c. 1140) is the figure with the most sophisticated account, but there is also an important treatise on the matter by Dominicus Gundissalinus (c. 1110–90, also known as a Dominicus Gundisalvi). This chapter concentrates on these two figures.

Equally misleading would be to translate '*scientia*' as 'science' if by that is meant something like modern, empirical science. There is nothing like modern science in the early Latin medieval period. There was, most probably, the development of different technologies for practical use, but that happened outside of the realm of philosophers. In fact, Hugh of St. Victor also happens to be one of the first thinkers to include what he called 'technical arts' (carpentry, husbandry, etc.) as part of the educational canon. Up to this point, education for intellectual elites aspired to copy the Greek and Roman ideal of the seven liberal arts: the so-called quadrivium of arithmetic, geometry, astronomy, and music, and the trivium of grammar, dialectics, and rhetoric. But almost all of the intellectual development happened in dialectics. Thinkers did not have access even to basic treatises in Greek mathematics and astronomy, for example. It is not surprising therefore that twelfth-century intellectuals were in fact more than eager to get their hands on whatever they could get of Arabic scientific treatises once some of them became available in the mid-to-late twelfth century.[2] There was thirst for knowledge, for sure, and, relatively recently, scholars have found texts that may be interpreted as the beginnings of a science of nature.[3] There was some preoccupation with how these scientific disciplines, also part of *scientia*, together with logic and dialectics, were to be conceived, used, and understood in the context of the Christian faith.

This preoccupation had a long history in the Christian Latin world. Boethius (480–c. 525), an important source for many twelfth-century thinkers, famously championed the cause of the liberal arts in Christian education by endeavoring to translate into Latin important works of logic, music, and arithmetic. There was also the so-called Carolingian renaissance in the ninth century, which resulted in widespread education reforms. It is not until the eleventh century, however, that we see in the Latin West a clear rebirth of original thought, especially in the field of dialectics and its application to the understanding of Christian faith and Scriptures. This resurgence, as is well known already, goes hand in hand with the development of cathedral schools and the apparition of masters more and more specialized in teaching and learning.[4] Abelard (1079–40) is perhaps one of the best-known examples of this new brand of masters that embraced dialectics completely. Certainly, by the twelfth century there is an ongoing debate about the role of dialectics, and in general of knowledge gained by reason – as opposed to knowledge gained by revelation – in the life of a Christian. It is in this context that discussions about *scientia* take place.[5]

The intellectual backdrop for these discussions is, however, Platonic thought, which twelfth-century Europeans gained mainly through Augustine, Boethius, and a number of anonymous treatises. Even though some of the details are taken primarily from Boethius, the bulk of the ideas and themes are explicit particularly in Augustine, who is perhaps the most influential figure in the early medieval Latin world. Part of this influence is owed to his prolific and rhetorically powerful pen, which he devoted to the cause of Christianity since his conversion around the year 386. The story of this conversion is told several years later in his *Confessions* (1981). There, he narrates how Christianity became intellectually viable for him after he read 'some books of the Platonists' (VII.9.13). What he found in those books marked him profoundly, to the extent that most of his positions on philosophical issues barely change in the course of his life, especially his view on what is the goal of man. This goal, according to Augustine, is to know and contemplate God, most probably with the help and guidance of faith. To this knowledge and contemplation of God, he assigns a distinct word: *sapientia*, that is, wisdom.

Augustine also manages to give intellectual support for the continuity of the classical, liberal arts program of study. The significance of the liberal arts for Augustine resides not in their practicality, but in their role as cultivators of the mind. The liberal arts are primarily concerned with theoretical knowledge. Whatever practical aspects they may have seem to represent, for Augustine, simply a snare to draw the student's interest into incorporeal, eternal things: 'desiring corporeal things to move towards and arrive at incorporeal things', he says in *Retractationes* (1984: II.I.6 (17:43–4)). Certainly, as is clear in *De Musica* (1969: I.4.8 (108)), the liberal arts for Augustine are strictly within the domain of knowledge (*scientia*), which in this early writing is already characterized as something ascribed to the soul and found only in the intellect, not in memory or sense perception.

Mathematics has a special role for Augustine. The goal, however, is not to engage in mathematical theorizing just to know some facts about numbers or geometrical figures. The idea is to get to know number itself, which for Augustine (1970: Bk II) is identical to *sapientia*. It is only as part of a path to *sapientia* that any discipline seems to have any intrinsic worth. In *De Trinitate*, a later work, wisdom is itself characterized as the essence of the divinity, and as something that can actually be attained by men. One of Augustine's main tenets here is that there is something similar to God in our soul. This is one of the major ideas that Augustine drew from his reading of 'the works of the Platonists', specifically the writings of Plotinus. God is an incorporeal being responsible for reason. He is, so to speak, Reason with a capital R, reason in the abstract, with perfect knowledge and infinite power. Our souls are endowed with the capacity to reason, and thus we depend on God. We are not parts of that Reason. We are reasoning beings for whom the standard of truth and rationality is God himself. We also have a material body, and in the interaction between our body and soul we have the capacity for deciding what to do. Instead of turning to God and the rational, we may turn to the body and carnal pleasures, and thus away from God. The key to getting to know God is, consequently, looking into ourselves and seeing Him there.[6]

There is therefore this inner struggle in man, according to Augustine (1968). It is due to the fact that, he says, reason can turn itself to the material instead of the purely intellectual. Man disgraces himself indeed 'when he neglects the love of wisdom (*sapientia*) which always stays the same, and lusts after knowledge (*scientia*) derived from experience with changeable things; [this knowledge] inflates but does not edify' (XII.11 (370)). Reason alone, therefore, cannot be trusted; *sapientia* should be its guide at all times. Augustine explains that *scientia* and *sapientia* form a kind of rational marriage between action – the accomplishment of the material functions of the body in the material world – and contemplation – partaking of the image of God. Things can go wrong in this interplay of functions, but not necessarily. The goal, in any case, is to fix the mind's gaze on the eternal things, even if we know that we have to live in a material world. *Scientia* thus has a positive aspect: if what *scientia* 'inflates', it does under the tutelage of the love for eternal things, then things go well. *Scientia*, in any case, is necessary, for we cannot live in this world without it. In fact, it is necessary for salvation (XII.14 (374–5)): 'For without [*scientia*] we cannot even possess the very virtues by which we live rightly and by which this miserable life is so regulated that it may arrive at eternal life which is truly blessed.' It is precisely the priority assigned to wisdom, and this essentially positive aspect of *scientia*, that thinkers in the twelfth century, and Hugh of St. Victor in particular, would adopt from Augustine when theorizing about the status of science and scientific disciplines.

Hugh has the most substantial account of *scientia* after Augustine and before the translation of the *Posterior Analytics*. There are two important works in which he deals with it. One is the *Didascalicon*, written in the 1130s. We could say that this is an update to Augustine's *De doctrina christiana* (1962), in the sense that it provides a curriculum for the Christian: a program of study covering both 'pagan' disciplines and the Scriptures. It is also an explanation of the classification and the origin of the sciences. The work is indeed radically different from Augustine's *De doctrina* in the way that those disciplines are set up, but in the end both Augustine and Hugh are aiming at the same thing.

The *Didascalicon* (1939) starts with a preface in which Hugh defends the idea of learning. He moves against those who think that learning may be impossible for the not so bright and simply futile for the rest. Here he is most probably responding to those contemporary voices contrarian to *scientia* and dialectics. To them, Hugh replies that the truth is that there is no excuse for not learning or at least for not trying to learn. Even the less talented can benefit from learning, if only so much, Hugh says. Those who can easily learn but decide not to do so are simply despicable: 'not knowing comes from weakness, but to hate knowledge comes from a wicked will' (preface, 1.16–17). The reason why acquiring *scientia* is important will become clear in the first chapters of Book I, as we will see later.

The work is indeed a manual for students. Its purpose is to teach Christians how to acquire knowledge. There are two ways, Hugh claims in the preface, in which someone can be instructed to acquire knowledge: reading (*lectio*) and meditation. The *Didascalicon* is about *lectio*, which includes in its meaning not only actually reading a text but also taking lessons, and which comes before meditation in teaching. The work is meant to give students the precepts for successful reading: a guide on what to read, in which order, and how. However, Hugh does not say at any point that reading is *required* to acquire *scientia*. *Scientia* may come also, for example, from natural intellectual activity. This can be gathered from Hugh's theory of knowledge, to which I now turn.

Hugh provides a detailed analysis of the process through which knowledge comes about in his short treatise *De Unione Corporis et Spiritus* (1980; also 1854). All knowledge is some sort of purification of being that happens at all levels, from the corporeal up to the divine. Hugh presents his theory by describing first how knowledge of the material is accomplished. The verse from Jn 3:6, 'What is born of flesh is flesh, and what is born from spirit is spirit', allows Hugh to introduce the idea that there has to be a medium between the material and the spiritual so that they can convene at some point, like they do, for example, in the normal activity of man. Since there is a great distance – Hugh does not say that it is an insurmountable distance – between body and spirit, there has to be something by means of which the body ascends (for the body is lower) to come near to the spirit, and something by means of which the spirit descends to approach the body.

Hugh indeed affirms that there is a scale of beings, starting with lower and higher bodies, then lower and higher spirits above bodies, and finally God as the supreme being. This is indeed a Platonic idea shared by Augustine, although it almost certainly comes to Hugh by way of Boethius' notion of the realms of the corporeal, the intelligible, and the intellectible. This is in Boethius' Commentary on Porphyry's *Isagogē*. The realm of the intellectible is actually the realm of the divine, and Boethius says he coined that word to translate the Greek *noēton*. Later, in the *Didascalicon*, Hugh uses these notions to account for the tripartite division of the theoretical sciences (physics, mathematics, and theology), claiming in conclusion that theology is the highest of them all precisely because it deals with the intellectibles.

For Hugh, however, entities in each of these realms – the material, the spiritual, and the divine – have different levels of being, and indeed there is something akin to an overlap in the ranks. Some bodies, for example, are of so high a rank that they are almost transcendent, almost spirit. Conversely, there are spirits of such a low rank that they are almost corporeal. It is the confluence of those high bodies and low spirits that makes possible the communication between the two kinds of entities. Also needed for that communication to happen is the capability of a particular entity or parts of an entity, be it corporeal, spiritual, or divine, to ascend or descend. According to Hugh, sense perception (*sensus*) is precisely that by means of which the corporeal ascends. Conversely, the spiritual descends to the corporeal by means of sensuality (*sensualitas*). What can happen between body and spirit can also happen between spirit and God. Spirits can also ascend towards God, and this they do through contemplation; God, in turn, can descend to spirits through revelation. To each of these faculties there is a corresponding instrument: theophany – that is, God's manifestation – in revelation, intelligence (*intelligentia*) in contemplation, imagination (*imaginatio*) in sensuality, and the instrument of sensuality in sense perception.

Hugh does not really explain what these instruments are, except for imagination. But, before doing that, he provides a deeper reason why, at least in the case of material entities, ascent and descent are possible. Indeed, Hugh explains, the different ranks of being are derived from the nature of the four basic elements out of which all material entities are composed. The elements themselves, in fact, can be ordered according to the rank of their properties. The more easily an element can be moved and the more difficult it is to contain it, the higher the element ranks in the scale. Thus, earth and water are of a lower rank than air and fire, because the former are more easily contained and less easily moved. Even though air is sometimes called spirit, Hugh notes, fire is the element that is closer to spirit. Fire, indeed, he says, is the most movable and the least containable element of the four. As a sort of confirmation for this view, he points out that, given that sense perception is what makes bodies ascend towards spirit, the more an element is like spirit, the farther it is from sense perception. So, for example, Hugh says, air has such subtlety that it cannot be seen that easily. Presumably, this should be even more applicable to fire.[7]

Sense perception – the first step towards knowledge, so to speak – is thus a purification of the material, a stripping-off of lowly elements. In Hugh's theory, it seems that the higher elements somehow serve to convey information about objects of knowledge. That information is decoded in the head.

Knowledge (*scientia*) of things, Hugh (1854) says, is a prerogative only of man and not of plants and other animals, and is possible because of the existence in the head of the faculty of creating imaginations (*vis imaginandi*). Imaginations are so elevated that they are the closest things to spiritual nature, and above them in the scale of being there cannot be anything but reason. An imagination is indeed a 'fiery' nature that is like the translation of what is formed outside the soul and that can be called a sense percept (*sensus*) (886.85-6 (287B)).

Hugh explains the process next using sense perception through vision as an example. First, the form of a sensible thing is drawn into the eyes by the vision rays. Sense perception is taken to be active: the eyes emit vision rays that hit the external things; the ray's reflections carry the sensible form back into the eyes. After this, the sensible form, still a corporeal entity, traverses the inner organs of vision, is purified once more, and is conveyed to the brain (*cerebrum*), where an imagination is formed. An imagination for Hugh (1854: 886.91-4 (287B-C)) is thus a corporeal thing that has gone through a process of purification so that it can participate in the crucial step that happens next: '[T]he imagination travels from the front of the head to the centre where it *touches* the very same rational substance of the soul and excites the capacity to discern, having been purified and made subtle so much already that it is *joined* together immediately with the same spirit' (my emphasis). This sounds very similar to Galenic theories of perception, and there is some evidence to suggest that Hugh knew early translations of medical treatises.[8] However, he rejects the idea of all of this happening at the material level. *Scientia* is not a purified material; it is completely intellectual. So, there cannot be any direct conversion from the corporeal to the intellectual. Hugh emphasizes later in the text that the soul itself is not material, it is not a 'material spirit', it is truly spirit. One important thing to note here is how Hugh is trying to integrate many different sources into a coherent picture. One of the challenges that he faces is to take into account these 'new' sources while retaining this overall Platonic framework. This is not a simple task. Gundissalinus does the same with many more new sources and, perhaps understandably, more clumsily.

So, again, there cannot be any direct conversion from the corporeal to the intellectual. This, of course, makes Hugh's theory very problematic. He does not say how the interaction actually occurs; he only says that the two realms almost touch. There is just some sort of interaction between two things that stand at approximately the same level of being even if belonging to different classes – an imagination in the corporeal side, and the soul in the spiritual side. Thus, after the interaction between the corporeal and the spiritual takes place, reason takes over and the spiritual thing that established contact with the imagination is purified even more. At some point, presumably, it would reach a level in which it would properly be *scientia*.

The process can continue even further up the ontological scale, for, according to Hugh, the soul can form purer thoughts and can reach a state, presumably of something still like *scientia*, that would be closer to God. Unfortunately, Hugh does not provide a detailed account of how the process goes. In principle, in any case, this process does not need to start always with thoughts or knowledge coming directly from the process of perception; it can start with anything that is already in the soul. As mentioned earlier, for Hugh, in this higher state called contemplation, the instrument would be intelligence. Later in the text, he succinctly explains this: an intelligence – the purest of thoughts, if we make the analogy to an imagination for the corporeal – is formed in the interior of the soul as the product of reason being concurrent with divine presence. That divine presence, Hugh says, informs reason to produce intelligence, which he now equates with wisdom (*sapientia*), in the same way that an imagination informs reason to produce *scientia*.

Making a parallel with the cognition of corporeal things, the process of acquiring wisdom may depend for Hugh not only on the soul having or producing purified thoughts, something that seems to be a natural ability, but also on God descending so that the soul grasps Him. There are indeed two main agents in Hugh's theory: the human soul and God. The bottom rung of the ontological scale, the material, is completely passive. Hugh calls God's descent 'revelation', as we saw, but he is probably not referring specifically to the kind of revelation given in the Scriptures.

The process with respect to corporeal things, in any case, also explains for Hugh why the contact with the corporeal can result in vice and degeneration of the soul. Certainly, in the same way that we can talk of an ever-increasing purification of the bodily material that makes its way up to the point where it is in contact with reason, Hugh says, we can talk of a descent of reason towards the body. The spirit has indeed its own mutability and it comes near the body by a process of vilification, putting aside its purity as if assuming the rougher properties of the corporeal. If this happens only according to nature, Hugh adds, there is only mutation and not corruption. If, however, it happens viciously and the soul finds a certain sickly delight in the contact with the body, the nature of the soul gets corrupted. Not, of course, that the soul loses its ability to acquire *scientia*, but, in a way, the soul would be going against the proper order of things in the ontological scale. The natural, and right, process seems then to be the ascent from the corporeal to the spiritual and upwards finally to God. The soul naturally would not dwell in that noxious part of reason that likes the corporeal. It is a degeneration of the soul that causes humans to forfeit looking for higher *scientia* and prevents them from arriving ultimately at intelligence and wisdom.

The process, then, is natural but it can be inferred that, for Hugh, there is the possibility, more or less common, of humans wanting to stay at the level of the sensible, just as, for Augustine, the body can be a nuisance. Thus the need for instruction, not perhaps to overcome the resistance to ascent per se, but to expedite the attainment of a certain level, and perhaps to instil a certain taste for the spiritual, so that real advance towards God can come about. Instruction, then, has one of the roles that Augustine gives to faith – of being a helper along the path to wisdom. For both Hugh and Augustine, this helper is purely intellectual.

Instruction, as said earlier, comes for Hugh in the form of reading, and in a second stage as meditation, but he does not say much about the latter. The only place in which he touches on it is in Book III of the *Didascalicon*, where it is characterized as 'sustained thought on the causes, sources, manner and utility of things'. Meditation, Hugh claims, starts with reading but is not subject to its precepts. Rather, meditation wanders, creating larger and larger spaces of knowledge, seeking wider, deeper, and less obscure things, seeking ultimately to contemplate the truth. Furthermore, we can meditate on three kinds of things: morals, God's mandates, and God's works. Hugh does not say which one of these three is most important at this stage, but probably the idea is to balance them, not to meditate more on one to the detriment of the others. A similar call for balance is stressed in other place in the text where he explicitly warns against passing up virtue for study, but also, conversely, against passing up study. The student should seek virtue but should not forget about other aspects of learning. Clearly, for Hugh, the door is open to the study of *all* sciences, including those of nature and mathematics. It seems, furthermore, that it is in fact mandatory for the Christian to engage in the study of scientific disciplines without necessarily having to see those as mere preparation for the study of the Scriptures, as it was for Augustine in *De doctrina christiana*. From what we have seen, scientific disciplines in this context should mean simply disciplines that can be read and through which we can reach higher and higher states of *scientia*, spirituality, and intelligence: that is, disciplines through which we can arrive at wisdom.

The final goal of both reading and meditation is, in fact, wisdom. Indeed, Hugh (1939: I.1, 4.4–5) starts the first chapter of the *Didascalicon* with an emphatic affirmation: 'of all things that ought to be sought, the first is wisdom, in which the form of the perfect good consists'. We saw that he equated wisdom with intelligence in *De Unione*, and that this was the instrument at the highest level of knowledge possible, the closest to God. Here, Hugh expresses again the thought that wisdom is the highest, but now with a clearer moral imperative that is supported by the identification of wisdom with the form of the perfect good. Hugh does not elaborate on this identity, most probably because the statement was surely familiar and indeed fairly acceptable to educated Christians of his time. The sentence most certainly implies something further: that wisdom is identical with God Itself, specifically with Christ, the second person of the Trinity. This identification could have come to Hugh from Boethius and the commentary tradition. In any case, Hugh subscribes to a view very similar to that of Augustine regarding wisdom, although his justification uses the Boethian tradition.

There is another point of similarity between Hugh and Augustine in the early pages of the *Didascalicon*. According to Hugh, in reality all that man needs to know can be gained by him from knowledge of his own soul. Wisdom, Hugh claims, illuminates man so that he should know himself, and tells him how unbecoming it is for him to look outside. This is not precisely Augustine's theory of illumination, which, to recall, is the theory that the mind is capable of 'seeing' eternal forms because those are illuminated in a way that is similar to how material things are illuminated by natural light. The illumination that Hugh is talking about is just the simple realization that what man needs to seek and know is already inside the soul. Here, Hugh is talking to something more like the idea of conversion in Augustine, the idea that there should be a turning oneself (*conversio*) in the direction of what is important within the soul.

The key for Hugh, in any case, is that the soul in fact carries the likeness of all things, and in a way can be said to be made of everything. This is not to say that the soul has the composition of all things, but rather that it has the reason (*ratio*) of that composition. The likeness of things that is in the soul, Hugh adds, is not something given to the soul from outside, but rather something that the soul has of its own power. The soul, he says, is not like a wall on which the likeness of things is painted; it is like a piece of metal on which an image is engraved. The metal indeed assumes the image of the impression and starts to represent the thing impressed on it – like, say, the image in a coin – by its own power and ability. That is, the metal does not need anything external to it – as, for example, the paint is needed in a wall – to represent whatever is imprinted on it. The soul, Hugh says, has the similitude of every other thing, but virtually and potentially.

This can also be understood if we consider again Hugh's description of the process of knowing. In the case of the perception of external corporeal things, there is indeed an interaction between the 'purified' corporeal forms of things and the soul; however, at all times higher knowledge occurs exclusively in the realm of the spiritual or rational. Since higher and higher knowledge entails further purification from whatever is left of that interaction with the corporeal, in principle, by its own activity, the soul could attain knowledge without needing any corporeal element whatsoever. The 'input' to the purification process could be, for example, the activity of the soul itself, although Hugh does not explain this. What is certain is that there is no explicit requirement by Hugh for *scientia*, let alone contemplation and wisdom, to be based exclusively on the sensible.

But, warns Hugh (1939), man is made asleep by the corporeal passions and, carried out of himself by sensible forms, forgets what he is. This is, again, why doctrine and learning are important. Ultimately, 'we are recovered by doctrine, so that we may recognize our nature and so that we may learn not to seek outside what we can find in ourselves' (I.1, 6.7–9). Learning – that is, the acquisition of *scientia* – is thus a crucial element of help in the quest for man's goal in life. It is not strictly speaking necessary, but in practice it probably is. In principle, we can use our mental powers to accomplish the necessary purification of thoughts that would create intelligibles so close to the divine that, when God reveals itself we would attain *sapientia*.

Hugh, then, subscribes to a fairly clear Platonic view of *scientia*, being preoccupied at the same time with the actual kinds of knowledge that humans can attain. Most surely, he was not at all familiar with Aristotle's works beyond the *Organon*, and instead he used Boethius, Augustine, and surely other Platonic materials as the basis for his treatises.

Right around the time when Hugh was writing his *Didascalicon*, close to the middle of the twelfth century, as is also well known, a translation movement started to take shape that would provide the Latin West with the rest of the Aristotelian corpus and a sizeable amount of Arabic commentary. From a thirteenth-century perspective, it seems as if European thinkers almost suddenly threw away the old sources and embraced Aristotle's corpus wholeheartedly, the problem being that of how to deal with the Christian authorities. From a twelfth-century perspective, however, we see in people like Gundissalinus (and perhaps even in Hugh) a much softer landing for the newly acquired material and a struggle to present the new material in terms of the older tradition.

Gundissalinus was an important translator of Arabic texts in Toledo, together with Gerard of Cremona and John of Seville. However, he not only translated texts but produced treatises that aimed at incorporating Arabic sources into the Boethian/Augustinian tradition exemplified by people like Hugh. Among his works we find two treatises on the soul, a short treatise on unity, a metaphysical account of creation (*De processione mundi*), and the most important work for our purposes, *De Divisione Philosophiae*.

De Divisione, which was written in the 1140s, is similar to Hugh's *Didascalicon*, not only in its subject matter, but also generally in the manner in which its author makes use of the materials available to him. Both treatises are, for the most part, extended, carefully selected quotations from a variety of sources, joined together and given coherence by original text from the author. At first glance, indeed, *De Divisione* appears to be nothing but a rehash of texts by al-Fārābī, Avicenna, and some other figures. Upon more careful reading, however, it is obvious that the material has not been simply copied, but that the author has selected texts according to his own original idea of how the subject matter needs to be arranged and presented. We can thus speculate that Gundissalinus was not satisfied with the account and division of the sciences given by, for example, al-Fārābī, whose work would be the closest Arabic model, or by Hugh, although we do not know if Gundissalinus read the *Didascalicon*. In any case, it is clear that he wanted to provide his own account.

The main difference between the work of Gundissalinus and that of al-Fārābī lies in the fact that Gundissalinus, unlike al-Fārābī, did in fact provide an explicit and thorough, although sometimes not very clear, account of philosophy and its subdivisions, in an extended prologue. It is in the prologue where we see most clearly that Gundissalinus, in spite of having translated and studied the 'new' works of the Greeks and the Arabs, still belongs to an intellectual environment similar to that of Hugh of St. Victor.

Al-Fārābī's text in question is the *Book of the Enumeration of the Sciences* (*Kitāb iḥṣāʾ al-ʿulūm*),[9] in which he provides his own classification of the sciences known in his time and cultural environment. This cultural environment was the Arabic writing (al-Fārābī himself was not a native Arabic speaker), Abbasid, intellectual society at the turn of the tenth century in what is called by Gutas 'the second beginning of philosophy in Baghdad'.[10] The work was translated at least twice into Latin in Toledo. One translation was done probably by Gundissalinus himself or perhaps by John of Seville.[11]

The book is composed of a short preface or introduction, and five larger sections or chapters, each one of which deals with a major subdivision of disciplines and sub-disciplines. The first chapter concerns the science of language (*'ilm al-lisān*) – essentially grammar, but also including other linguistic knowledge such as prosody and correction in reading (a non-trivial matter in Arabic) and writing – while the second chapter is about logic (*'ilm al-manṭiq*). Both disciplines are presented as being instruments to the rest of the sciences. The next two chapters correspond, more or less, to the three major branches in the Aristotelian subdivision of the sciences. The third chapter is about mathematics (*'ilm al-ta'līm*), which includes not only the disciplines of the quadrivium, but also others such as optics, the science of weights and mechanics. The fourth chapter deals with the two other Aristotelian branches: physics (*'ilm al-ṭabī'ī*) and metaphysics (*'ilm al-ilāhī*), both essentially understood in the Aristotelian sense. The fifth and final chapter is about politics (*'ilm al-miḥnī*), law (*'ilm al-fiqh*), and Islamic theology (*'ilm al-kalām*). Gundissalinus uses a good deal of text from the first four chapters, and completely omits the preface and final chapter in *De Divisione*.

Al-Fārābī (1991) does not explain why he chose to present the sciences in this order, and with these subdivisions. The treatise might have been intended as the description of a curriculum for students, not as a philosophical defence or explanation of Aristotle's division of the sciences, or indeed of the author's modifications to it. One would expect the prologue to say something about this, but it does not. The short prologue, in fact, simply states the alleged purpose of the treatise: namely, to let the person who wants to learn and observe (*naẓara/speculor*) the sciences know where he is going, what kinds of things he is going to be looking at, and what will be the profit and excellence of the enterprise. The student can then compare the different sciences, and determine which one is more excellent, which more useful, which more solid and true, and which is weaker and more problematic. Also, al-Fārābī continues, the book serves to distinguish the pretenders from both those who are studious, as well as those who are truly wise. The pretenders cannot answer questions about the parts and contents of a science, while others who may be studious, although knowledgeable in one part or area, may not know the rest (prologue, ar:7, fr:43–5).

The idea is thus, in essence, to map out the different sciences within the presumably well-known and accepted Aristotelian division, which now includes other sciences developed in the Medieval Islamic world. Gundissalinus has a different goal for his *De Divisione*, so he does not use anything at all from al-Fārābī's prologue, and instead provides his own.

Gundissalinus begins his prologue by asserting the motivation for the treatise. This motivation is altogether different from al-Fārābī's, for in Gundissalinus' work there is an overarching goal: essentially, it has to do, in fact, with wisdom (*sapientia*). Gundissalinus begins by stating that, in ancient times, many wise men illuminated the darkness of the world in the same way that stars do. Those men left us the sciences, which, like little torches, illuminate the ignorance of our minds. Because people now are more preoccupied with worldly things, some people put their efforts into eloquence, while others are inflamed by temporal vanity. Gundissalinus laments that the study of wisdom is waning, as people now, like blind men, do not pay attention (*attendunt*) to the light. Thus the need for establishing what wisdom is and what are its parts, even if only expressing it superficially and showing it to people as a sort of degustation of the different parts. The hope is, Gundissalinus (1993: 1.4–17) says, that people will get a taste of supreme wisdom and, seduced by the flavour of its parts, demand the whole thing for themselves.

The idea is thus to entice men to attend to the light of wisdom, with wisdom clearly identified as being opposed to the mundane. This is, of course, in the same line as Augustine's views. The idea of the sciences illuminating men, and making them turn their attention away from the material to wisdom, is a powerful rhetorical device for readers accustomed to Augustinian fare. Gundissalinus transports the whole enterprise of the sciences, so that it comes to reside under the umbrella of wisdom. This is not to say that Gundissalinus is Augustinian, someone who, overall, follows Augustine's views; he is not. The point is simply that he is still well within an intellectual environment in which Augustine and Platonism in general are important.

The prologue continues with an account of the types of things to which man is attracted. This defines the main subdivisions of the sciences. Man is indeed primordially divided into flesh (*caro*) and spirit (*spiritus*). It is clear that man is attracted to some things on account of the flesh. Some of those things are attractive because they are necessary, others because they give pleasure, and others because of man's curiosity. Of these carnal things, Gundissalinus seems to hold the view that only those things that are strictly necessary for the body are good. In any case, these types of matters will not be referred to again in the treatise. Indeed, for Gundissalinus, philosophy and the sciences have to do only with the spiritual part of man, which, of course, is also Hugh's view. Man's spirit,

Gundissalinus continues, is attracted to three types of things as well. Of these, some are nocive, some are vain – magic and secular honours, for instance – and some are useful.[12] The latter are divided into virtues and 'noble science' (*scientia honesta*), and in fact, Gundissalinus affirms, 'the whole perfection of the human being' consists of these two (5.1).[13]

Noble science is divided into two main branches: divine and human science (*divina et humana scientia*). Divine science is none other than the Scriptures, but Gundissalinus will not mention this again in the treatise. When he talks of divine science later in the text, he is clearly and unequivocally referring to Aristotle's theology. There is no room for confusion, because the context in each case is very clear. It is clear as well that the Scriptures are taken to be, as was the case for Hugh, one of the major parts of knowledge as a whole, and that the essential distinguishing attribute between divine and human science is the source of that knowledge – that is, God directly, in the case of the Scriptures, and man, in the case of human science. Therefore, it is not necessarily of consequence which faculty in the soul is at play when a human accesses that knowledge.[14] Human science, however, is the proper subject matter of the work, and is characterized as that knowledge that 'is recognized to be discovered by human reason, like all arts that are called liberal' (5.8–11). The liberal arts do not constitute *all* of the sciences for Gundissalinus, as is clear from the fact that he dealt with many other disciplines outside the trivium and quadrivium, but they seem to be paradigmatic examples of what a science is. Furthermore, arts, including the liberal arts, are of two kinds: those that deal with eloquence, like grammar, poetics, rhetoric, and human law; and those that are concerned properly with wisdom, that is, those that either illuminate the human soul towards the knowledge of truth, or kindle the love of goodness. Those arts, in fact, constitute the sciences of philosophy (5.14–16). Gundissalinus does not explain the exact nature of the relationship between these two kinds of science. It is not, in any case, the main aspect of subdivision of the sciences that he wants to propound, and thus, perhaps, he only wanted to emphasize again the primacy of wisdom. Some disciplines would then have a higher status, resulting from how significantly they contribute to that ultimate goal.

Next in the prologue is an account of philosophy itself, which Gundissalinus takes from Isaac ben Solomon Israeli's (c. 832–c. 932) *Liber de Definicionibus*. Isaac Israeli was a Jewish thinker who wrote in Arabic, and about whom we do not know many biographical details. Besides a number of medical works, there are several extant philosophical works preserved in a number of manuscripts in Arabic, and in translations into Hebrew and Latin. He was quoted by Jewish and

Latin philosophers even in the thirteenth century. The *Liber de Definicionibus* was apparently translated twice in Toledo by the same people who translated al-Fārābī's *Enumeration of the Sciences* and in similar circumstances: there is an incomplete translation attributed to Gundissalinus, and then a complete one by Gerard of Cremona. Quotations drawn from these works are found even in works of thirteenth-century writers such as Albert the Great and Thomas Aquinas.[15] The passages selected by Gundissalinus serve only to support the general thesis that he did not, in fact, want to deviate from the traditional line, even if Isaac's work belongs to a different tradition. Gundissalinus could have chosen to stress the differences between the new texts and the textual tradition that he inherited – Boethius, Augustine, Isidore, and others – but he did not.[16]

Gundissalinus begin his quotation of Isaac's account of philosophy with the affirmation that there are indeed two kinds of definitions to be given for philosophy, one from its effect (*ex effectu*), the other from its properties (*ex proprietate*). According to the latter definition, philosophy is the 'assimilating (*assimilacio*) of the human to the work of the creator according to human virtue' (Gundissalinus 1993: 6.1–2; = Israeli 1937–38: 303.4–6). The assimilating of something to the work of the creator is defined, without further explanation, as the perception of the truth of things – the truth of the cognition of the things, Isaac says, and of their operation according to what agrees with the truth (1993: 6.2–4; = Israeli 1937–38: 303.6–8). It is not exactly clear how this *assimilacio* is related to a perception of the truth, but in any case Isaac immediately adds that this perception amounts to grasping the four natural causes of things. Staying with Isaac's text, Gundissalinus then provides an account of the four causes: material, formal, efficient, and final. Each one, except the material cause, he says, is of two modes, corporeal and spiritual. A corporeal final cause is like, for example, that of a house, which is made so that somebody can live in it; a spiritual final cause is like that of the union of body and soul in man, which, Isaac says, is made so that truth is manifested to the man, and so that he can discern between right and wrong (Gundissalinus 1993: 6.24–7.3; = Israeli 1937–38: 304.10–20). This distinction, very puzzling in itself, is useful for Gundissalinus, because it lets him stress the idea of *scientia* as having to do fundamentally with man being the union of flesh and spirit. The corporeal part of man has a role to play in *scientia*, because a part of *scientia* is in fact about man's corporeal life. After introducing Isaac's definitions, Gundissalinus can then, relatively smoothly, refer back to one of Isidore's (1911: II.24.1–9) definitions: namely, that philosophy is the knowledge of human and divine things, together with the study of living well. Philosophy *ex effectu*, however, is, as Gundissalinus (1993: 7.17–18) states next (quoting anew from Isaac), the integral cognition by a human being of himself.[17] This is so because man, being a conjunct of body and soul, has, in principle, a sort of immediate access to all that is, both substance and accident. This is, of course, the same idea put forth by Augustine and Hugh, that is, that wisdom can, in principle, be attained by following the traditional motto: 'Know thyself.' Gundissalinus certainly found in Isaac a source that is to some extent continuous with ideas of this kind.

Something similar can be gathered from the explanation that Gundissalinus brings up, again quoting from Isaac, as to how philosophy is called 'love of wisdom'. The key obviously lies in what we take wisdom to be. Here Isaac, and thus Gundissalinus, characterizes wisdom, as he had done with philosophy, *ex effectu* and *ex proprietate*. According to its property, wisdom is described as 'the truth of knowledge (*scientia*) of first sempiternal things' (Gundissalinus 1993: 8.18–19; = Israeli 1937–38: 307.3–4). The first sempiternal things are, in turn, characterized as things that are eternal by their nature 'such as the species, which are the end and the complement of generation, the genera, which are superior to them, the genera of the genera, until one reaches the truly first genus which is created from the power of the Creator without mediator' (Gundissalinus 1993: 8.19–22; = Israeli 1937–38: 307.4–9). Truth, for its part, is simply that which is (*id quod est*), as opposed to falsehood, which is that which is not some thing (*id quod non est aliquid*). The passage is obscure, yet we can gather at least that wisdom is, for Isaac, ultimately intellectual in nature, and has to do with getting as close as possible to the Creator. For Gundissalinus, of course, the Creator must be God; therefore wisdom is, again just as for Augustine and Hugh, getting as close as possible to God, which in turn implies knowing the first genera of all things. There is still a gap between the wise man and God, for the wise man in this account is acquainted not with God Himself, but with the first, eternal, immediately created genus. Wisdom is not, therefore, actually partaking in God's nature; it is one's maximally approximating Him – a state of contemplation, not of identification.

Wisdom *ex effectu* is described as the completion of intellectual virtue, so that it arrives at correct judgements, say, of truth and falsity, or of what is possible, impossible, and necessary, without any type of sophism (Gundissalinus 1993: 9.14–17).[18] Gundissalinus' text here is difficult to decipher. Here again we have an obscure passage that he takes from Isaac, but this time as a close paraphrase instead of a direct quotation. In Isaac's text, as translated by Gerard of Cremona, there follows an account of eight different kinds of sophisms that the wise man should be able to recognize and avoid. This account is not in

Gundissalinus. It is made clearer in that account that the idea is that whoever has wisdom has that extra capacity to sort out propositions, and thus to be able to tell right from wrong.

Thus wisdom also serves to make the person more intellectually virtuous. One of the implications of this view seems to be that, for Gundissalinus, the wise man is not 'up there', entranced, so to speak, with knowledge of the first eternal things – in the contemplation of God. Rather, the wise man continues to live, and wisdom causes there to be this particular virtuous effect on him. Isaac's texts may have served Gundissalinus precisely because they convey an idea of wisdom that is much more integrated with *scientia*, since, in some way, wisdom is both a looking up to God, yet also entails keeping one's feet on the ground. It is not surprising then, that, in winding up this section on philosophy in his prologue, Gundissalinus states that the intention of philosophy is to grasp the truth of all the things that are, to the fullest extent that is possible to man (Gundissalinus 1993: 9.21–2). Gundissalinus has thus established that philosophy is noble *scientia* of the human type – as opposed to divine *scientia*, that is, the Scriptures – and that it is primarily about gaining knowledge of first eternal things, the mission requirement being to know all things as well as possible.

He then begins his general account of how the different disciplines are classified. The general classification is none other than Aristotle's division into practical and theoretical sciences, each of which is in turn divided into three types – natural, mathematical, and divine, in the case of the theoretical. Before stating that classification scheme, however, Gundissalinus tries to explain how this classification originates, with the help mainly of sporadic quotations from al-Ġazālī, Avicenna, and Boethius.[19] The sciences are divided just as things are divided, and since things can be made by humans or not made by humans, one part of science is about human action, the practical, and other about the rest, the theoretical.

The theoretical sciences get much more attention than the practical, but Gundissalinus seems here to be struggling with the collation of his sources. His goal seems to be that of explaining Aristotle's tripartite division of the theoretical sciences as originating from a division of things, just as he had done with the practical-theoretical distinction. He starts with a long quotation from Avicenna. However, Avicenna's division does not seem to help him to arrive at what he wants in a straightforward manner; so he chooses to present an alternative view, taken from al-Ġazālī's *Metaphysics*, in which things are distinguished, first, on the basis how they actually exist, whether inside or outside of matter and motion, and, second, in how they are understood, whether they are associated with matter or not. Gundissalinus then ties this to Aristotle's tripartite division of the theoretical sciences, by quoting again from Avicenna: one part of the sciences, physics, is speculation about those things that are not separated from their matter, either in being or in understanding (*in intellectu*); another, mathematics, is speculation about things separated from matter in understanding but not in being; and yet another one, theology or metaphysics, is speculation of things separated from matter both in being and in understanding (Gundissalinus 1993: 14.19–15.6). He then brings up Boethius to back this up, but, surprisingly, misquotes him to make it appear as though Boethius, Avicenna, and al-Ġazālī agree completely.[20]

The subsection on the theoretical sciences ends with a short account of their utility. It is new text taken from al-Ġazālī, but it should not sound discordant to ears accustomed to hearing from the likes of Augustine and Boethius. The utility of the theoretical sciences is, Gundissalinus quotes, to know the dispositions of all the things that have being, so that the forms of everything get traced in our souls according to their own order, just as visible form is traced in a mirror. That tracing or drawing of forms into our souls is supposed to be of the same perfection as the soul itself, because the soul's ability to receive that image or tracing is in fact one of its properties (Gundissalinus 1993: 15.16–23; = al-Ġazālī 1933: 2.3–9). This account, in fact, resembles the idea that Hugh brought up in the *Didascalicon* – and also, in a general sense, in his theory of knowledge – of the soul being capable of receiving and internalizing the forms of things as some sort of imprint.

This, in any case, completes the theoretical sciences, and so brings us next in the prologue to an account of the practical sciences. These are, however, quickly taken care of, simply by stating that they are divided into ethics, family affairs, and political science. Hugh (1939: II.19, 37–8) also dispensed with explaining the practical sciences in great detail, and instead presented them in essentially the same terms as Gundissalinus does. The prologue ends with a short introductory discussion of logic, the technical details of which will be discussed at greater length later in *De Divisione*. The rest of the book is a fairly detailed description of the different scientific disciplines following mainly al-Fārābī, as pointed out before.

Both Gundissalinus and Hugh, as we have seen, try to give support to a Platonic view of *scientia*. Hugh develops a more explicitly Platonic theory of knowledge, involving the purification of being across the material and spiritual realms, stressing the material/spiritual distinction in spite of the philosophical problems that it entails. Hugh may have already had access to materials newly available to the Latin West, but, in any case, his theory is firmly grounded in the Platonic tradition of the likes of Augustine and Boethius. Gundissalinus, however, was a major figure in the translation of Arabic texts into Latin, but he also, in his own treatises, defends the Platonic tradition by carefully adding his own views and selecting the material in such a way as to try to give the impression that thinkers as diverse as Avicenna, al-Ġazālī, and Boethius would all agree. In the end, the twelfth-century view of *scientia* as an important intellectual requisite to the attainment of wisdom, with the body a given but itself the cause of problems, is never challenged.

Notes

1 An English translation can be found in Aristotle (1984: vol. 1).
2 For a general account, see Crombie (1995: ch. 1).
3 See, for example, the case of the so-called School of Chartres (Speer 1997). The Chartrians, who probably were not really part of any school, talk about 'scientific' topics, but do not offer any particularly influential view on *scientia*. For more on the School of Chartres, see Ellard (2007).
4 For a general account, see Pedersen (1997).
5 Abelard is, however, notoriously absent from these discussions.
6 For a thorough explanation of this, see Menn (1998: esp. 144–66).
7 Hugh's discussion has some similarities with Augustine's discussion of the elements in *De Genesi ad litteram* III.4–5. Augustine also claims that the elements are somehow implicated in the process of sense perception. Fire, being the most volatile, is also for him the closest to the spiritual. Just like Hugh, Augustine claims, however, that the realm of the spiritual and the realm of the corporeal are two separate kinds.
8 This passage seems to include also both an appropriation of, and a response to, newly translated medical texts. There were translations of Arab and Greek works already in the mid-eleventh century in places like Salerno, Italy. According to Liccaro (1979), Hugh in *De Unione* is indeed responding to one of those translations – namely, a collection of ten books on medicine attributed to Isaac ben Israeli and translated by Constantine the African in Salerno. In book IV of this collection, it is said that every spirit is of three kinds: natural, spiritual, and animal. Most of the functions usually attributed to parts or aspects of the soul are explained as the movement of animal spirit, which is identified as moving through the nerves and that seems to belong squarely within the realm of the corporeal, throughout the different parts of the brain: memory in the back, sense and fantasy in the front, and reason and intellect in the middle. Hugh retains this idea of the localization of

the activities in the brain. Authors such as William of Conches, Liccaro says, would embrace this kind of theory as well, and would try to take such theories into account in their own views about issues such as the relation between the world-soul and the human soul. Hugh, however, wants to make it very clear that there is no conversion from the corporeal to the intellectual.

9 Arabic versions with translations into French and Spanish can be found in al-Fārābī (1953, 1991).

10 The 'first' beginning happened a century earlier and has al-Kindi as its main figure (Gutas 2009: 24–5). For a general introduction to al-Fārābī, see Fakhry (2002).

11 John of Seville is also known as Johannes Hispalensis. His version does not translate all the Arabic text. González-Palencia (1953: xi–xii), whose edition includes both Latin versions, ascribes this first translation to either Gundissalinus or John of Seville, based only on the fact that Gundissalinus' own *De Divisione Philosophiae* includes extended literal quotation from it. The second translation is by Gerard of Cremona and is very literal and complete. Gerard of Cremona is also an important translator of Aristotle's works from Arabic sources; he lived in Toledo, where he died in 1187. See Dod (1982: 58).

12 Hugh of St. Victor (1939: III.2, 49–52) also talked briefly about magic, distinguishing it from astronomy, and providing arguments to show that it was indeed a vain discipline. Although Gundissalinus does not say anything substantial about the issue, he agrees with Hugh on its 'moral' status. Hugh's remarks made it into Kilwardby's *De Ortu Scientarum* (1976: ch. 67, 225–6) more than a century later.

13 Gundissalinus does not explain what he means by *scientia honesta*. He seems to imply that there is some other kind of science with negative connotations, but there is no mention of this in the text.

14 Some scholars have insisted on seeing in this main division a radical distinction between a human, rational, philosophical wisdom, and a theological, Christian wisdom. For instance, Fidora (2003: 27–8) seems to agree with van Steenberghen. For Gundissalinus, as well as for Hugh and Augustine, as should be clear, there is only one wisdom. There are, however, two kinds of *scientia* for Gundissalinus, but, as previously stated, they are distinguished by their source, and not by the human faculty or methods involved. Furthermore, we cannot really affirm that only human science is rational. Gundissalinus does not say anything about the methods of divine science, which is still referred to as *sacra pagina* and not yet as theology, as it would be in the thirteenth century. Nevertheless, he probably agreed with both Augustine and Hugh, in that the main method at play is the interpretation of texts in which human reason is indeed important, not for the actual generation of the contents of that knowledge – since God is taken to be the author – but presumably for the discovery of what God actually meant.

15 A thorough account of Isaac's biography and the textual tradition of most of his extant philosophical works, together with an English translation and commentary on his most significant writings, as well as a study of Isaac's philosophy, can be found in Altmann and Stern (2009). Gerard of Cremona's translation is in Isaac Israeli (1937–38). In what follows, I give references to that edition.

16 Isaac's major influence is al-Kindi (Altmann and Stern 2009: xviii). Obviously, there could have been other factors involved in choosing this text in particular. For example, it could have been the only one available to him for this particular doctrine. However, Isaac's text can in fact be seen as an elaborate Aristotelian account of some of the ideas that we saw deployed by Hugh as well, thus confirming a certain continuity of thought with Gundissalinus.

17 This corresponds to Isaac Israeli (1937–38: 306.2–3). Here, Isaac's text in Latin translation differs minimally.

18 This corresponds roughly to Isaac Israeli (1937–38: 307.27–308.3).

19 From al-Ġazālī, Gundissalinus uses the work that is generally known as al-Ġazālī's *Metaphysics* and that he translated – probably with the help of John of Seville – from the original Arabic *Maqāṣid al-falāsifa* (or *The Aims of the Philosophers*). For some time there were doubts among scholars regarding the status and authorship of this work, because its contents go against al-Ġazālī's philosophical commitments in other works. The work is, in fact, al-Ġazālī's exposition of the ideas of the philosophers whom he will attack in his *Tahāfut al-falāsifa* (Salman 1935: 103–27). The Latin translation appears in al-Ġazālī (1933). Gundissalinus' quotations from Avicenna come from the *Logic*, which is part of Avicenna's massive treatise *Kitāb al-Shifāʾ*. The Latin translation can be found in Avicenna (1961).

20 The passage in question is from *De Trinitate* II.5–16 (Boethius 2005). Gundissalinus subtly changes a few words in the text so that the quotation agrees with Avicenna and al-Ġazālī, but in fact this would be the opposite of Boethius' view. Where Boethius says that mathematics is without motion unabstract (*sine motu inabstracta*), Gundissalinus writes that, for Boethius, mathematics is abstract with motion. This passage from Boethius, in fact, was seen as problematic by other thinkers of the twelfth century. Thierry of Chartres, Gilbert of Poitiers, and Clarembald of Arras were puzzled by Boethius' use of the words 'abstracta' and 'inabstracta'. It seems odd to say that mathematics is unabstract. For a detailed discussion of these authors regarding this issue, see Fidora (2003: 40–1). Merlan (1953: 71–3) also deals with different medieval interpretations of Boethius.

References

al-Fārābī (1953), *Catálogo de Las Ciencias*, trans. Á. González-Palencia, Madrid: Maestre.

al-Fārābī (1991), *Iḥṣā' El-ʿulūm*, trans. Ilham Mansour and Ra's Bayrut, Lebanon: Markaz al-Inmā' al-Qawmīk.

al-Ġazālī (1933), *Algazel's Metaphysics: A Mediaeval Translation*, ed. J. T. Muckle, Toronto: St. Michael's Medieval Studies.

Altmann, A. and Stern, S. M. (2009), *Isaac Israeli: A Neoplatonic Philosopher of the Early Tenth Century*, Chicago: University of Chicago Press.

Aristotle (1984), *The Complete Works of Aristotle: The Revised Oxford Translation*, ed. J. Barnes, Princeton: Princeton University Press.

Augustine (1962), *De doctrina christiana*, ed. J. Martin, Corpus Christianorum Series Latina 32, Turnhout: Brepols.

Augustine (1968), *De Trinitate*, ed. W. J. Mountain and Fr Glorie, Corpus Christianorum Series Latina 50–50a, Turnhout: Brepols.

Augustine (1969), *De Musica*, ed. G. Marzi, Firenze: Sansoni.

Augustine (1970), *De Libero Arbitrio*, ed. W. M. Green, Corpus Christianorum Series Latina 29, Turnhout: Brepols.

Augustine (1981), *Confessiones*, ed. M. Skutella, H. Juergens, and W. Schaub, Stuttgart: Teubner.

Augustine (1984), *Retractationvm Libri II*, ed. A. Mutzenbecher, Corpus Christianorum Series Latina 57, Turnhout: Brepols.

Avicenna (1961), *Opera Philosophica*, Louvain: Edition de la bibliotèque S.J.

Boethius (2005), 'De Trinitate', in Claudio Moreschini (ed.), *De Consolatione Philosophiae, Opuscula Theologica*, 2nd edn, Munich: K.G. Saur Verlag, 165–81.

Crombie, A. C. (1995), *The History of Science: From Augustine to Galileo*, New York: Dover.

Dod, B. G. (1982), 'Aristoteles Latinus', in N. Kretzmann, A. Kenny, and J. Pinborg (eds), *The Cambridge History of Later Medieval Philosophy*, Cambridge: Cambridge University Press.

Ellard, P. (2007), *The Sacred Cosmos: Theological, Philosophical, and Scientific Conversations in the Twelfth Century School of Chartres*, Scranton and London: University of Scranton Press.

Fakhry, M. (2002), *Al-Fārābī, Founder of Islamic Neoplatonism*, Oxford: One World.

Fidora, A. (2003), *Die Wissenschaftstheorie des Dominicus Gundissalinus*, Berlin: Akademie Verlag.

González-Palencia, Á. (1953), 'Prólogo', in *Catálogo de Las Ciencias*, Madrid: Maestre.

Grosseteste, R. (1981), *Commentarius in Posteriorum Analyticorum Libros*, ed. P. Rossi, Firenze: L.S. Olschki.

Gundissalinus (1993), *De Divisione Philosophiae*, ed. L. Baur. Münster: Aschendorff.

Gutas, D. (2009), 'Origins in Baghdad', in R. Pasnau (ed.), *The Cambridge History of Medieval Philosophy*, Cambridge: Cambridge University Press.

Hugh of St. Victor (1854), *De Unione Corporis et Spiritus*, ed. J. P. Migne, Patrologia Latina, 175, Paris: Garnier, 285–94.

Hugh of St. Victor (1939), *Hugonis de Sancto Victore Didascalicon: De Studio Legendi*, ed. C. H. Buttimer, Washington, DC: Catholic University Press.

Hugh of St. Victor (1980), *Il 'De Unione Corporis et Spiritus' Di Ugo Di San Vittore*, ed. A. M. Piazzoni. Studi Medievali, 3rd Series, 1: 861–8.

Isaac of Israeli (1937–38), *Liber de Definicionibus*, ed. J. T. Muckle, Archives D'histoire Doctrinale et Litteraire Du Moyen Age, 12.

Isidore of Seville (1911), *Isidori Hispalensis Episcopi: Etymologiarvm Sive Originvm Libri XX*, ed. W. M. Lindsay, Oxford: Clarendon Press.

John of Salisbury (1929), *Ioannis Saresberiensis Episcopo Carnotensis Metalogicon Libri IV*, ed. C. C. J. Webb, Oxford: Clarendon Press.

Kilwardby, R. (1976), *De Ortu Scientiarum*, Toronto: The Pontifical Institute of Mediaeval Studies.

Liccaro, V. (1979), 'Ugo Di San Vittore Di Fronte Alle Novita Delle Traduzioni Delle Opere Scientifiche Greche E Arabe', *Actas del V congreso internacional de Filosofía Medieval*, vol. II, 919–26.

Menn, S. (1998), *Descartes and Augustine*, Cambridge: Cambridge University Press.

Merlan, P. (1953), *From Platonism to Neoplatonism*, The Hague: Martinus Nijhoff.

Pedersen, O. (1997), *The First Universities*, Cambridge: Cambridge University Press.

Salman, D. (1935), 'Algazel et Les Latins', *Archives d'Histoire Doctrinale et Littéraire Du Moyen Age*, 10–11: 103–27.

Speer, A. (1997), 'The Discovery of Nature: The Contribution of the Chartrians to 12th Century Attempts to Found a "Scientia Naturalis"', *Traditio*, 52: 135–51.

3

Averroes on the Attainment of Knowledge

Richard Taylor

1. Introduction

The Muslim philosopher, jurist, and physician Ibn Rushd of Cordoba, known to the Latin world as Averroes (d. 1198 CE), is perhaps best known to modern students of the history of philosophy of knowledge as an Aristotelian thinker who professed the shockingly novel and seemingly bizarre epistemological doctrine of a single, separately existing, immaterial substance shared by all humankind. It is easily evident that he meant to be Aristotelian through and through in his various commentaries on the works of Aristotle, for he simply held that of all human beings Aristotle was unsurpassed: 'I believe that this man was a model in nature and the exemplar which nature found for showing the final human perfection in the material realm.'[1] That there are well-reasoned arguments for his doctrine of the separate material intellect is no less apparent in his late *Long Commentary on the* De Anima *of Aristotle* (c. 1186, translated by Michael Scot in Sicily at the Court of Frederick II c. 1220), in which that precise doctrine is first spelled out in detail. Yet Averroes was a dynamic thinker whose thought shifted and changed with further study and reflection over many years. He wrote seven or more works touching on issues concerning human intellect and the attainment of knowledge, including an early *Short Commentary* or *Epitome of the* De Anima (1160s) and a later paraphrasing *Middle Commentary on the* De Anima (perhaps c. 1174 or later), with these two works presenting very different accounts. However, the *Long Commentary on the* De Anima *of Aristotle* and his early *Commentary on the* Parva Naturalia (1170) were the only works on epistemology by Averroes known to European thinkers of the thirteenth century such as Thomas Aquinas. Well known for his critique of Averroes in his *On the Unity of the Intellect Against the Averroists* (c. 1270) and in other works, Aquinas nevertheless developed much of his earliest account of natural epistemology from study of Averroes and Avicenna under the influence of his teacher, Albert the Great.

In what follows, I first provide accounts of the early theories of knowledge set out by Averroes in his *Short Commentary on the* De Anima and *Commentary on the* Parva Naturalia and in his *Middle Commentary on the* De Anima. I then turn to his famous *Long Commentary on the* De Anima *of Aristotle* to explain his mature theory and the philosophical issues that it was meant to address and resolve. I follow this by setting out an account of the importance of his mature *Long Commentary* for the development of the natural epistemologies of Albert and Thomas. I conclude with some brief remarks on intellectual abstraction in the medieval Arabic tradition and its influence, and with a question about the price of abstractionism.

2. Averroes' *Short Commentary on the* De Anima

Leading philosophical predecessors such as al-Farabi (d. 950) and Avicenna (d. 1037), as well as Averroes himself and many others of the philosophical tradition in the lands of Islam, were powerfully influenced in their study of natural epistemology in Aristotle by the interpretations of the Aristotelian Greek commentators Alexander of Aphrodisias (fl. c. 200) and Themistius (d. 387). Decisive in this was Alexander's imposition of a doctrine of intellectual abstraction onto the teachings of Aristotle. Aristotle had explained that sensation apprehends particular things of the physical world by separating them from matter.[2] However, the complete separation of the essence of a thing intelligible in potency from its matter and particularity, such that the mind could grasp the intelligible in act as universal and predicable of many, is another consideration altogether. To support the affirmation of human attainment of scientific knowledge, Aristotle (1984: 3.5) proposed that the making of what is intelligible in potency (the experienced particulars) into intelligible in act required the assistance of an immortal and eternal intellect itself in act. Yet just how this takes place remained underdetermined and never sufficiently explicated by Aristotle.[3] This lacuna, however, was filled by Alexander who proposed that the intellect in act provides the power for separating the essence to be received into the receptive mortal human mind that he labelled 'material intellect'. That separating (*chōrizōn*, Arabic *yufridu-hā*) he labelled abstraction (*aphraisesei*, Arabic *ifrād*), and attributed to the intellect in act which he identified with God in his *On the Intellect* (1887: 106–13).[4] In his *Paraphrase of the* De Anima *of Aristotle*, Themistius adopts the notion of intellectual abstraction set out by Alexander as central to his account of Aristotle. For him, however, it is not God, but a separate productive or agent intellect already full of forms or ideas as intelligibles in act, that supervenes and penetrates the human being's collection of particular intelligibles in potency to guide and assist the human being in the abstraction of intelligibles in act.[5] The teachings of Alexander on abstraction deeply influenced the reading of the works of Aristotle for the entire Arabic tradition and those in the *Paraphrase* of Themistius were perhaps important for Avicenna and most certainly foundational for Averroes,[6] though both these philosophers thoroughly rethought the issues for themselves.

In his *Epitome* or *Short Commentary on the* De Anima, Averroes crafted an account of human intellectual understanding largely under the influence of Alexander of Aphrodisias and the Andalusian philosopher Ibn Bajjah (d. 1138), a novel account spelled out to some extent in his *Commentary* or *Epitome of the* Parva Naturalia. The reports of the external senses are gathered and unified in the common sense to produce particular images in the imagination. The human power of imagination, however, differs from that in other animals because it has a receptivity for intelligibles. Hence, '[t]he imaginative soul is distinguished by the fact that it does not need an organic instrument for its activity'.[7] Nevertheless, though the imagination is not an organ, it is still a bodily power gathering in itself images that are particular and still bearing the affects of materiality. Consequently, there is need for the agent intellect to be 'in the soul' in a way as a formal actuality[8] for the abstraction or separation of the content of the imagination and to create intelligibles in act which are the content of human knowledge of eternal essences. Yet those essences as abstracted cannot be received into the imagination itself without being immediately particularized by their subject, the particular imagination. Following Alexander and Ibn Bajjah, Averroes then conceives of the material intellect, the required receptive power belonging to the human subject of these intelligibles, not to be the imagination but rather a disposition (*istiʿdād, epitēdeiotēs*) of the particular images or forms in the imagination. The sense of this is that the so-called material intellect can be receptive of abstracted intelligibles in act because its existence is epiphenomenal upon the mixture of bodily parts and not directly in itself constructed of matter. This notion, derived from Alexander's *De Intellectu* and developed by Ibn Bajjah, allows the intelligibles in act to be received into an immaterial subject as required by their own immaterial natures (Alexander 1887: 112.11–16).[9]

This teaching, or something close to it, is set out in Averroes' *Epitome of the* Parva Naturalia, in his discussion of dreams and how separate intellects that know only universals could possibly send universal intelligibles in act into particular human minds. Averroes handles it in a way that is similar to what he does in the *Short Commentary on the* De Anima. Since universals sent from any separate and immaterial intellect cannot be received as universals without becoming particularized images in the particular human imagination belonging to the human knower, the universals could be received into the imagination only as particulars. The solution used seems to be a version of the account in the *Short Commentary*. The universal coming from the Agent intellect is received by the soul as particular in the individual soul but 'is related to that universal' (Averroes 1972: 80.6; English translation: 1961: 47). In the *Short Commentary*, this means that the material intellect is a disposition of the forms in the particular human imagination. Perhaps we can describe this by saying that the particular in the imagination comes to have a qualification relating to universality, such that the particular can be seen under a mode or consideration of universality, though Averroes does not spell all this out here or in the *Short Commentary*. What is in the imagination, then, can in some way stand for the universal, though the universal as such cannot be received into a particular human imagination without being particularized and no longer being universal. Universals in this way are received as particulars into the particular imagination and its particular circumstances. What is received is received in the mode of the recipient. So, what the individual receives is an individual spiritual (*ruḥānī*) form that is similar to the intelligible which, it seems, must function as a representation of the intelligible while also bearing some content similarity to what is in the intelligible (Averroes 1972: 81–2; English translation: 1961: 47–8). Averroes was well aware that this theory entailed that, with the death of the body and end of a functioning imagination, the epiphenomenal material intellect drops out of existence. That is, he was aware that this philosophical account left no room for philosophical reasoning in favour of a post-mortem existence of the human being or its soul or intellect.

This account is interesting today, since it verges on denying for human beings the reality of intelligibles in act or universals as real entities or real accidents in the mind, and proposes that for human beings these exist only as a mode of consideration regarding images in a perishable mind. To have knowledge of the universal is to be able to predicate something of many particulars, and a non-realist account would seem to be satisfactory. However, such a notion was too far ahead of its time for Averroes. Instead of moving towards a novel nominalist conception, he returned to the notion of the material intellect as a true intellect.

3. Averroes' *Middle Commentary on the* De Anima

For the most part, the *Middle Commentary* consists of a paraphrasing account of Aristotle's *De Anima*, although there is an intriguing excursus on intellect. Here Averroes (2002: 116 [sec. 297–8]) sets forth a view of the agent intellect that is similar to that of the *Short Commentary*, insofar as the constitution of the human intellect involves a composition of the individual human material intellect and the shared agent intellect with this latter coming to be 'in' human beings as 'form for us'. It is through the intellectual abstractive power of the agent intellect that individual human beings are able to come to understand the worldly essences presented to the internal senses through sense perception:

> It is clear that, in one respect, this intellect is an agent and, in another, it is form for us (*ṣūrah la-nā*), since the generation of intelligibles is a product of our will. When we want to think something, we do so, our thinking it being nothing other than, first, bringing the intelligible forth and, second, receiving it. The individual intentions in the imaginative faculty are they that stand in relation to the intellect as potential colors do to light. That is, this intellect renders them actual intelligibles after their having been intelligible in potentiality. It is clear, from the nature of this intellect – which, in one respect, is form for us (*ṣūrah la-nā*) and, in another, is the agent for the intelligibles – that it is separable and neither generable nor corruptible, for that which acts is always superior to that ¯ which is acted upon, and the principle is superior to the matter. The intelligent and intelligible aspects of this intellect are essentially the same thing, since it does not think anything external to its essence. There must be an agent intellect here, since that which actualizes the intellect has to be an intellect, the agent endowing only that which resembles what is in its substance. (116 [sec. 297]; translation modified)

This understanding takes place through the reception of intelligibles in act into the receptive material intellect. However, the conception of the material intellect in this work is very different from that of the *Short Commentary*.

Averroes provides a new analysis of the nature of the material intellect as a subject for intelligibles in act and of its relationship to the human soul, in his account of rational power corresponding to *De Anima* 3.4–8. Disregarding the *Short Commentary*'s understanding of the material intellect as identified with a disposition of the forms in the imagination, Averroes insists that, insofar as it is a real intellect, the material intellect 'cannot be mixed with the subject in which it is found.' The reason is that, if that were so, 'the forms of things would not exist in the intellect as they really are – that is, the forms existing in the intellect would be changed into forms different from the actual forms. If, therefore, the nature of the intellect is to receive the forms of things which have retained their natures, it is necessary that it be a faculty unmixed with any form whatsoever' (Averroes 2002: 109 [sec. 278]). That is, the nature of intellectually understood intelligibles in act dictates that they be received into a subject that is unmixed with the body or powers of a body or any other form. Consequently, the material intellect cannot be a disposition of the forms of the imagination but must rather be immaterial and yet also receptive. Averroes writes:

> Both approaches to the material intellect have thus been explained to you – that of Alexander and that of the others – and it will have become clear to you that the truth, which is the approach of Aristotle, is a combination of both views, in the manner we have mentioned. For, by our position as stated, we are saved from positing something separate in its substance as a certain disposition, positing [instead] that the disposition found in it is not due to its [own] nature but due to its conjunction with a substance which has this disposition essentially – namely, man – while, in positing that something here is associated incidentally with this disposition, we are saved from [considering] the intellect in potentiality as a disposition only. (112 [sec. 285])[10]

That is, the material intellect is not merely a disposition attached to the forms of the imagination; rather, it is an immaterial disposition belonging to a human being who comes to be knowing through the actualization in being of that disposition by the abstractive power of the separate agent intellect. But how is that attachment of an unmixed and immaterial power, the material intellect, to the human being to be conceived?

For his understanding of the relationship of the human being to the material intellect, Averroes considers it to be analogous to his understanding of celestial entities – namely, the celestial bodies which the celestial souls are 'in' (scil., intrinsically associated with) and the intellects which are the causes of the movement of the celestial bodies by their souls – as Marc Geoffroy has rightly pointed out (Averroes 2001: 64–5, 71ff.). In the case of the eternal heavens, the moving body and its soul are not composed hylomorphically as are transitory sublunar beings. Rather, the soul is 'in' the celestial body without forming a single hylomorphic composite from the two, each of which is an eternal being. In the case of humans, the material intellect is not literally 'in' the body, the soul or the human composed of the two, since the material intellect must remain unmixed to be receptive of intelligibles without distortion by preexisting formalities or matter, taken literally. Hence, an individual material intellect belongs to and exists 'in' the human soul. To this extent, the power of soul called 'material intellect' has its existence and individuation through its relation to and association with the individual soul existing in the body. Although Averroes chooses not to draw the conclusion explicitly, it is clear that the perishing of the composite of soul and body also entails the loss of individualization and existence for the associated material intellect. Hence, as was the case for the *Short Commentary*, here too in the *Middle Commentary* there is no provision or rational argumentation supportive of post-mortem existence of individual human beings. That is, in the *Middle Commentary on the* De Anima, the ontology of the soul and its powers entails that the human soul and intellect perish with the death of the body.

4. Averroes' *Long Commentary on the* De Anima

In his major work on human knowledge, more familiar because of the wide dispersion of its Latin translation in medieval Europe, Averroes again confronted the issue of the nature of intelligibles in act, and the character of a subject suitable for them for the sake of human intellectual understanding. Critically reflecting on the teachings of Themistius in the latter's *Paraphrase of the* De Anima, Averroes brought his mind to bear on a notion he had not dealt with at length in either of the two earlier commentaries: namely, a unity of knowledge that makes shared science and intersubjective intellectual discourse possible. In both of those works, Averroes held that each human being possesses his or her own personal material intellect. In the *Long Commentary*, however, he adopts a view that he had explicitly rejected in the *Middle Commentary* (2002: 111 [sec. 282]) and that he had raised as worthy of further consideration in a short work called *Epistle 1 on Conjunction* (2001: 210) – namely, the material intellect as a single separate entity shared by all human beings. In forming this new understanding, Averroes found the *Paraphrase of the* De Anima, by Themistius, a powerful stimulant.

In the Arabic text of Themistius (1973: 188.17–189.4) Averroes read,

> There need be no wonder that we all are as a group composites of what is in potency and of what is in act. All of us whose existence is by virtue of this one are referred back to a one which is the agent intellect. For if not this, then whence is it that we possess known sciences in a shared way? And whence is it that the understanding of the primary definitions and primary propositions is alike [for

us all] without learning? For it is right that, if we do not have one intellect in which we all share, then we also do not have understanding of one another. (My translation.)[11]

This unity of intellect for the sake of 'understanding of one another' Averroes applied to his conception of human intellectual knowledge, to form his novel understanding of the unity of the material intellect. It is a view inspired by his third reading of Themistius' *Paraphrase*, though not held by Themistius himself.[12] For Averroes, this understanding of the material intellect satisfied the need for the unity of understanding on the part of distinct human individuals, since this entity is the repository of abstracted intelligibles in act to which all particular acts of understanding and scientific discourse refer. This is possible only insofar as the nature of the material intellect is such that it is a unique reality constituting a distinct immaterial species, so that intelligibles received are not particularized as they would be were it to be truly material or one among many individuals of a species. Averroes was well aware of the difficulty of asserting that something without matter, and itself actual as immaterial, could be. Nevertheless, to solve the complex array of issues involved in accounting for the phenomenon of intellectual understanding on the part of transitory human beings, Averroes (2009: {409}, 326) crafted this new account while being explicitly conscious of the metaphysical commitments entailed, something evident in his description of the material intellect as 'a fourth kind of being' in addition to matter, form, and matter-form composites.

With this new teaching, Averroes called upon the familiar notion that individual human beings employ the external senses and the common sense to produce intentions in the imagination. These are then refined and stripped of the extraneous by the cogitative power yielding denuded intentions placed in memory, ready for transference from the mode of being of particulars to the mode of being of intelligibles in act.[13] This takes place, thanks to the presence of the separate agent intellect 'in the soul' as 'form for us' effecting the abstractive transference. It is also thanks to the presence of the material intellect 'in the soul', as well as its being the immaterial subject receptive of the intelligible made in act by the agent intellect, no longer an intelligible in potency as it was in the external and internal powers of the individual soul. For the individual human knower, this brings about the theoretical intellect as a positive disposition of knowing (*al-'aql bi-l-malakah, intellectus in habitu*) in the soul which accounts for the human experience of knowing the intelligibles in act which Averroes had reasoned could only exist in the material intellect, the shared immaterial subject of intelligibles. In this teaching, the presence of the two separate intellects 'in the soul' provides the connection with the individual knower's cogitative power responsible for human acts of will in making pre-noetic preparations for abstraction. This is the gathering of images intelligible in potency through the external and internal senses. The realization of knowledge in that individual is coordinated with abstracted intellectual content in the material intellect to yield the theoretical intellect of individual human knowing. On this account, the theoretical intelligibles exist in act in the separate material intellect since they require an immaterial substrate, but they also exist in the individual human knower through a connection with the separate material intellect apparently forged in the process of abstraction. In this way, the individual human knower can be called the subject of truth insofar as the individual provides from sense perception the content intelligible in potency. This comes to exist as intelligible in act in the material intellect – the subject of the existence of the intelligible in act – by way of the abstractive and elevating power of the agent intellect. In his *Commentary on the* Republic, Averroes (1974: 86–8) explains that the end of humans as natural beings is the attainment of ultimate perfection and happiness through the intelligibles of the theoretical sciences.

The most challenging section of the *Long Commentary* is in Book 3, Comment 36, where Averroes critically reviews the responses of Alexander, Themistius, al-Farabi, and Ibn Bajja to Aristotle's famous remark at the end of *De Anima* 3.7, 431b17-19 (1984: 686): 'Whether it is possible for [the human mind] while not existing separate from spatial conditions to think anything that is separate, or not, we must consider later.'[14] It was commonly known that there was no extant text in which Aristotle returned to explicate his meaning. These two Greek philosophers took the text to refer not to mathematics and mathematical abstraction but to the issue of whether real intellectual knowledge of eternal and unchanging essences can only come through a connection to higher intellectual substances, and in this these two predecessors of Averroes in the Arabic tradition followed their lead. Averroes found that those who held the material intellect to be a body or a power in a body could find no way to provide a satisfactory account of human intellectual understanding of immaterial intelligibles. Alexander had been right to hold that the activity of the separate agent intellect as 'form for us' is required for the abstraction of intelligibles from human experience of the world, and that the intellect must somehow be 'in the soul'. But he was wrong to think that the material intellect could be epiphenomenal on a mixture of bodily parts and elements. (Yet, as explained earlier, this is not far from Averroes' own position in the *Short*

Commentary.) Such a thing could never be the receptive subject of eternal intelligibles in act. Themistius was wrong to think, in a Platonic fashion, that the intelligibles preexist in the agent intellect and that each human individual has his or her own intellect to be actualized as immaterial in an abstractive process of its own under the guidance of the separate agent intellect. Al-Farabi, Averroes reports, apparently questioned his own view and raised the question of whether there really could be a connection between transcendent intellect and human experiences of the world of particular beings to allow for a real science of intelligibles in act to be generated in some way in human beings. And Ibn Bajjah had set out to explain the connection to transcendent intellect, by proposing a rising tree of abstractive processes that would lead human beings finally to a single intellect, the agent intellect containing all the intelligibles in act. This Averroes rejected, since abstraction alone by itself cannot attain to anything beyond initial experience with which the abstraction began. Abstraction of sensibles cannot lead by its continued use to something as generically different as a purely immaterial intellect. For Averroes, none of these methods lead to a post-mortem existence for human beings consisting in conjoining with separate intellect for highest human fulfilment and ultimate happiness. Rather, for Averroes, the highest fulfilment available to human beings is perfection in the theoretical intelligibles – that is, in scientific knowledge. The existence of human knowledge of eternal intelligibles of science gives witness that human beings are naturally constituted to attain knowledge. What is required for this is that it be the natural condition of human beings that they use their external and internal senses to apprehend the world and its forms and essences that are intelligible in potency. To make the transference from the mode of being of a particular to the mode of being as an intelligible in act (which makes the predication of universals possible), Aristotle's assertion of the agent intellect is also required. And to make available the needed subject for intelligibles in act, there must be asserted a separate material intellect which (unlike the views of Averroes in the two earlier commentaries) is not a determinate particular but is instead a unique entity shared by all human beings for the unity of science and of intersubjective discourse. Hence, to return to the issue of Aristotle's text at *De Anima* 3.7, there is a kind of uniting with separate substances that must take place for the sake of human knowledge – namely, the uniting with the separate agent intellect and the separate material intellect. In this way, the end of human beings is to be found in knowledge and not in uniting with a separate entity; rather, uniting for the short period of a transitory human lifetime is a means to the fulfilment and happiness gained in the attainment of knowledge.[15]

The foregoing reflects the issue of the ontology of the soul, since the philosophical reasoning must be focused on the natures of the intelligibles in act and natures of the subjects into which they are received. For Averroes, human intellectual understanding comes about when the two separate substances, the agent intellect and the material intellect, are intrinsically present in the human soul by a form of sharing or participation. But the human soul is the first actuality of a natural body having organs, while those intellects are separate from body. In light of this, Averroes determines that the term 'soul' is equivocal and that intellect is not properly part of the essence of the human soul. With this, Averroes provided his own response to the issue raised by Aristotle in *De Anima* 2.2 as to whether intellect is another kind of soul distinct from the soul that is the form of the physical body. Explaining his understanding of Aristotle, Averroes (2009: {160–1}, 128) writes thus:

> [I]t is better to say, and seems more to be true after investigation, that this is another kind of soul and, if it is called a soul, it will be so equivocally. If the disposition of intellect is such as this, then it must be possible for that alone of all the powers of soul to be separated from the body and not to be corrupted by [the body's] corruption, just as the eternal is separated. This will be the case since sometimes [the intellect] is not united with [the body] and sometimes it is united with it.

That is, the human being's soul is the actuality of body responsible for the formation of the hylomorphic composite. The rational part of soul or intellect is not properly soul as form of the body; it can be called 'soul', but only in a wholly equivocal sense. Intellect, then, does not belong properly and per se to this hylomorphic composite in virtue of itself, but rather is only shared through the presence of the agent and the material intellect during the earthly life of the human individual. Hence, no argument for personal immortality can be based on the per se presence of an intellectual – and thereby immaterial – power of the soul that is fully intrinsic to each individual human. The consequence is that, while the agent intellect, the material intellect, and also the human species can be reasoned to be eternally in existence ({407}, 322), there is no basis in argument for a continued existence of the individual human soul after the death of the body. For Averroes in the *Long Commentary*, then, the ontology of the human soul does not entail any post-mortem existence for individual human beings, nor does it entail a rising of the human soul or intellect to some sort of extranatural contemplation of separate substances in which they are united in ultimate happiness. This, however, was not what the Latin tradition found in reading Averroes. Thomas Aquinas thought that Averroes held that, through a connection with the agent intellect, humans could rise by natural powers to see and know other higher separate substances, something that he fully rejected in his own teaching.[16] Siger of Brabant reasoned that, for Averroes, the material intellect is the most receptive of all entities.[17] Consequently, since human beings unite with the material intellect, through that uniting they could come to knowledge of all other separate intellects. The language for both views is present in Comment 36 and elsewhere in the *Long Commentary*, but as parts of the analysis and refutation of the views of others.

5. Averroes, Albert the Great, and Thomas Aquinas

It is well known that Thomas Aquinas and his teacher, Albert the Great, both vehemently rejected the teachings of Averroes in a number of works, and they each wrote a work on the unity of intellect in refutation of Averroes and his Latin followers.[18] What has remained nearly unknown[19] and certainly unheralded is the important role of the *Long Commentary on the* De Anima in the development of the natural epistemology of Aquinas as set out in his first major work, his *Commentary on the Sentences of Peter Lombard* written in 1251–53/54. (Aquinas 1929)

Aquinas came into contact with Albert at Paris in 1245, and was later taken to Cologne to be Albert's assistant before returning to Paris in 1250/51. Some years earlier (c. 1242), Albert had composed a large treatise on human nature, generally following the account of Aristotle, albeit with some significant differences. With this work, his *De homine*, Albert provided a rich and up-to-date philosophical treatise drawing on Aristotle and all the philosophical resources available to him in Latin translation. In this work, Albert drew extensively and explicitly on the thought of Avicenna in his *De Anima* and *Metaphysics*, and on that of Averroes in the *Long Commentary on the* De Anima. Regarding the doctrine of the intellect, Albert is particularly forthright in citing his sources, often with extensive quotations, and in detailing the precise way in which he read their texts.

From Avicenna, Albert embraced the general teaching that the human soul is by nature an imperishable rational entity that employs the body, and its external and internal sense powers, to enrich itself intellectually. The Latin tradition generally understood Avicenna to teach that the efforts of individual human beings to form a pre-noetic grasp of things intelligible in potency is a preparation of the soul to receive an emanation of intelligibles in act from the separate Agent intellect which is itself replete with forms. Further, it was clear in the texts of Avicenna that the Persian philosopher also held that individual human beings do not have intellectual memory, and so require access to those intelligibles in the agent intellect. The agent intellect, on this account, is not an intellectualizing power that merely aids human beings in their efforts at abstraction; it is also the efficient cause of the forms of natural things in the world, emanating forms when the materials are suitably prepared. As Albert (2008: 402.40) puts it, '<Avicenna> expressly accepted that the agent intellect is the separate intelligence of the tenth order of the separate intelligences.' This notion that the agent intellect is the immediate efficient cause of things of the world is extended in the common Latin tradition to the notion of the formation of intellectual understanding. That is, the content of intellectual understanding is provided, not by the individual human being experiencing and analysing things of the world, but rather by the emanations coming from the agent intellect. The various abstractions or separations that the human being moves through, from sense perception to image formation, are mere preparation for the soul's reception of an abstraction or immaterial form from the agent intellect.[20] But this account of individual human intellectual understanding is something that Albert says he will have nothing of.[21] Rather, for him 'the agent intellect is part of the soul ... And on account of this we say that the agent intellect is part of the potential soul flowing from it as "that by which it is" or act; but the possible <intellect> on the part of the soul flowing from it as "what is" or potency' (416). Curiously enough, however, Albert derived this notion of agent intellect and possible (scil. material) intellect as parts of the individual human soul from his study of Averroes.

From his close examination of Averroes' *Long Commentary on the* De Anima, Albert understood something quite different from what has been explained above about the teachings of the Cordoban. He writes, 'For following Aristotle and Averroes ... we say that the human agent intellect is conjoined to the human soul, is simple and does not possess the intelligibles but brings them about in the possible intellect from phantasms, as Averroes expressly says in <his> Commentary on De Anima' (412.69). That is, for Albert, the agent intellect and possible (material) intellect are not separate entities, but are in us as intrinsic powers of the soul, and this he understands to be the teaching of Averroes. Recall that earlier I noted the language of Averroes, as he explained that both the agent intellect and the material intellect come to be 'in the soul' in the formation of the human theoretical intellect or the intellect in a positive disposition (*al-'aql bi-l-malikah/intellectus in habitu*). In his explanation of how human willing efforts bring about intellectual knowledge, Averroes said that the agent intellect becomes 'form for us' as an actualizing power 'in the soul'. And through the connection forged in the activity of intellectual abstraction, the receptive material intellect also comes to be 'in the soul', as our voluntary efforts at knowledge attainment make evident. For after the initial abstraction involving the transference of the intelligible in potency into an intelligible in act deposited in the material intellect, the individual human being qua theoretical intellect is able to reconnect and make use of the abstracted intelligible now in act in the unique material intellect. But Albert reads the text of Averroes very literally:

> Averroes <writes>: 'Every intellect existing in us has two actions. One is of the genus of affection and it is to understand; the other <is> of the genus of action. And this is for abstracting these from matter, which is nothing but to make them understood in act after they were understood in potency.' Since, therefore, one of these is the agent intellect and the other the possible <intellect>, each of those intellects will be existing in us and not a separate substance. (411.46–53)

With these words, Albert revealed the existence of two interpretations of Averroes current in his day, the view that the intellects are separate substances and the view that the intellects are 'existing in us' as powers in each human soul.[22] For Albert, the correct reading is that 'the agent intellect and the possible intellect are intrinsic parts of the rational soul' (416). Further, he remarks that 'we take it that the intellect is in potency to the species of the agent <intellect> and to the intelligible species' and goes on to say that the meaning of 'the species of the agent <intellect>' is 'the act of the intelligible species, as light is the act of color' (438). For Albert, the human power of agent intellect abstracts the forms and intelligibles from the images or phantasms, and 'the possible intellect receives the forms and intelligibles and retains them' (442). These, which Averroes called 'theoretical intelligibles', are for Albert the abstracted intelligibles in act in the individual material / possible intellects of human beings, and are denominated as intelligible species (*species intelligibiles*), scil. intelligible forms.

   Although Albert misunderstood the complex texts of Averroes containing the Cordoban's unique account of a single shared separately existing material intellect, his misreading of phrases such as 'in the soul' and 'existing in us' led him to craft a new account of human intellectual processes in his early *De homine*. And it is fundamentally this novel account that appears in Thomas Aquinas' first account of natural human epistemology in his *Commentary on the*

Sentences, Book 2, distinction 17, question 2, article 1, 'Whether there is one soul or intellect for all human beings.'[23]

When Thomas undertakes his analysis of his predecessors and sets out his own teachings on the issue of human knowledge and its attainment, he follows the custom of his day by not mentioning the work of his teacher, since citation of living authors was commonly avoided. What is more, by the time of his writing, it was evident that Albert's initial interpretation of Averroes, rejecting the notion that the agent and material/possible intellects are separate substances, was wrong. This alone surely prompted Aquinas to undertake his own thoroughgoing study of Averroes and the thinkers of the Greek and Arabic traditions available to him at the time. Still, he and his teacher are in agreement on the intellects as powers of the individual human soul and on the intelligibles in act as intelligible species, multiplied according to the number of human knowers. That is, the teaching of Aquinas is largely the same as Albert's, even though Aquinas set out his own account of the Arabic sources by sometimes drawing on texts different from those used by his teacher.

In the *solutio* of the article in the first part, he makes extensive use of Averroes' *Long Commentary on the* De Anima to review, critique, and reject the teachings of Alexander, Theophrastus, Themistius, and Ibn Bajjah, and then turns to refute Averroes himself. As he sees it, '[N]early all the philosophers after Aristotle are in agreement that the agent intellect and the possible [intellect] differ in substance and that the agent intellect is a certain separate substance' (trans. from Taylor 2013b: 283). In the second part he sets out his own teaching, accepting from Avicenna that the possible (scil. material) intellect is multiple, in accord with human bodies, and does not perish with the death of the body. Further, he explains that the agent intellect differs in different human beings. Hence, these are diverse powers found in each human individual:

Therefore, since receiving understood species which belongs to the possible intellect and making them intelligibles in act which belongs to the agent intellect cannot [both] come together in the same thing, but receiving belongs to something insofar as it is in potency and making [belongs to something] insofar as it is in act, then it is impossible that the agent [intellect] and the possible [intellect] not be diverse powers. (291)

Hence, for Aquinas,

the soul has a power by which it makes sensible species to be intelligible [species] in act, and this power is the agent intellect. And [the soul] has a power by which it is in potency for being made in the act of determinate knowing brought about

by a sensible thing's species made intelligible in act, and this power or potency
is called possible intellect. Upon the operations of these two powers follows all
our understanding. (292)

This account, first set out in Albert's *De homine* grounded in his misinterpretation
of the texts of Averroes, provided for Thomas the principles and a model for
the formation of his own account of the foundations of human intellectual
understanding through intellectual abstraction.

6. Conclusion

Though many modern scholars of Aristotle's own writings (e.g. Wedin 1988;
Burnyeat 2008) make little or no mention of an account of intellectual abstraction
transferring the intelligible content of sensory experience to the level of intellect
and scientific universals, the Arabic tradition, under the interpretive spell of the
account of Alexander confirmed by Themistius, read this back into the texts of
Aristotle and worked to craft coherent accounts of human knowledge. As Aquinas
notes, the notion of the agent intellect separate in substance was commonplace
and accepted by 'nearly all the philosophers after Aristotle'. Averroes himself
struggled over the issues throughout his career. He first conceived an account
holding human beings to have knowledge through forms in the imagination,
certified in some way by the agent intellect. Rejecting that because of its material
entailments, he set out a second conception, holding that the receptive power
that Alexander called 'material intellect' must be a receptive power free of matter
and forms in its own right, in order to receive abstracted intelligibles in act.
Third, rethinking the arguments of Themistius for a final time, he tailored a new
theory to the notion that there must be one set of intelligibles, referenced by
all human beings for the unity of knowledge and discourse. This final theory,
with its explanation of the agent intellect and the material intellect as separately
existing substances, was largely rejected by thinkers of the Latin tradition such
as Aquinas, the later Albert, Bonaventure, and others, with the exception of a
small number of so-called Latin Averroists and some others later who found
value in parts of Averroes' teachings. Nevertheless, through the arguments of
his *Long Commentary on the* De Anima, Averroes remained a significant player
in the later discussions of human intellect among European Christian thinkers.
And, as spelled out above, through the misinterpretation of Albert, that work
played an important role in the formation of the thought of Thomas Aquinas.

Yet it remains the case that this entire tradition owes much more to Alexander of Aphrodisias for his interpretation of Aristotle than to the Stagirite himself, particularly in the case of the Arabic tradition and its influence on the later Latin tradition through translations of philosophical works from Arabic. It may be worthy of some reflection to consider whether the price of abstractionism itself is too much to pay, with its assumption of the nature of human knowing as necessarily and essentially immaterial, therewith requiring an ontology of soul involving an immaterial agent and an immaterial recipient, be they individual, or unitary and shared. That one must assert the existence of a separate agent intellect, or of a special immaterial power of intellectual transference and apprehension of abstracted essences that exists in the human soul, from a modern perspective seems to be more than a little burdensome if not fantastic. Could it be that this entire endeavour was in fact a wrong turn in the history of human knowledge, one that Aristotle himself never took? That is the view of some later thinkers which may be well worth considering.

Notes

1 Averroes (1953: {433}; 2009: 345). References to this text will be to the Latin pages enclosed in brackets ({}) and the English translation without brackets, as employed in this note. Also see Taylor (2004).
2 See Aristotle (1984: Bks 2.5, 2.12). The form of the stone, not the stone itself, is in the eye through the sense of sight (3.8).
3 See Burnyeat (2008). The notion of intellectual abstraction of intelligibles, so central to the thought of thinkers of the classical rationalist philosophical tradition in Arabic and a number of Greek predecessors, is not at all discussed by Burnyeat, since he simply does not find it present in Aristotle.
4 See also Alexander (1887: 108.3–7, 108.14–15, 111.15–19). Arabic text: Alexander (1956: see 185.1–6, 193.24, 185.15–16); Alexander (1971: 34.4–7, 38.16–18; see also 34.10–11). English translation: Alexander (2004: 28, 36; see also 29).
5 See his rich account of *De Anima* 3.5 in Themistius (1899: 98.12–104.3). Arabic: Themistius (1973: 169–90). English: Themistius (1996: 122–34).
6 See Taylor (2013a, forthcoming).
7 Averroes (1950: 74.9–10; 1985: 108.14–15). Some translations are from Taylor (2013a).
8 For the notion that the agent intellect is 'in the soul' and 'form for us', see Taylor (2005). Also see Averroes (2009: xxiv ff.).

9 'This instrument is said to be intellect potentially, supervening on this sort of blending of bodies as a suitable potentiality for receiving the intellect that is in actuality' (Alexander 2004: 39–40). For a modern version of this theory about the meaning of Aristotle's thought, see Wedin (1988). Regarding Ibn Bajjah, see Averroes (2009: intro., xxv–xxvii, lxxxix–cxiii).

10 Note that I change Ivry's «substantively separate» for *mufāriqan fī jauhari-hi* to 'separate in its substance'.

11 This Arabic text, based on an incomplete manuscript, is missing Greek pp. 2–22 and some other passages. This corresponds to Themistius (1899: 103.36–104.3; 1996: 129). Cf. Averroes (2009: {411–12}, 328–9).

12 For more detailed discussion of this, see Averroes (2009: intro.) and Taylor (2013a).

13 The intention 'is transferred in its mode of being from one order into another' (Averroes 2009: {439}, 351).

14 Whether Aristotle meant this text to concern mathematical or separate substances is not altogether clear. The Arabic seems to express the issue as more definitely being about separate substances rather than magnitudes. 'We will investigate later whether it is possible for the intellect while in the body to apprehend something of the things separate from bodies, or this is not possible' (Aristotle 1954, 78). We find this in Averroes' (2009: {480}, 382) alternate translation as 'Later on we will investigate whether or not the intellect, when existing in the body, not as separate from it is able to apprehend any of those things which are separate from bodies'. In the lemma for his main text, he has this: 'Our reflection later will concern whether it can understand any of the separate things while it is separate from magnitude, or not' ({479}, 381, translation modified). Averroes cited his alternate Arabic translation here because he was suspicious about the soundness of his main Arabic text of Aristotle.

15 In the Latin tradition, Book 3, Comment 36, was misunderstood by Thomas Aquinas and also by Siger of Brabant. For the latter, see Steel (1998a, 1998b; cf. 2001).

16 In his *De Veritate*, Aquinas (1972: q. 18, a. 5, ad 8, 549.348–50) writes that for Averroes 'when the production of such intelligibles takes place in us, then the agent intellect is united with us as form. And in this way we will be able to know separated substances through the agent intellect'.

17 See Steel (2001: 229ff). Siger was apparently fixating on two texts (2009: {437}, 350; {489}, 390) in which Averroes says that the material intellect has understanding of all things.

18 Albert's *De unitate intellectus contra Averroem* (1263) was written before Aquinas' *De unitate intellectus contra averroistas* (1270).

19 This is noted by Miller (1954), but the purpose of his article is to show differences between Aquinas and Albert across other works.

20 Avicenna's actual teaching is that the content of human intellectual understanding comes from sensory experience of the world, with the rational soul being assisted

by the supervening presence of the agent intellect. On this issue, see Hasse (2000, 2001, 2013), Gutas (2001, 2013), Alpina (2014), and Taylor (forthcoming).

21 *Nos nihil horum dicimus.* See Albert the Great (2008: 412.57ff.).

22 On the confusing issue of First and Second Averroism, see Averroes (2009: intro., xcix ff.).

23 For an analysis and complete translation of this article, see Taylor (2013b). This translation is based on an unpublished version of this article provided by Dr. Adriano Oliva, president of the Commissio Leonina in Paris, responsible for the preparation of the critical edition of this work.

References

Albert the Great (2008), = Albertus Magnus, *De homine*, eds. H. Anzulewicz and J. R. Söder, in *Alberti Magni Opera Omnia*, t. XXVII, Pars II, Münster: Ashendorff.

Alexander of Aphrodisias (1887), *De Anima Liber Cum Mantissa*, ed. I. Bruns, Berlin: George Reimer, Commentaria in Aristotelem Graeca, Suppl. II, pt. 1.

Alexander of Aphrodisias (1956), 'Texte arabe du PERI NOU d'Alexandre d'Aphrodise', in S. J. Finnegan (ed.), *Mélanges de l'Université Saint-Joseph*, 33: 159–202.

Alexander of Aphrodisias (1971), *Commentaires sur Aristote perdus en grec et autres épitres*, ed. ʿA. Badawi, Beirut: Dār al-Mashriq.

Alexander of Aphrodisias (2004), *Alexander of Aphrodisias. Supplement to On the Soul*, trans. R. W. Sharples, London: Duckworth.

Alpina, T. (2014), 'Intellectual Knowledge, Active Intellect and Intellectual Memory in Avicenna's *Kitāb al-Nafs* and Its Aristotelian Background', *Documenti e studi sulla tradizione filosofica medieval*, 25: 131–83.

Aristotle (1954), *Aristotelis De Anima (Arisṭūṭālīs fī an-Nafs)*, ed. A. Badawi, Cairo: Imprimerie Misr S.A.E. (Reprint: Beirut and Kuwait, 1980).

Aristotle (1984), *On the Soul (= De Anima)*, trans. J. A. Smith, in J. Barnes (ed.), *The Complete Works of Aristotle: The Revised Oxford Translation*, Princeton: Princeton University Press.

Averroes (1950), *Talkhiṣ Kitāb al-Nafs*, ed. A. F. El-Ahwani, Cairo.

Averroes (1953), *De Anima: Averrois Cordubensis Commentarium Magnum in Aristotelis De Anima Libros*, ed. F. S. Crawford, Cambridge, MA: Medieval Academy of America.

Averroes (1961), *Averroes. Epitome of the* Parva Naturalia, trans. H. Blumburg, Cambridge, MA: The Medieval Academy of America.

Averroes (1972), *Averrois Cordubensis Compendia Librorum Aristotelis Qui Parva Naturalia Vocantur, Textum Arabicum*, ed. H. Blumberg, Philadelphia: The Medieval Academy of America.

Averroes (1974), *Averroes on Plato's Republic*, trans. R. Lerner, Ithaca, NY: Cornell University Press.

Averroes (1985), *Epitome de Anima*, ed. S. Gomez Nogales, Madrid.

Averroes (2001), *Averroès. La Béatitude de l'âme. Éditions, traductions et études*, ed. and trans. M. Geoffroy and C. Steel, Paris: Librairie Philosophique J. Vrin.

Averroes (2002), *Averroes: Middle Commentary on Aristotle's* De anima. *A Critical Edition of the Arabic Text with English Translation, Notes, and Introduction*, ed. and trans. A. L. Ivry, Provo, Utah: Brigham Young University Press.

Averroes (2009), *Averroes (Ibn Rushd) of Cordoba. Long Commentary on the* De Anima *of Aristotle*, trans. and ed. R. C. Taylor, ed. Th-A. Druart, New Haven, CT: Yale University Press.

Burnyeat. M. (2008), *Aristotle's Divine Mind*. Milwaukee: Marquette University Press.

Gutas, D. (2001), 'Intuition and Thinking: The Evolving Structure of Avicenna's Epistemology', *Princeton Papers. Interdisciplinary Journal of Middle Eastern Studies*, 9: 1–38.

Gutas, D. (2013), 'Avicenna's Philosophical Project', in *Interpreting Avicenna. Critical Essays*, Cambridge: Cambridge University Press.

Hasse, D. N. (2000), *Avicenna's De anima in the Latin West: The Formation of a Peripatetic Philosophy of the Soul 1160–1300*, London: The Warburg Institute, Turin: Nino Aragno Editore.

Hasse, D. N. (2001), 'Avicenna on Abstraction', in R. Wisnovsky (ed.), *Aspects of Avicenna*, Princeton: Markus Wiener Publishers.

Hasse, D. N. (2013), 'Avicenna's Epistemological Optimism', in P. Adamson (ed.), *Interpreting Avicenna: Critical Essays*, Cambridge: Cambridge University Press.

Miller, R. (1954), 'An Aspect of Averroes' Influence on St. Albert', *Mediaeval Studies*, 16: 57–71.

Steel, C. (1998a), 'Siger of Brabant versus Thomas Aquinas on the Possibility of Knowing the Separate Substances', in J. A. Aertsen, K. Emery, and A. Speer (eds), *Nach der Verurteilung von 1277: Philosophie und Theologie an der Universität von Paris im letzten Viertel des 13. Jarhunderts. Studien und Texte*, Berlin: Walter de Gruyter.

Steel, C. (1998b), 'Medieval Philosophy: An Impossible Project? Thomas Aquinas and the "Averroistic" Ideal of Happiness', in A. Speer and J. A. Aertsen (eds), *Was ist Philosophie im Mittelalter? Akten des X. Internationalen Kongresses für mittelalterliche Philosophie der Société International pour l'Étude de la Philosophie Médiévale 25. bis 30. August 1997*, Berlin: Walter de Gruyter.

Steel, C. (2001), *Der Adler und die Nachteule: Thomas und Albert über die Möglichkeit der Metaphysik, Lectio Albertina, Albertus-Magnus-Institut Bonn*, Münster: Ashendorff.

Taylor, R. C. (2004), 'Improving on Nature's Exemplar: Averroes' Completion of Aristotle's Psychology of Intellect', in P. Adamson, H. Baltussen, and M. W. F. Stone (eds), *Philosophy, Science and Exegesis in Greek, Arabic and Latin Commentaries*, vol. 2, London: Institute of Classical Studies.

Taylor, R. C. (2005), 'The Agent Intellect as "Form for Us" and Averroes's Critique of al-Fârâbî', *Topicos* (Universidad Panamericana, Mexico City), 29: 29–51. Reprinted, with corrections, in *Universal Representation and the Ontology of Individuation: Proceedings of the Society for Medieval Logic and Metaphysics* 5 (2011): 25–44.

Taylor, R. C. (2013a), 'Themistius and the Development of Averroes' Noetics', in R. L. Friedman and J.-M. Counet (eds), *Medieval Perspectives on Aristotle's De Anima* (Philosophes Médiévaux, LVIII), Louvain-la-Neuve/Louvain-Paris-Walpole MAa, Editions de l'Institut Supérieur de Philosophie/Peeters.

Taylor, R. C. (2013b), 'Aquinas and the Arabs: Aquinas's First Critical Encounter with the Doctrine of Averroes on the Intellect, *In 2 Sent.* d. 17, q. 2, a. 1', in L. X. López-Farjeat and J. Tellkamp (eds), *Philosophical Psychology in Arabic Thought and the Latin Aristotelianism of the 13th Century*, Paris: Vrin, 142–83, 277–96.

Taylor, R. C. (forthcoming), 'Avicenna and the Issue of the Intellectual Abstraction of Intelligibles', in *The Routledge History of the Philosophy of Mind*, Routledge.

Themistius (1899), *In Libros Aristotelis De Anima Paraphrasis*, ed. R. Heinze, Berlin: G. Reimeri [Commentaria in Aristotelem Graeca, 5.3].

Themistius (1973), *An Arabic Translation of Themistius' Commentary on Aristotle's De Anima*, ed. M. C. Lyons, Columbia, SC: Bruno Cassirer.

Themistius (1996), *On Aristotle's On the Soul*, trans. R. B. Todd, Ithaca, NY: Cornell University Press.

Thomas Aquinas (1929), *Commentary on the Sentences of Peter Lombard*. Latin text: *Aquinatis, Scriptum super libros Sententiarum magistri Petri Lonbardi epsicopi Parisiensis*, t. 1 and 2, ed. P. Mandonnet, Paris: P. Lethielleux, 1929; t. 3, ed. M. F. Moos, 1956; t. 4, ed. M. F. Moos, 1947. These texts are incomplete since they include only half of Book 4, A full version can be found at http:/www.corpusthomisticum.org/opera.html.

Thomas Aquinas (1972), *Quaestiones Disputatae De Veritate*, in *Sancti Thomae de Aquino, Opera Omnia*, tome 22, v. 2, Rome: Ex Typographia Polyglotta S.C. de Propaganda Fide.

Wedin, M. V. (1988), *Mind and Imagination in Aristotle*, New Haven: Yale University Press.

4

Robert Grosseteste on Demonstration

John Longeway

Robert Grosseteste's *Commentary on the* Posterior Analytics (1981) is, it seems, the earliest full commentary on that work to attain complete distribution in the Latin West. It was published around 1220–30. The central goal of the *Posterior Analytics* is to provide a technique for coming to scientific knowledge, demonstration, and this fact suggests that only that of which there is a demonstration is known; but it also argues that the conclusion is known because the premises are known, so that the ultimate premises, the first principles of a science – which there must be, of course, the root of all the demonstrations in it – are *also* known, but *not* through demonstration. So, Grosseteste suggests, in chapter 2 of his commentary, that in the strictest sense, principles are not known at all, since they are not demonstrated: that is, the cause of their being so is not identified, and indeed, insofar as it differs from them or their parts, such a cause is not to be found. This motivates, in chapter 2 of the text, arguments to the effect that demonstration is either circular, or else there is no knowledge at all. The way out of these absurd conclusions, Grosseteste suggests, is to recognize that the word 'knowledge' can be used in a wider sense to cover cognition of principles as well as cognition of the conclusions of demonstrations, and it is in this wider sense that principles are better known than are the conclusions of demonstrations.

The first principles are known through knowledge of their terms, which are contained within them, and this without any contact with the rest of the world, and so there are at least two ways to know a proposition – through a demonstration, and through knowledge of the terms of a proposition.[1] John of Salisbury in his 1159 *Metalogicon* (1955), one of the earliest works in the West showing some familiarity with the *Posterior Analytics*, suggests that it primarily concerns mathematical knowledge, which is known to us even in this life as necessary truth, and not at all the knowledge of sensibles *as such*, that is, as they are sensed (Grosseteste 1981: IV, 6).[2] This view is acknowledged by Grossesteste. Knowledge of sensibles as such will always involve, according to him, a contingent proposition, true when the observation of it occurs, false, perhaps, at other times. Knowledge is to be had only of what must be true, and that knowledge depends on knowledge of principles.

Grosseteste begins his argument with a confession that we know the premises (in the sense in which we know them) even more than we know the conclusions of demonstrations (in that sense). We know, he says, (1) broadly, (2) strictly, and (3) more strictly (I, 2). (1) Broadly, we know when we have a comprehension of the truth, and this covers cases in which we have an erratic contingent knowledge, provided by what is commonly called a demonstration. We may have 'knowledge' that a cat is in the room, based on our visual impression of the cat. We are, reasonably, quite certain about this, but the demonstration, merely gesturing, say, towards the cat, is an appeal to the senses, not to reason. We may know that the Pope is sitting, similarly, despite the fact that the action is a free one, and cannot be known at all in a strict sense.[3] (2) We know, speaking strictly, when we have knowledge of things that are always, or are for the most part, and thus we know natural things, again through demonstration; but in natural things we know only those things that are necessarily true of a given substance. If one knows that scammony produces the discharge of red bile, then we know something that is necessarily true. We do not know that it *always* produces the discharge, though, for any causal tendency can be blocked by opposing causal tendencies in nature. We only know that the drug induces the discharge due to an innate causal tendency, and, in the absence of any countervailing circumstances, will therefore produce it. Can we *know* that it produces it at a particular time? Only, it seems, with the aid of the senses, and so not at all in this second sense. (3) We can know those things that are always the same, and thus we can know mathematics, both its principles and conclusions (I, 2: 9–28). Demonstration is a syllogism producing knowledge, so that we also know in this sense in having the demonstration (I, 2: 38–40). And finally, as we have seen, (4) we can know in the sense that we have a demonstration, but this sense seems to overlap both (2) and (3), and so does not belong in the sequence of more and more narrow senses of the term represented in (1) through (3).

Now, the scientific knowledge produced is of the cause of a thing, which is immutable in itself and in its causing; and the other sorts of knowledge, Aristotle insists, are sophistical and incidental (71b9–10). He is interested in scientific knowledge in the *Posterior Analytics*, not simply a certain cognition of some fact. That means understanding the cause of the thing (the situation) known, and that not an accidental cause, but the cause of it that is always effective, and is required for the production of the situation known in that sort of thing. So, if we know scientifically that a triangle has three angles equal to 180°, we must know something about its being a triangle that implies that its angles have 180°. Knowing something about its being a particular sort of triangle won't do; nor will something known about its being a plane figure.

And so there follows the first of Grosseteste's conclusions: Demonstrative knowledge is from the true, and first, and immediate, and prior and better known, and what is causative of the conclusion (Grosseteste 1981: I, 2: 40–2). Here the material definition is proved from the formal definition, 'syllogism producing knowledge', in accord with the demonstration, 'Every demonstration is a syllogism producing knowledge, every demonstration producing knowledge is one that is from true premises, from what is first etc., therefore every demonstration is a syllogism that is from what is true, first, etc.' Also, Conclusion 5, a demonstration is a syllogism from necessary premises, since only such a syllogism can produce a necessary conclusion, and knowledge is always of the necessary (I, 4: 4–5). Conclusion 2 is that premises in demonstrative syllogism are known more than their conclusions (I, 2: 67–9). Conclusion 3 is that no one can know conclusions more than the principles of the conclusion (I, 2: 77–8). Conclusion 4 is that nothing is better known than the principles.[4]

There are three notions of truth at work here. (1) Most generally, truth is whatever is. This is quite consistent with contingency in a proposition, and this general notion of truth underlies the general notion of knowledge, awareness of what is. This general truth is also applicable to mathematical propositions, and to propositions we would nowadays say express natural laws. (2) The truth that expresses natural law is present in a proposition when the premises expressing the law are such as to *make* the conclusion true, as long as nothing gets in the way. For instance, the heating produced by fire is supposed to occur as long as the natural activity of the fire is not blocked in some way, but not always – rather, only for as long as nothing ruling out the fire's heating occurs in the course of natural causation. The cause known here in the demonstration will be an efficient cause. As for (3) – the truth applicable to those that are always the same – some truths of this sort can be known by demonstration. In producing scientific knowing of these truths, demonstration works by comparing concepts, taking note when one situation causes another formally, not efficiently, and so takes no notice of sensory observation of how the world is. The natural world is composed of opposed powers, and so any efficient causal principle will be true, but only as long as no other power interferes and prevents the effect. (The principle will always be true, but not always effective, and so it has to have the qualification stated in it – that no other power interferes so as to prevent the production of the effect.)

Now, this narrow definition of scientifically knowable truth introduces a gap between scientific truth and the truth about the world to which we hope to apply it. We can only know unchanging truth that is never false, the sort in mathematics, and the world is full of truths that last but a moment, and so are not knowable at all, truths about nature. There seems to be no way to get to nature from mathematics, though Grosseteste, notably, is convinced that mathematics – that is, geometry, through the use of optics, for him the central science – is the key to understanding the world. The gap, he might be supposed to claim, is filled by the natural laws governing the operation of the various material things that are found in the world. These laws are unchanging, and always true, so that fire always has the capacity to heat, but they are hampered by the fact that they are conditioned, so that fire heats what is adjacent to it, unless it is already hot, or there is something cold just on the other side that cools it, or whatever.

But nowadays we must observe that there is in fact no such thing as fire. If we must identify something as fire, it would be, say, an exothermic chemical process (*not* a kind of stuff), but even so general a thing as that, which can occur with any number of entirely different substances, will not do as the sole source of heat in the world. There are also subatomic processes, which produce the heat of the earth's interior, and that of the sun (different subatomic processes do these two things). So fire, in the medieval conception of the thing, does not in fact exist, at all. If it did, it would do the trick, I suppose, of explaining why things are heated, but the world would not be at all the world in which we find ourselves living. Perhaps it is necessarily true that fire heats things, but the real reason why they are heated is not captured at all in that dictum. And one can go through the entire science of the time, with similar observations. So the principle in the demonstration referring to fire is simply wrong, not because fire would not heat, and that necessarily, but because there is no fire. We need to know, not simply what necessarily heats, but what actually exists that necessarily heats. Moreover, what we now understand as the source of heat in the world is not something that we understand by surveying the ideas provided to us by God, or at least nothing that we can recognize as surveying those ideas seems to have occurred in the history of their discovery. If that is the process lying behind scientific discovery, it is a hidden process.

Or we could try something more complex. Are there wolves, which necessarily (except when conditions blocking the causal action of the wolf nature are present) seek to eat sheep? It seems so, and perhaps from this observation we could argue that these animals must have sharp teeth and be fast and wily. But unfortunately there is more than one way to skin a cat, which means that wolves, to be efficient consumers of sheep, don't have to be almost anything in particular. They could be slow, but good at staying hidden, or have powerful front paws, or any number of other things, and still catch sheep to eat. It seems very hard to set up a demonstration of the wolf's material definition on the basis of its formal definition.

Perhaps it is actually not so bad as that. In fact, the sharp teeth of wolves do enable them to eat sheep, even if they might have done it in some other way, so we might argue that this is the reason why they have them. A science, we are told by the Aristotelian, does not prove the existence of its subject matter, but instead presupposes it. The science of animals simply assumes that animals exist, animals of the sorts that it studies, drawing on sensory cognition to understand and define them. The concepts of animals that we have each define a certain way of making one's living in the world (its formal definition), and the physical properties of animals (their material definitions) can be deduced from these concepts. (Grosseteste says that the 'material definition' is demonstrated through the 'formal definition'. So the formal definition of wolf specifies how it gets its food, and in this world it will therefore eat sheep.) So if the world must reflect some set of forms realized within it, we can draw information about the world from the senses, and make guesses at what forms are being realized. Perhaps none of our guesses are so sure that they would constitute knowledge, but some are sure enough that we can suppose that something like certain forms are realized in the world. The first move in establishing a science stands outside the science itself, and is to establish that the subject of the science exists. The *Posterior Analytics* does not do this part of the job, and it is presumably covered by the senses, which tell us what the world is like. If all that we had were the senses, that would be as far as we could get; but we also have the intellect, and a set of forms provided to us by God. Of course, we don't have these forms in any clear and distinct fashion, but they no doubt dispose us to interpret the world in one way rather than another, and perhaps, if our rational faculty were working right (no sin), it would lead us to recognize those forms when we saw them reflected in the world. That recognition would lead to the establishment of a principle about the natural world, one always true – say, that fire heats as much as it can whatever is adjacent to it, or that wolves eat sheep – that we would then know, and that could serve as a foundation for a syllogism. We see the world, and it reminds us of the forms of things, which we have to some degree already, but not at all clearly.[5] So the procedure is to make guesses at what exists, with the aid of the senses, and work out through demonstration the consequences of each of our proposals, holding on to what works.[6]

Now, lambs fear wolves, instinctively, because they eat sheep. It is a natural fact that lambs do this, and they do not fear other possible destroyers of lambs that do not exist. This fear has a natural expression in their sensory systems, for they are capable of sensing wolves as such, and recognizing through their senses that wolves are real and exist. So, it seems a necessary fact about the world that sensory systems include a list of the sorts of things that are likely to be encountered in it, and information about these things that will govern the behaviour of the animal with the system in a way that comports with their basic strategy for surviving. Moreover, this will be due to God's provision for these things, to God's providence, not to, say, evolution. This natural recognition of the causal properties of things, which are necessary to them, will be present in all animals. An animal is designed to live in the world that it is in, not in any other, and so it has the natural cognitive (not, notice, *rational*) functions needed to survive in that world. So a sheep has some way available to it to recognize wolves, which generally works – not a definition of wolf (which belongs only to a rational animal), but something along those lines, which, for the most part, enables it to identify wolves, and to remember and apply its memories to current experience. It will never happen that sheep should consider whether they are well-adapted to survive or not; but they are, because of (among other things) this way of recognizing wolves, though, of course, they have no language, no concepts, and do not speak or reason. It is not clear, outside mathematics, if human beings are any better off than sheep in their knowledge of the world, but at least human beings are poised, ready to advance into scientific knowledge of the world if they should get a chance to do so. Right now, though, they know nothing scientifically except mathematics.

Next, let us look at how Grosseteste himself does his science under these difficulties. He notes that the concept of wolf, intensely practical as it may be, is not particularly simple. In fact, the defining functions of a wolf fail to mention anything (or at least anything much) about how they are realized in this world. Wolves eat sheep, but what is this eating? How does it occur? Well, wolves must have parts, and so do sheep, and wolves take parts from the sheep, absorb them, and transform them into wolf, or use them as sources of energy, and so on, and so continue to live. Matter is basic, and one might wonder what the form of

matter is. I can understand this well enough without considering the details –
the fact that wolves are three-dimensional, and so on – but in addition wolves
can only be realized, it seems, in a world in which there are the right sorts of
parts to make up a wolf. Now, this sort of thing led Aquinas to say that the idea
of a wolf includes within it the ideas of all that is required to fill out our account
of the wolves' life, but Grosseteste fights shy of that. He thinks that the form of
wolf is far simpler than that, and is applied in the natural world to something
already made up of the requisite sorts of matter, organized in such a way as to
reveal the functioning of wolf, as that is detailed in the form of wolf, *but that*
the form of wolf does not contain this information as to how it is to be realized in
the world. It is necessary to realize it in this way, and so we can argue from the
form of wolf to these facts about its matter and the way in which it is found in
the world, but it is not specified in the form of wolf. So wolves eat sheep. What
sheep are, what it is to eat, how the sheep matter is converted to wolf matter, and
otherwise used in the wolf: all of these are facts, not about the nature of wolf, but
about how wolves' natures are realized in *this* world.

In his *On Light*,[7] Grosseteste (1912) gives an account of the origins of the
universe that lays out some of this necessary background about the world.
Light, he claims, is the first form of matter, which provides it with geometrically
ordered extension. As Form, Light contains no structure in itself, and so, if it
is to be realized, it can only be realized in a single point, without parts, and,
insofar as the Light realized in it is concerned, unrelated to any other point in
the world. But light has a natural causal power, which it must exercise – the
power to reproduce itself.[8] It produces new instances of light, distinguished from
itself only by its position in space, in a straight line extending outward. The light
thus extends itself into a sphere of light and matter. (Each point in the sphere is
occupied by an instance of light – i.e. the form of light present in matter – but
light cannot occupy more than a point, as was just observed.) In doing so, it
reproduces itself infinitely – that is, an infinite number of times. It must, because
it cannot make a new light anywhere except adjacent to itself, or as close as
possible to that, for there are no two adjacent points. So, it must make a new
light by making light at *all* points between itself and a second point – that is, at
an infinite number of points.[9]

Before we go on, consider this sphere of matter. The matter is not light, even
if it can only exist due to the light at every point that it occupies in space. The
matter is, in a sense, constituted by light, and it is the matter that guarantees the
existence of the sphere.[10] How does this light constitute matter? Well, it provides
a spatial structure to matter (and things made of matter, too), so that the light, in

the aggregate, acts like matter, occupying space, displaying shape, and so on, in accord with Euclidean geometry. We note that matter and light come together, so that there are no places that are not occupied by matter, since no-light means no-matter, and no-matter means no-light.[11] Perhaps this light can even move. That light should move makes no sense in itself, but once we imagine the light in a space, generated by an infinitely numerous light, it can move from one place to another in it. The light takes on new properties through its generation of light, among them location in space, and so light, or a collection of light can move from one place to another.

Now consider the outer surface of this sphere of light. It is fully actualized, for it is rarefied as much as it can be while still being light at all. (It is obvious, somehow, that light has a lowest possible level. Moreover, stronger light can reproduce, while lowest light cannot do so without some help.) This outer sphere of light is intelligible, intelligent, and remains quite capable of reproduction, but there is no place, and can be no place beyond it, where it can do so, since it cannot reproduce itself sufficiently strongly to be light at all where there is no light at all already. If light had originally been of this sort, then nothing would have happened at all! The created light must be stronger than it needs to be – that is to say, less fully actualized. So the universe begins, it seems, from something created as capable of further actualization through reproduction, and, being capable, it immediately sets out to do this.[12] The more perfectly actualized light is, the less powerful it is. So, the perfectly realized light at the outer surface of the sphere reproduces inwardly, where there is light somewhat stronger than necessary to be light, and so there is less work to be done to make light, and a new wave of light spreads to the centre. This can happen since the more interior light is not fully actualized, and so becomes more actually light when new light is added. This light, now twofold, has its outermost portion fully actualized, of the lowest intensity. The second sphere then illuminates the light below it, and the process repeats itself as often as it can, forming a series of nine spheres, each, in its outer part, of the lowest intensity of light. The lowest sphere (that of the Moon?) now has below it light that is so unactualized (i.e. dense) that the fully actualized light of the lowest sphere cannot bring it to fullness (cannot cause it to expand any of it to its minimal density), and so it remains incomplete, despite the light shining down upon it. This light shining into the sphere below the moon is continuous, since the light above is capable of producing new light below, and below the moon the light is insatiable, and cannot be provided with enough light to fully actualize it. This lowest matter thus becomes fully matter, ranked in order as fire, air, water, and earth. Fire receives light (continually) to the extent that it is capable of physically illuminating other things, and air, though not so much light as that, is still capable of expanding outwardly, though less so than fire is. Water retains only weight, being incapable of outward expansion, and earth, least mobile, and most powerfully material of all, occupies the center.

Elsewhere, we are told, in *On Lines, Angles, and Figures* (Grosseteste 1912: 59–60), that 'the consideration of lines, angles and figures is of the greatest utility since it is impossible for natural philosophy to be known without them ... All causes of natural effects have to be given through lines, angles and figures, for otherwise it is impossible for the reason why (*propter quid*) to be known in them'.[13] This round assertion of the importance of mathematics in physical science seems to be rooted in the production of an Euclidean geometry by the initial expansion of light. All motion and change is due to the analogous transmission of properties from matter to matter, in straight lines to adjacent matter, and so optics provides the prototype of physical science. The transmission, by the way, is affected by the nature of the recipient, and so, when the power of an object 'is received by the senses, it produces an effect that is somehow spiritual and noble' (60),[14] as, of course, the original of light is.

What do we learn from this exposition of the development of the world from light? We come to perceive a way in which the world might (if there is in fact light of the sort envisioned) have developed from a simpler world in which there was nothing physical at all. Light provides a convenient springboard here, for it can be viewed simply as the ability of the intellect in a non-physical being, a mind, to spread its knowledge to other intellects, as in the illumination of one angel by another. Indeed, in this illumination the light of intellect seems, as it were, to generate new lower beings, ending in a being right at the edge of the physical, the intelligence of the moon, that spreads its illumination only to physical beings below it. So, the exposition addresses the most critical problem in the Neoplatonic view of the creation, the transition from immaterial to material things, moving from light, the form of matter, but not itself material, existing only at a single point, to corporeal matter, spread through space, in a barely intelligible move from finite to infinite.[15]

Let us consider how knowledge of all this might occur. First, we note the knowledge of definitions. The definition of light is that which can reproduce itself in another place or thing. The definition applies, in a way, it seems, to everything, though we restrict our consideration of it to those cases in which we are particularly interested in this property. This property expresses itself variously in various sorts of light. So, it may express itself in the mind's *irradiatio spiritualis* (Grosseteste 1981: I, 17: 38–47)[16] which makes another soul know, or in a more physical spread of heat from fire or any effect imagined to spread from one thing to another. The nature and conditions of the thing that is the light determines how that light manages to spread itself about in its situation. God, of course, is at work in all things, illuminating them so that we can understand them, and is, in his creation, the prime example of this spread. The use of Platonic metaphor here is irreducible and fundamental – light creates itself in other things, in whatever way might be made out in each situation in which it occurs, and this gives rise to all sorts of things in the world.

The definition of which we have knowledge, then, in coming to knowledge in definition, is not of the underlying structure and its operations, but is rather of the end of the thing, a formal definition. The material definition, which expresses the materials making it up and its arrangement, may be used, with the aid of mathematics, in making out how the end is accomplished, but it is not that definition that is fundamental to demonstration. It may be used in working out the consequences of the situation, but it can only be used to the extent that it is grasped in relation to the formal definition, to the end sought. Thus, the definition per se of the subject is the formal definition, and the material definition is demonstrated of this formal definition as its realization in the material at hand.[17]

An axiom is a very general principle, so general as to stand outside all the sciences, which does not actually enter into demonstration as a premise. It is perceivably true because its subject and predicate are identical, eliminating any need for a demonstration, with a connecting middle term, to establish them (I, 8: 186–9). These principles take several different forms. One states that the genus can always be predicated of its species. This is not to say that animal can be predicated of rabbit, which is much too specific to count as an axiom, but rather that from which this follows – namely, that a genus can always be predicated of its species. No particular species or genus is mentioned in the axiom. From this principle it does follow that rabbits are animals, but only on the assumption that animal is the genus of rabbit. That assumption must be established first, and it is, of course, a much more interesting project than the establishment of the axiom. We must determine the definitions of animal and rabbit to do it, which means definitions applying to things that we sense.

Now, such a vision is not applicable merely to one science. Take, for instance, the principle that equals to a single thing are equal to one another. One might apply it in extremely varied sciences, such as biology, and the science of diplomatics. In both sciences one can identify things, animals and diplomatic missions, and speak of their identity, or lack of it, to one another, and the equality or lack of it of different animals or missions. There is something in common in both sciences, a structure of equality, say, or a form of unity. But this is only because animals and diplomatic missions are both 'things', not because they are two instances of any given sort of thing. There is no common kind to which both belong, beyond an 'existent'. They have nothing in common, save existence. But 'existent' is not a kind of thing at all, since anything consistently conceived can be existent. So, our axiom that two things equal to the same thing are equal to one another tells us nothing about diplomatic missions, except perhaps this: if we are to find them equal to one another, we will have to find standards of identity for them that live up to the notion of equality, including this axiom. What those are might be entirely mysterious in any particular case, but if they cannot be found then we cannot speak of two diplomatic missions as identical to one another. We have to already know something about diplomatic missions, something expressed in their definitions, before we can begin to talk about them.

One consequence of this is that if we are to use the notion of equality in the science of diplomatic missions, we must use a form of the axiom already adapted to it by a specification that it can apply there. We have to use 'diplomatic missions that are the same mission as another are the same as one another', or 'if one mission is the same as another, and a third mission is the same as well, then the two missions the same as the third are the same as one another'. In that way, the standards by which two missions are the same as one another are drawn on, standards we have established exist, and the whole procedure, though parallel to the procedure in biology, is not the same, for equality of species of animal is a different notion from equality of diplomatic missions, with a different underlying causal basis.

Knowledge of a causal principle is neither knowledge of a definition, specifying what a thing is for, nor of an axiom, laying out the general shape that a picture of the world must take to count as a picture at all. A causal principle connects the existing things we are studying to one another, specifying how they interact with one another. Causal principles establish ways in which things affect the rest of the world, and thereby change it, and so they imply that the world outside the cause is not unchanging, and not therefore knowable. With the exception of God, everything that causes anything is itself changeable due to the effects of other causes upon it. So the realm of the natural world would seem to be unknowable. But Grosseteste considers these causal entities not as they are sensible, or as they act in the world, but rather as they are subject to an unchanging nature, which specifies exactly their causal activities. He assumes that a natural being will have causal principles that apply to it in such a way that it acts *as long as nothing prevents it* from doing so.[18] So, fire may heat something, as long as the something is not simultaneously affected by something cool, does not have an insulator between it and the fire, and so on. *Every* action is considered to work in this way, so that the law applying to something that acts naturally is that it will act as long as nothing else, in accord with natural causal principles, prevents it from doing so. This means that a causal principle may state that fire, say, will produce heat in something with which it is in contact *as long as nothing else prevents it from doing so*.[19] That is not an empty statement, for it insists that the fire *produces* the heat. Moreover, if the fire produces the heat through the agency of something else, then it is not a principle. The fire must be the immediate source of the heat, or else we must look for a more fundamental principle underlying this principle, referring to the actual source of the heat. Given all of that, the principle will *always* be true, whether the cause is active or not.

Now, this means that to know the principle, we must know that it will always be true, and this means that it cannot be known through the evidence of the senses. Nonetheless, it is cognized through the senses, for we come to form the concept that lies behind the principle through the senses, as we have seen. When it is cognized, so that we have a reasonably strong argument that it is so rooted in sensation, we suppose that we know the causal power by which the action happens. We 'know' that fire heats, or at least, if we come to have an immediate perception through reason of the nature of fire sufficient to support this conclusion, we might know that fire heats. The perceptual cognition leads to real knowledge in that case, which is similar to the knowledge of a definition. That is not to say, though, that knowing the definition of fire simply means that we know it heats. Rather, if we know its definition, we are capable of coming to perceive that it heats, if we perceive that it must heat if it is to exist in the natural order. Fire is the active element in the natural order, and, to be so, it must therefore heat. If the natural order were different, perhaps it would do something else, but, as it is, it heats, and this we know through the senses.[20]

So the certainty of the principle is from the intellectual vision of the form, even though the principle involves the attribute, which is not essential, or part of the definition. Perhaps we want to say that the attribute is part of the interaction between form and surrounding circumstances in which it is realized. The moon comes in line with earth and sun, and, given the sizes, opacity of the earth, and distances, the moon is eclipsed. The definition of the moon in no way contains this information, and one might have expected it always to be illuminated, but, given its nature, in that situation it is not, and we know this through the senses.

But consider the case of scammony. We know, with the aid of the senses leading to the universal, but through a universal nonetheless, that scammony produces a discharge of red bile, as long as nothing prevents its doing so. That is to say, we know that something must actively oppose its production of the discharge, or else it will occur, for scammony drives such a discharge if it is not actively opposed. Now, this knowledge is necessarily to some degree vague, for we probably do not know all the ways that the discharge could be prevented. Moreover, it may be that it is not scammony, but something else associated with it, that produces the discharge, but we have not been able to tease out that component, and won't notice this until we obtain some scammony that does not produce the discharge even under the best conditions, lacking that component. Or perhaps it is some more general sort of thing, of which scammony is one sort, that produces the discharge. So our knowledge, though not exactly wrong, still does not amount to knowledge, strictly speaking, through demonstration (Grosseteste 1981: I, 14: 247–71). But it may also be correct, and formed by a perfectly good demonstration. So it seems that we may have knowledge of which we are not certain, for we cannot be reasonably certain that such knowledge is correctly formed, at least not before we receive a proper illumination from God, which we can recognize as such. But still we have what certainty one can have in this life concerning the matter.

If we move on to the fourth area in which knowledge is possible, mathematical knowledge, this is all changed. Here the form of which we have knowledge, the form of triangle or circle, say, is not a form that we encounter in the world, it seems, or detect with the senses. Rather, we understand the form precisely through its definition, from which we deduce its relations, following reason alone, to other forms of a like sort. There is nothing here that we do not know, nothing hidden; and nonetheless there is knowledge, and ignorance, of complex relations among these individual items that goes as far, it seems, as anything in the natural world. The question here is not that of what these things are; it is of whether or not they exist. The difficulty is not in the discovery of the definitions; it is in working through and grasping the complexity of the relations among them. The natural world is a collection of machines, formed in an Euclidean space, realizing, as do all machines, certain goals – namely, the existence of certain sorts of things with certain aims, and aiming ultimately at the existence of a world in which human beings can live their lives. At one end of this collection of machines is their aim, the human essence itself, which exceeds natural means, and through reason shapes the whole of creation into an expression of humanity, itself the invention of the God who made it all. At the other end are the bits and pieces combining to make up the machine, arranged in a mathematically defined space/time. Through demonstration, reason knows these machines as they must be, spatially. In the end, it seems, we must realize – to know the whole – that the way the world is put together is the only way that it could be put together to express the human essence, including its supernatural goals.

To know is to know why it must be so. To know this is to know why God has to create the world thus, and that means knowing why God's aims for the world require this. That means, in the case of natural science, knowing what features of the world are the ones that God aims to realize, what features of it comport to God's ends. Nothing short of this would suffice to establish with certainty the principles of a science. The world is the way it is because it is best that it be that way. When we turn from natural science to mathematical science, we find in geometry the necessary matrix in which the world is formed. Space is necessary to the formation of compound unities, and time is necessary to their change. These things can be known simply from a contemplation of what they are, for they are complex, the first of complex things, and their structure can be captured in the formal apparatus of reasoning. In fact, unlike the natural laws, which are bound by an infinite complexity of inhibiting factors in their operations in the world, they can be captured perfectly. Thus, the demonstration of mathematical principles is the most perfect exemplification of demonstration that is possible.

Now, Grosseteste's theory of scientific knowledge is an externalist theory, arguing that one has scientific knowledge as long as one believes what is in fact true on the right basis, because one understands the causal matrix, efficient or formal, that in fact makes it true. Given his syllogistic logical theory, this means taking it to be true because it is the conclusion of a demonstration. One needs only the principal cause; all the rest of the matrix, enabling that cause's operation, can be only partly grasped. Unlike people today, he does not think that scientific knowledge is the highest kind of knowledge there is, reserving for that place knowledge arising from a view of the form on which scientific knowledge could be based, were it fully known by us, and taking it that such a view is the gift of the God responsible for the form, and denied to us in this present life, due to our sins. This view, of course, has certain resounding scientific consequences. The world is made for the sake of the good, and all things in the end happen for the best. The ultimate cause for any scientific law is the fact that it works out for the best, and so is the end for which the law was established by God. In practice, this view subordinates science to theology and faith, by which theology is known. The modern view of mathematics as laying somehow the foundation of scientific theory is maintained, and the metaphysics driving the view also insists on freedom of will.

As for the methods by which a scientific view of the world can be developed and defended, Grosseteste does a good job of defending the more obvious points, but does not develop any very philosophically interesting picture. He allows that a weakened sense of the forms of things that God made underlies our everyday view of the world, and sees science as a development from this everyday view. The view of science that has emerged in the past 400 years or so, with, for instance, its introduction of evolution and reduction of biology to physics, would hardly have been suggested by Grosseteste's principles, but is not, perhaps, necessarily opposed to them. In his view of scientific method, Grosseteste seems to have absorbed Aristotle's *Posterior Analytics*, but not to have gone beyond it or to be aware of challenges to it.

Notes

1   Knowing a proposition through the knowledge of its terms is knowing it to be true from its terms' meanings, and so true necessarily. Nothing outside the proposition's terms, like the time of day, for instance, affects its truth. So the proposition is imagined to be relatively simple, consisting of two terms connected by a copula. Moreover, knowledge of a term is supposedly not acquired through a sensory impression of its object. It is known only through knowledge of what it means, as it is expressed in an essential definition, which is known quite independently of sense impressions. In particular, an essential definition is known through direct knowledge of the concept associated with the term, which is in the soul independently of sense impressions (though it is associated with sense impressions – someone who knows what a wolf is through knowledge of its essence, and has encountered wolves and observed them a little, also (often) knows what one looks like). If it turned out there were no such concepts, then there would be no knowledge of the term, and no knowledge at all of any proposition. In all of this, Grosseteste assumes, with Augustine, that knowledge proceeds downward from God. It is only because God illumines the mind that it has these concepts, and can know the eternal truths demonstrable from them. Aristotle, given his somewhat different frame of mind, assumes that one can have gained knowledge of the term only from sensation and self-knowledge. Concepts are formed from experience.

2   See also Grosseteste (1912: IV, 8; II, 3).

3   A demonstration that the Pope sits would have to run, 'The Pope does X, whatever does X sits, therefore the Pope sits.' That the Pope does X would have to

be known to be true at all times. Say that it was not. Then what is known is that the Pope usually sits, say. Does this provide the cause for why the Pope sits when he does? No, since we need to include in any such explanation of the cause the reason why the Pope sits *now*, and not at some other time, and no such explanation is provided. Do we perhaps deduce 'the Pope sits' from 'the Pope sits now' and many other such statements about different times? Only if the Pope always sits, which he does not. Could we even deduce that the Pope usually sits, or is capable of sitting, always? Only if sitting is, instead of a mere accident adhering to the Pope, the direct outcome of some action that the Pope takes, *an action directed at sitting*, and this not as a result of its being directed at anything else. The action of sitting has to be done per se. But sometimes such a per se action fails because the Pope simply chooses not to sit. Instead, the Pope walks. He acts, not naturally, but freely, and can omit action if he chooses to – again, not naturally, but freely. The complete understanding of the situation is not to be had, it seems, or else it is what has just been explained, and in the natural course of events it can never be known that the Pope sits at all. It requires awareness of his doing it, and that awareness is not gained by reason, but only through the senses.

4   'Behold what elegant order. First it was demonstrated that a demonstration is a syllogism from true statements. Now the first division of the true is through contingent and necessary, and from this it demonstrates next that demonstration is from the necessary; Now necessity first and mostly is found in propositions having these three conditions, universality, namely, as much from the part of the subject as from the part of time, and what is predicated is said of subject per se, and what of the subject first. On this account it is demonstrated next that demonstration is from propositions which have three conditions in which they connect with one another. But before this it is demonstrated that these three things are to be defined, because without definitions they will not be sufficiently understood. Therefore, it is defined first 'it is said *de omni*', because that is more universal than 'it is said *per se*', next it is said *per se* is defined, because that is more universal than 'universal' and 'said about the first'. The definition of 'that which is said *de omni*' plainly is not in need of explanation' (Grosseteste 1912: I, 2: 103; I, 4: 31).

5   This is the burden of *Posterior Analytics* II 19, in which it is argued that experience of the world, which is due to reason, arises from particular sensory observations, common sense, imagination, and memory, all available to animals, and from experience arises the universal, known by *nous* in such a way as to ground the first principles of science.

6   Alternatively, we might decide that wolves and fire exist, and leave in question *what* they are, and just how extensive their powers are. So, fire turns out to be a process

after all, despite looking at first like a substance, and one that only produces some of the heat in the world, not all of it. And wolves turn out to be something subject to evolutionary processes.

7   McEvoy (1982: 151) comments that this work (Gosseteste 1912) is 'perhaps the only scientific cosmogony, written between the *Timaeus* and modern times'.

8   How do we know this? Do we *know* what general sorts of things there are in the world? Do we *know* the world to be spatial, with three dimensions, and temporal with one? Grosseteste (1981: 215) says that we arrive from the senses 'at an experiential (*experimentale*) universal principle', and the adjective *experimentale* indicates that the universal principle is not known scientifically, not even as a principle, but still is known in a general way, through reason. Compare Immanuel Kant's *Critique of Pure Reason*, specifically the Transcendental Aesthetic on space, which resolves the problem here by postulating that space is an a priori necessary representation, which is the ground of all further outer sensations.

9   This seems questionable. Might it not be better to conclude that it makes no new points at all, since there are no adjacent points at which it might make it? But then we get no cosmology. No doubt, Grosseteste considered that light must expand outward from a point, and in a straight line. That was the only resource that he had to produce a spatial order, and so the difficulties here must be accepted, and are to be resolved when one has a better understanding of the matter. The fact that the expansion is instantaneous makes it all the more mysterious.

10 Indeed, matter is, by definition(?), what exists. It has no other property in itself. Light is by definition what reproduces itself.

11 Matter is in space, which is provided by light, one point at a time, and a quantity of matter can apparently be said to occupy a region of space – a sphere, say. So matter, unlike light, in itself has quantity. If there were only light, we could not speak of anything except points of light. But a quantity of matter allows us to speak of breadth, width, and depth of a shape.

12 Moreover, it also begins from light so unactualized that it can support all the rest of the process of producing the universe, without ever becoming even less actualized. So the coarsest and least actualized matter at the center of things, the densest of earth, was the first light produced.

13 In *On the Nature of Places*, a continuation of *On Lines, Angles and Figures*, Grosseteste (1912: 65) says that 'the diligent investigator of natural phenomena can give the causes of all natural effects, therefore, in this way by the rules and roots and foundations given from the power of geometry'. The intensity of the effect will depend on the angle at which it strikes an object, its distance, and the figure within which it operates (a cone or sphere), as well as distance.

14 Note that this means that the senses receive in some way the form of the thing transmitted to them, so that, through an aggregation of sense in memory and the

repetition of memory in *experimentum*, a universal may emerge. The universal is not invented or contrived by us, but is actually in what we receive from the senses, and so is guaranteed to be a real universal, found in nature, and it can serve as a principle in a science.

15 It is to be noted that God himself is light, inasmuch as he is a Trinity, for he begets splendor from himself (Grosseteste 1982: VIII, 3.1).

16 The eye emits a ray when it sees (McEvoy 2000: 336), and the soul is imagined to emit a ray as well. The soul or eye is a little sun, in Platonic terms.

17 The distinction between formal and material definition occurs at *Posterior Analytics* II 9, 93b22, in the translation of James of Venice, which says that 'some definitions made in accord with species, have no middle term by which they are demonstrated, but definitions made in accord with matter can have such a middle term'. This interpolation in the text captures a Neoplatonic distinction, upon which Grosseteste (1981: II: 620–60) seizes.

18 He also distinguishes free from natural actions, allowing freedom of will in human beings and angels. A free act can be omitted purely by the will of the being that can commit it, with no external circumstance bringing about the omission. Grosseteste does not consider free acts in connection with the *Posterior Analytics*. Although a free act has a reason, the reason need not be effective, the will itself having the ability to set it aside.

19 This would not be true if fire were a free agent, of course.

20 Or, somewhat less plausibly, following the example provided in Aristotle (who is *not* evidently committed at all to this approach), thunder is the extinction of fire in a cloud (formal definition) *because of* continuous sound in the cloud (material definition). See *Posterior Analytics* II 9–11. Aristotle does specify that the sound in the cloud is perhaps the final cause here, intended to frighten those in the underworld (11, 94b31-4), though it seems that he makes the claim at least partly in jest. He does say that the extinction of fire is the efficient cause, and the definition of thunder is 'noise in a cloud', but it is not at all clear that he means to make anything more of this than one way in which the four causes connect up with one another in a demonstration. Following the Neoplatonic line of interpretation, Grosseteste makes this the model of the highest sort of demonstration in natural affairs.

References

Cunningham, J. (2012), *Robert Grosseteste: His Thought and Its Impact*, Toronto: Pontifical Institute of Medieval Studies.

Grosseteste, R. (1912), *Die philosophischen Werke des Robert Grosseteste, Bischofs von Lincoln*, ed. L. Baur, Münster i. W: Aschendorff.

Grosseteste, R. (1981), *Commentarius in posteriorum analyticorum libros*, ed. P. Rossi, Florence: Olschki.

Grosseteste, R. (1982), *Hexaëmeron*, ed. R. C. Dale and S. Gieben, trans. C. F. J. Martin, London: Oxford University Press.

John of Salisbury (1955), *The Metalogicon of John of Salisbury: A Twelfth-Century Defense of the Verbal and Logical Arts of the Trivium*, trans. D. D. McGarry, Berkeley: University of California Press.

McEvoy, J. (1982), *The Philosophy of Robert Grosseteste*, Oxford: Clarendon Press.

McEvoy, J. (ed.) (1995), *Robert Grosseteste: New Perspectives on His Thought and Scholarship*, Instrumenta Patristica, 27, Turnhout: Brepols.

McEvoy, J. (2000), *Robert Grosseteste*, Oxford: Clarendon Press.

5

Thomas Aquinas on Knowledge and Demonstration

Alexander Hall

1. Introduction

The twelfth-century Latin West experienced a renaissance as the Reconquest of the Iberian Peninsula provided direct access to classical pagan thought lost since the fall of the Western Roman Empire in fifth century CE.[1] Whereas Plato's writings garnered little attention despite his indelible influence on medieval thought via thinkers such as Augustine (354–430 CE), by the close of the twelfth century CE all of Aristotle's writings were available in Latin; prior to this, medievals had only his *Categories* and *On Interpretation*, and a few texts from late antiquity, including Porphyry's *Isagoge* (a brief introduction to *Categories*), works comprising what medievals termed the old logic (*logica vetus*). Hence, by the time that Thomas Aquinas and his thirteenth-century colleagues take up discussing human knowledge, they have a direct access to Aristotle that is nevertheless mediated by the Islamic commentary tradition that shaped the initial reception of the texts. Aquinas finds in Aristotle an account of knowledge whereupon it admits of degrees of certainty, the highest of which is absolute, of what 'belongs to the subject according to the essential nature of the subject' (*Commentary on the 'Posterior Analytics of Aristotle'* [In PA] 1.11.3).[2] Aquinas adheres very closely to Aristotle on this matter, who, for his part, worked to supplant Plato. A brief discussion juxtaposing the three may clarify Aquinas' views.

1.1 *Locus classicus*

Plato and Aristotle believe that knowledge admits of degrees of certainty, ranging from probable to necessary, with '*epistēmē*' sometimes used to signify the latter.[3] In this connection, '*epistēmē*' is often translated into English as 'scientific knowledge', in line with the Latin translation of the term with '*scientia*'. Aristotle and Aquinas recognize at least two types of *epistēmē*: (1) necessary *epistēmē* (Greek: *anagkaiōn*/Latin: *necessarium*) and (2) *epistēmē* that is true for the most part (Greek: *epi to polu*/Latin *ut frequenter*).[4] Broadly construed, (1) pertains to axiomatic systems such as geometry, indemonstrable principles of demonstration (such as the principle of non-contradiction or a mental grasp of an entity's essence through understanding), and perhaps even to certain natural phenomena such as eclipses.[5] However, (2) concerns natural phenomena where like causes do not always produce like results, as in the process of generation that does not always lead to healthy birth outcomes.[6]

Whereas Plato and Aristotle agree that *epistēmē* may be necessary, they differ over its object. For Plato, what is known in this way are the forms, entities that exist outside space and time as unique and perfect instances of qualities (e.g. beauty), natural kinds (e.g. human being), or perhaps even artefacts (e.g. bed).[7] Forms are imperfectly copied by individuals that instantiate characteristics (essential or otherwise) in this act of participation.[8] Aristotle agrees, in his *Metaphysics* (*Metaph.* 7), that individuals within a natural kind somehow share an essence, which he terms 'the what it was to be (*to ti ēn einai*)', but he denies that essences exist apart from particular substances, which he views as hylomorphic (i.e. matter-form) composites,[9] granting ontological primacy to the substances in which forms inhere (*Categories* 14b1-13), effectively inverting Plato's scheme: 'All the other things are either said of the primary substances as subjects or in them as subjects. So if the primary substances did not exist it would be impossible for any of the other things to exist' (5, 2b4-6).[10]

As regards Aquinas' understanding of *scientia*, what Plato (at least in his middle-period) and Aristotle agree on is as important as why they differ. They agree that we possess necessary or certain knowledge of universal definitions,[11] but differ over the source of this knowledge, offering nativist and empiricist accounts, respectively. Nativism (or 'innativism') holds that innate concepts, categories, ideas, and so on make up some part of what we know. In *Meno* (80a-86c), Plato advances the nativist theory of anamnesis (the recovery of knowledge through recollection) to resolve the paradox of inquiry, which asks how one who does not know the correct answer to a question could recognize it as such when it is given. Other, middle-period, dialogues such as *Phaedo*, *Phaedrus*, and *Republic* link anamnesis to the forms, known by us in the interims between reincarnations. In *De Anima* (*DA*) 3.5, Aristotle leaves little room for personal immortality, and advances the empiricist thesis that knowledge is through experience: we have universal definitions via a psychological process of abstraction from particulars (An. Post. 2.19; *DA* 3.4–5). However, Aristotle's break with Plato does not signify any doubt on his part that we possess knowledge that is necessary:

> The proper object of unqualified scientific knowledge [*epistēmē haplōs*][12] is something which cannot be other than it is. (An. Post. 1.2, 71b15-16)
>
> Since the object of pure scientific knowledge [*epistēmē haplōs*] cannot be other than it is, the truth obtained by demonstrative knowledge will be necessary. (1.4, 73a21-23)

Aquinas' commentary on these passages recognizes the necessity of *scientia*, and correlates this necessity with certainty:

> To know something scientifically is to know it completely ... to apprehend its truth perfectly ... Because *scientia* is also sure and certain knowledge of a thing ... It is further required that what is scientifically known could not be otherwise. (In PA 1.4.5)
>
> Since the definition of *scientia* spoke of that which cannot be otherwise, that which is scientifically known through demonstration will be necessary ... Demonstrative science [*demonstrativa scientia*] is ... what we acquire through demonstration. Consequently, it follows that the conclusion of a demonstration is necessary. (In PA 1.9.2)[13]

Moreover, Aquinas reads Aristotle's project as an attempt to retain certainty in the absence of forms and anamnesis:

> Plato ... held that *scientia* in us is ... of an impression upon our minds of ideal forms from which ... are also derived the natural forms in natural things ... In like fashion he postulated that *scientia* in us [arises] ... when man is brought to recall things which he naturally understands in virtue of an imprint of separated forms ... Aristotle's view is opposed to this on two counts. For he maintains that natural forms are made actual by forms present in matter ... He further maintains that *scientia* is made actual in us by other *scientia* already existing in us ... through a syllogism or some type of argument. (In PA 1.1.8)

Aristotle does not think that, in eliminating transcendent forms, one must sacrifice knowledge of what cannot be otherwise.[14] *Posterior Analytics* supplants Plato's anamnesis with induction and thereby answers the *Meno* paradox, which introduces Aristotle's work: 'All teaching and all intellectual learning come about from already existing knowledge ... Before the induction, or before getting a deduction, you should perhaps be said to understand in a way – but in another way not ... Otherwise the puzzle in the *Meno* will result; for you will learn either nothing or what you know' (1.1, 71a1-30). Aristotle asks us to imagine a person, asked whether he knows that all pairs are even-numbered, being confronted with something that he did not immediately recognize as a pair: for example, one-third of six. In a sense, the person knew that it was pair, by means of previous principles gathered by induction. Aquinas notes of this example: 'The conclusion ... was already known, not absolutely, but as it was virtually known in its principles ... However, according to Plato's theory the conclusion was pre-known absolutely, so that no one learns afresh but is led to recall by some rational process of deduction' (In PA 1.3.3).

1.2 The scope of knowledge: certainty and induction

Aquinas, then, views *Posterior Analytics* as a theory of knowledge that can preserve necessary truths without reliance on Plato's forms. This deserves attention, as Eleonore Stump (2005: 226–7) in her influential *Aquinas* concludes that there is no guarantee that, for Aquinas, *scientia* comprises knowledge rather than error. Stump bases this claim on what I take to be an overly circumspect reading of Aquinas on induction.[15] Stump is concerned about warding off a foundationalist interpretation on which Aquinas restricts the scope of knowledge to a small set of propositions known with certainty and those derived from these (221). I too would reject such an extreme foundationalist reading. I take it rather that Aquinas' understanding of knowledge makes room for probabilistic justification that correlates with a variety of epistemic attitudes that are differentiated with respect to their various degrees of certainty (all of which fall short of *scientia*), ranging from mere fancy, on the low end, to belief, at the apex (In PA preface).[16] Moreover, *scientia* itself is one of five intellectual virtues concerned with universal knowledge and directed at truth. The complete list is: *scientia*, art, wisdom, prudence, and understanding.[17] But Stump seems to go too far in her move away from foundationalism when she suggests (231) that on Aquinas' view every proposition that one takes as certain may be wrong owing to the possibility that we are deceived or mistaken. Certainly induction may go awry. Likewise, we may think that we grasp a necessary truth, and be wrong. Nevertheless, worries such as these do not stop Aquinas from stating that by induction we can grasp the essence.[18] Again induction furnishes true premises (In PA 1.4), with universal predicates (In PA 2.20), that tell what belongs to the essence of a thing (In PA 1.11), such that the resultant knowledge is necessary, that is, for such knowledge 'it is not possible to fall short of the truth' (In PA preface). As regards foundationalism, I take it that Aquinas' account of *scientia* is foundationalist inasmuch as scientific demonstration requires indemonstrable principles (In PA 1.4; see Section 3.1 below); but, along with Scott MacDonald (1993: 177), I believe that 'it is a mistake ... to suppose that his epistemology is coextensive with his account of strict *scientia*'. *Scientia* is, it appears, one of a variety of cognitive attitudes that Aquinas would count as knowledge.

1.3 Précis

A study of Aquinas on the art of logic, especially its judicative and investigative branches, discloses the aim of *scientia* relative to other types of knowledge. I then take up the definition of the demonstrative syllogism as a syllogism productive of *scientia*, the assertions of per se inherence that comprise its propositions, and its types: *propter quid* and *quia*. Finally, I discuss the relationship between demonstration and definition, revisit necessity as regards natural phenomena, and close with a brief discussion of the types of definition that are furnished by the scientific syllogism.

2. The art of logic

Aquinas classifies logic as an art. An art is a practice designed to facilitate an activity – in this case, deliberation. Arts are products of reason, hence logic as the art that directs reason is 'the art of the arts' (In PA 1.1.2).

2.1 The branches of logic

The branches of logic are mapped onto the three acts of reason: (1) understanding, by which we form a mental representation of the essence of a thing; (2) combining and dividing, that is, forming affirmative and negative propositions that are either true or false; and (3) advancing from known to unknown. The acts are ordered. (2) requires (1) and is in turn required by (3) (2004 preface; In PA preface). Aristotle's *Categories* and *De Interpretatione* consider the first two acts; the remainder of his logical writings, the third. The third act admits of a threefold division. (3A) Judicative logic explains the inherence of properties via the essence of the subject of inherence. Judicative judgements possess the certitude of *scientia*. *Scientia* is necessary (*necessitas*) and cannot be other than true (*non est possibile esse veritatis defectum*) (In PA preface). Judicative judgements are arrived at by syllogism. Aristotle's *Prior Analytics* concerns formal validity, the

Posterior Analytics both formal validity and the nature of the propositions of the scientific syllogism. (3B) Investigative logic is a logic of discovery (as opposed to the analysis of judicative logic) (ST 1.79.8c). Here, certainty is not always (*non semper*) had. Rather, we may arrive at a degree of assent ranging with increasing certainty from mere fancy (*existimatio*) to faith or opinion (*fides vel opinion*). Aristotle's *Topics*, *Rhetoric*, and *Poetics* belong to investigative logic as a division of (3), which advances from one thing to another. (3C) Fallacies are treated in Aristotle's *Sophistical Refutations*.

2.2 Judicative and investigative logic

Discovery (the province of investigative logic) is from the first principles to which judicative judgements return via analysis: 'Human reasoning, by way of inquiry and discovery (*inventionis*), advances from certain things simply understood – namely, the first principles; and, again, by way of judgement returns by analysis to first principles, in the light of which it examines what it has found' (ST 1.79.8c).

Investigation then may look to judgement to confirm its findings: 'To the second process of reason [i.e. where it succeeds for the most part, viz. (3B)] another part of logic called investigative is devoted. For investigation is not always accompanied by certitude. Hence in order to have certitude a judgement must be formed, bearing on that which has been investigated' (In PA preface). Aquinas does not expand upon this comment. But we may speculate. Investigation sets out to acquire truths: for instance, that a lunar eclipse results from a privation of light caused by the earth's interposition between moon and sun (An. Post. 2.8). Judicative logic links these principles to their effects via the scientific syllogism, which we can think of as a syllogism whose statements capture traits that belong to its subject by means of its definition, which is a formulation of its essence; hence:

> A privation of light is a lunar eclipse
> The moon suffers a privation of light
> Therefore, the moon is now eclipsed

Judicative logic would then lend certitude to investigative logic by syllogisms that place the principle (i.e. cause) discovered via investigation as a middle in a scientific demonstration that relates it to its effects. We will consider the nature of these links in Section 3. At any rate, *Posterior Analytics* is philosophy of science from an Aristotelian moderate realist perspective that prioritizes primary substances as the loci of the forms, and insists that correct explanations be in terms of unchanging factors tied to the definitions of the causes at play. So, it appears that judicative logic organizes the findings of investigative into a framework that illuminates the various types of causality at play, thereby broadening the field of inquiry and establishing new connections, a process that Aquinas discusses when comparing the various types of inquiry:

> Questioning occurs one way in demonstrative sciences and another way in dialectics [which belongs to investigative logic]. For in dialectics not only the conclusion but also the premises are open to question; but in demonstrative sciences the demonstrator takes premises as *per se* known or proved by such principles. Hence, he asks only about the conclusion. And when he has demonstrated it, he uses it as a proposition to demonstrate some other conclusion. (In PA 1.21.3)

3. The scientific syllogism: its definition, elements, and species

3.1 The definition of the scientific syllogism

Scientia is, as it were, rigidly designating inasmuch as it picks out essential predicates. At *Posterior Analytics* 1.2, Aristotle defines *scientia* and the scientific syllogism. At this juncture, he is speaking only of *scientia propter quid*, which is of an effect in terms of the essence of its cause. He terms this *scientia* 'unqualified' relative to *scientia quia*, which lacks an unmediated grasp of an essence and thereby fails to meet the criteria for strict or unqualified *scientia*.[19] Regarding *scientia propter quid*, Aristotle notes:

> We suppose ourselves to possess unqualified scientific knowledge of a thing, as opposed to knowing it in the accidental way in which the sophist knows, when we think that we know the cause on which the fact depends, as the cause of that fact and of no other, and, further, that the fact could not be other than it is. (71b8-11)

Aristotle defines the scientific syllogism in terms of its end (the acquisition of *scientia*) and matter (scientific premises):

> What I now assert is that at all events we do know by demonstration. By demonstration I mean a syllogism productive of scientific knowledge (*sullogismon epistēmonikon*), a syllogism, that is, the grasp of which is *eo ipso* such knowledge ... The premises of demonstrated knowledge must be true, first,

immediate, better known than and prior to the conclusion, which is further related to them as effect to cause. (71b17-21)[20]

True. Aquinas spells out the truth requirement in terms of the medieval doctrine of the transcendentals, which has it that truth, goodness, and unity are convertible properties of being: 'What is not true does not exist, for to be and to be true are convertible' (In PA 1.4.14).[21]

First and Immediate. A proposition is first if it states the cause of an effect and immediate if it is indemonstrable. Immediate propositions include various axioms, some particular to a science – for example, arithmetic posits that a unit is quantitatively indivisible (An. Post 1.2, 72a22) – others regulative of demonstration – for example, the law of the excluded middle (An. Post 1.11, 77a30-31; In PA 1.7.8).[22] Again, knowledge of an essence arrived at by induction is immediate. As immediate propositions are requisite for proof, the An. Post. account of *scientia* is foundationalist (as noted in Section 1.2). No demonstration can proceed with principles that require proof.[23]

Better Known and Prior. Premises are better known than and prior to the conclusion when the premises construe the essence of the subject as the cause of effects concomitant with that essence.[24]

Causes. 'The propositions of a demonstration are the causes of the conclusion, because we know in a scientific manner when we know the causes' (In PA 1.4.15). *Scientia* is of essential predicates viewed as causes of concomitant properties. We designate the essence with *per se* propositions. Every scientific proposition is a *per se* proposition.

3.2 *Per se* propositions

Propositions that map onto the essence of the subject are termed 'per se' (Greek: *kath'hauto*). Aristotle describes four types of *per se* proposition in the *Posterior Analytics*, three of which Aquinas identifies as relevant to demonstration (An. Post 1.4, 73a35-b17)[25]:

[PS1] *Per se* attributes are such as belong to their subject as elements in its essential nature (e.g. line thus belongs to triangle, point to line ... These elements ... are contained in the formulae defining triangle and line).

[PS2] [*Per se* attributes are] such that, while they belong to certain subjects, the subjects to which they belong are contained in the attribute's own defining formula. Thus straight and curved belong to line, odd and even ... to number ... The formula defining any one of these attributes contains its subject – e.g. line or number as the case may be.

[**PS4**] What belongs of itself to something is *per se*.[26] ... [For instance], the predication is *per se*, e.g. if a beast dies when its throat is being cut, then its death is also essentially connected with the cutting, because the cutting was the cause of death, not death a 'coincident' of the cutting.[27]

The term 'per' designates a causal relationship, either extrinsic, when one entity acts on another, or intrinsic, whereby an entity is viewed as the cause with respect to what belongs per se to it. The sense relevant to the investigation of the *Posterior Analytics* is the latter. Aquinas links Aristotle's account of per se belonging to Aristotle's four causes: formal, material, efficient, and final:

> There are four genera of causes ... One of these is the *quod quid erat esse*, i.e. the formal cause, which is the completeness of a thing's essence. Another is the cause which, if placed, the caused must also be placed: this is the material cause ... The third is the cause which is the source of motion, i.e. the efficient cause ... The fourth is that for the sake of which something is performed, namely, the final cause. And so it is clear that *through the middle in a demonstration all these causes are manifested, because each of these causes can be taken as the middle of a demonstration.* (In PA 2.9.2; emphasis added)[28]

Aristotle's four causes factor into demonstrations through formulations of per se belonging.

PS1 propositions designate the essence of the subject by means of its definition and thereby instance formal causality. 'The first mode of that which is *per se* is when the definition itself or something expressed in the definition is predicated of the thing defined' (In PA 1.10.3). We shall see that the minor premise of the paradigmatic scientific demonstration is PS1. Hence the predicate term of the minor premise is a definition of the subject in terms of any one of Aristotle's four causes, each of which 'can be taken as the middle'.

PS2 propositions concern properties. In this technical sense, a property is an essential trait whose definition incorporates the definition of the subject of its inherence (as the definition of 'snub' mentions nose) (In PA 1.14.2). PS2 designates material causality, through which the subject is the ontological ground of the inherence of a predicate: 'That that to which something, is attributed is its proper matter and subject.'

PS4 propositions comprise any way that a subject can act as a per se cause with respect to itself. PS4 propositions can designate any one of Aristotle's four causes. Hence any instance of PS1 or PS2 is an instance of PS4. As some scholars would dispute this broad construal of PS4, comment is required. Here is the text in full:

[Aristotle] gives the fourth mode, according to which the preposition *'per'* designates a relationship of efficient cause *or of any other*. Consequently, he says that whatever is attributed to a thing because of itself, is said of it *per se*; but whatever is not so attributed is said *per accidens*,[29] as when I say, 'While he was walking, it lightened.' For it is not the fact that he walks that causes lightning, but this is said by coincidence. But if the predicate is in the subject because of itself, it is *per se*, as when we say, 'Slaughtered, it died.' For it is obvious that because something was slaughtered, it died, and it is not a mere coincidence that something slaughtered should die. (In PA 1.4.7; emphasis added)

Aquinas states that PS4 designates efficient causality or any other type of causality. Yet John Longeway (2007: 2, 142; 2009: 17; 2011: 1065) and John Jenkins (1997: 23) both suggest that PS4 designates only efficient causality. Longeway glosses PS4 as 'true *per se* due to an efficient causal connection' (2007: 2), notes that 'the fourth way indicates an efficient causal connection' (2011: 1065), and speaks of PS4 as 'indicating efficient causation' (2009: 17). None of this commits him to the claim that PS4 designates only efficient causality, though his comments suggest that this is his view. Jenkins (1997: 23), however, translates Aquinas' *'Haec praepositio per designat hatitudinem causae efficientis vel cuiuscunque alterius'* with 'This preposition *per* denotes a relationship to an efficient cause, even to some other thing'. Aquinas did mention at the outset of this *lectio* that *'per'* can designate an extrinsic cause. Jenkins may wish to accommodate this; yet, at this juncture, Aquinas has explicitly excised this sense from consideration. It seems that *'vel'* functions not as an adverb but rather as a conjunction, allowing PS4 to designate any of the four causes, as we shall see it must do on Aquinas' account of the scientific syllogism. Both Larcher's and Berquist's translations read *'vel'* as a conjunction.

Aquinas follows his account of per se belonging with a discussion that notes how such belonging figures into the scientific syllogism: 'The scientifically knowable are, properly speaking, the conclusions of a demonstration wherein proper attributes are predicated of their appropriate subjects. Now the appropriate subjects are not only placed in the definition of attributes, but they are also their causes. Hence the conclusions of demonstrations involve two modes of predicating *per se*, namely, the second and the fourth' (In PA 1.10.8).[30]

Later, Aquinas expands on these comments in a discussion that takes in the premises and conclusion of the paradigmatic scientific syllogism:

Furthermore, it should be noted that, since in a demonstration a proper attribute is proved of a subject through a middle which is the definition, it is required that the first proposition (whose predicate is the proper attribute, and whose subject is the definition which contains the principles of the proper attribute) be *per se* in the fourth mode, and that the second proposition (whose subject is the subject itself and the predicate its definition) must be in the first mode.[31] But the conclusion, in which the proper attribute is predicated of the subject, must *be per se* in the second mode. (In PA 1.13.3)

We may schematize Aquinas' description of the paradigmatic scientific syllogism thusly[32]:

[Major Premise]	Definition of the subject – Proper attribute	[PS4]
[Minor Premise]	Subject – Definition of the subject	[PS1]
[Conclusion]	Subject – Proper attribute	[PS2/PS4]

Recall that the middle is a definition of the subject construed broadly, so as to admit of formulation in terms of any of Aristotle's four causes (In PA 2.9). So, for example, Aquinas demonstrates that stones are corruptible by means of the material definition of a stone as something that is composed of contraries: 'If one middle which is the material cause be taken in two propositions, a conclusion follows of necessity; as if we were to say: "Everything composed of contraries is corruptible; but a stone is such: therefore, a stone is corruptible"' (In PA 2.9.4).

The middle is the material rather than the efficient cause of the attribute, as it would have to be on Longeway's and Jenkins' readings. This and other such examples throughout the text require that PS4 encompass all four causes.[33] It then appears as if Aquinas settles on PS4 in the major premise in order to secure this outcome, thereby ensuring that the scientific syllogism is capable of getting at its subject from a variety of perspectives.

Scientia is necessary, as it is of concomitant properties:

If an accident inheres necessarily and always in a subject, it must have its cause in the subject – in which case the accident cannot but inhere. Now this can occur in two ways: in one way ... it is caused from the principles of the species, and such an accident is called a *per se* attribute or property. (In PA 1.14.2)

Conversely, because *scientia* is of attributes of this type, 'demonstration cannot be from anything or of anything but what is *per se*' (In PA 1.14.6). Hence, as regards the form and parts of the scientific syllogism, it comprises *per se* propositions that are 'true, first ... immediate ... better known than, prior to, and causes of, the conclusion' (In PA 1.4.10).

3.3 Types of scientific syllogism

Aquinas picks up his consideration of the qualified type of scientific syllogism with the reminder that, in its strictest sense, *scientia* is *propter quid*, that is, through causes that are first and immediate (In PA 1.23). Here the discussion turns to *quia* proof, cases where one or both of these criteria are not met. By way of introduction to *scientia quia*, we should note that variations of *that* (*quia*) and *why* (*propter quid*) questions make up the entirety of what we seek via the scientific syllogism: 'The number of questions is equal to the number of things that are scientifically known ... But there are four things that we ask, namely, (1) *quia*, (2) *propter quid*, (3) *si est*, (4) *quid est*. To these four can be reduced whatever is scientifically inquirable or knowable' (In PA 2.1.2).

We ask (1) whether this or that is the case, (2) why this or that is the case, (3) whether something exists, and (4) what a thing is. When we discover whether this or that is the case (1), we may inquire why it is so (2); and when we know whether something exists (3), we may ask what it is (4). So, (1) and (2) are paired, as are (3) and (4). What sets the types of questions apart is that (1) and (2) are composite questions, whereas (3) and (4) are simple.[34]

In every one of these cases, we seek a middle: 'One is either asking whether there is a middle, namely, in the question (1) whether this or that is the case and in the question (3) whether something exists, or what the middle is, namely, in the question (2) why is this or that the case and in the question (4) what is the thing' (In PA 2.1.8).[35] (1) and (3) are *quia* questions. They seek a middle that is an effect linked to the essence of a thing, such that the existence of the middle discloses that of the subject.[36] Aristotle uses the example of thunder. When we hear rumbling in the clouds, we know *that* thunder (defined as an extinguishing of fire) is in the clouds,[37] though we may not know *why* there is thunder in the clouds (in case we do not yet know that it is an extinguishing of fire in the clouds):

> There is a rumbling in the clouds
> Thunder is a rumbling in the clouds
> Hence, there is thunder in the clouds. (In PA 2.7)

Recall that *scientia* is analytic. It either explains an effect in terms of the essence of its cause or accounts for our knowledge that something is the case. This is especially clear here. No one who hears the rumble of thunder requires proof that the thunder whose effect she hears exists. Instead, the demonstration shows what makes us aware that there is thunder, namely, the sound that it generates. Conversely, (2) and (4) do tell us *why* something is the case. Accordingly, they seek a middle that designates the essence of the subject by means of a definition in order to account for the inherence of a property that is a concomitant with that essence, for example:

The extinguishing of fire is in the clouds is thunder
In the clouds, fire is extinguished
Therefore, in the clouds there is thunder. (In PA 2.7)

A *propter quid* demonstration 'proceeds from the causes both first and immediate of a thing'. That is, demonstration *propter quid* is (1) from causes and (2) from immediate causes. *Quia* demonstration differs from *propter quid* demonstration on two fronts, relative to these criteria. (Q1) demonstration is not through immediate principles, and as a consequence does not employ the first cause. As we shall see, (Q1) proofs are, as it were, defective *propter quid* proofs. (Q2) demonstration, although through immediate things, is not through the cause but through effects.

(Q1) demonstrations rely on propositions wherein the major is 'set outside (*extra ponitur*)' (In PA 1.24.1), as in negative propositions or when the middle has a broader extension. In these cases, the demonstration relies on a mediate major premise. Here is Aristotle's example:

Whatever breathes is an animal
No wall is an animal
No wall breathes. (In PA 1.24)

'Animal' is of broader extension than 'whatever breathes'. The proximate cause of not breathing is not having lungs, so a prosyllogism would be required to establish the major premise, for instance:

Whatever has lungs is an animal
Whatever breathes has lungs
Whatever breathes is an animal

Since the major premise of the initial proof was not immediate, it did not employ the first, that is, proximate, cause. If we had the proximate cause as the middle, Aquinas states that we would have a demonstration *propter quid*:

Whatever has lungs breathes
Walls do not have lungs
Therefore, walls do not breathe. (In PA 1.24)

Quia and *propter quid* demonstrations are often characterized in terms of a movement towards, or away from, an essence viewed as a cause, respectively.[38] But the true difference seems rather to be that *quia* proofs do not employ the first, that is, proximate, cause.

(Q2) demonstration is not from a cause but, rather, is through an effect designated by immediate propositions in a proof that discloses the existence of the cause of the effect, for example:

> Whatever does not twinkle is near
> The planets do not twinkle
> Therefore, the planets are near. (In PA 1.23)

The effect is concomitant with the essence of the cause, and hence the expressions used to designate either are convertible. Convertible terms are counter-predicatable. A, B, and C are counter-predicatable when 'A is in every B and in every C, and these, namely, B and C, must inhere in each other, so that every B is C and every C is B, and also inhere in A so that every A is B and every A is C' (In PA 1.8.8). Because the effects from which we gather knowledge of the cause are convertible with that cause, a (Q2) demonstration can be turned into a *propter quid* (PQ) proof. The new proof switches the minor premise and the conclusion, keeping the major where it is but reversing the order of its subject and predicate terms (In PA 1.23).

(Q2) Proof	(PQ) Proof
Whatever does not twinkle is near	Whatever is near does not twinkle
The planets do not twinkle	The planets are near
Therefore, the planets are near	Therefore, the planets do not twinkle

The (Q2) proof reveals that the planets are near, by means of an effect of their proximity, namely, that the planets do not twinkle. When the proximity of the planets is revealed as the cause of the fact that the planets do not twinkle, the proximity can serve in (PQ) as a definition of the subject with which the effect is concomitant.

Finally, Aquinas speaks of a type of (Q2) proof for which only some of the principles are convertible. This is a variant of (Q2), so let us name it (Q2b) and refer to what was termed '(Q2)' as (Q2a). A (Q2b) demonstration is not always valid, for example (ibid.):

(Q2b) Valid	(Q2b) Invalid
Whatever does not twinkle is near	Rapid pulse is a sign of fever
Venus does not twinkle	John has a rapid pulse
Venus is near	John has a fever

The considerations put forward in this section result in the following scheme[39]:

	Effects that are first	Effects that are convertible
(PQ)	Yes	Yes
(Q1)	No	No
(Q2a)	No	Yes
(Q2b)	No	Yes and No

4. Scientia *and* definition

In connection with the four questions that comprise all scientific inquiry, we noted that when we learn (1) that something is the case, we ask (2) why it is so; and when we learn (3) that something exists, we ask (4) what it is. In each case, the answer to the question is a middle. For (1) and (3), the middle designates an effect tied to the essence of the thing; for (2) and (4), a definition that designates an essence. As (1) and (3) are concomitants of an essence, it is clear that in every case what we want is a definition. Having at the outset of Book II shown how scientific inquiry is reduced to these four questions and that each is tied in with definition, Aristotle turns to the relation between demonstration and definition. Hence Aquinas notes that Book II concerns definition, 'the middle from which the demonstrative syllogism proceeds' (In PA 1.4.1).

The opening chapters sort out how definition figures into the scientific syllogism. We learn that a definition expresses what a thing is, whereas a demonstration presupposes this (In PA 2.2); moreover, three possible ways of demonstrating a definition – via convertible terms, division, or supposition – are all question-begging, to one degree or another.[40] Hence, the conclusion of the scientific syllogism cannot itself be a definition that designates the essence of the subject.

Aristotle then turns to the role of definition vis-à-vis demonstration: 'We must now start afresh and consider ... what is the nature of definition, and whether essential nature is in any sense demonstrable and definable or in none' (An. Post. 2.8, 93a1-3). He takes up first what Aquinas terms the way of 'logical proof' (In PA 2.7.2). Like the question-begging proofs of In PA 2.3, this proof works with a formulation of the essence to demonstrate a formulation of the essence. But, unlike with those earlier proofs, Aquinas believes that the logical proof is not question-begging. He provides an example of the definition of a house in terms of its end, from which we may construct a definition in terms of its matter.[41]

Shelters meant for habitation are composed of wood and stone
<u>A house is a shelter meant for habitation</u>
Houses are composed of wood and stone

Unlike the question-begging proofs from In PA 2.3, the various terms of this proof are not wholly convertible, presumably as they are taken from different causes (final and material). Nevertheless, Aquinas rules this out as a demonstration, on the ground that 'by this method it is not sufficiently proved that what is concluded is the essence of the thing of which it is concluded, but merely that it is in it' (In PA 2.7.3). Aquinas does not elaborate. But it seems that if we assume that the major designates the essence of the minor term, we will have assumed what we set out to demonstrate, namely, that the major term belongs to the definition of the minor term.[42] This immediately precedes Aristotle's positive account of demonstration and definition, and may constitute the dismissal of a tempting candidate for *scientia*, the demonstration of one designation of the essence by means of another in terms of various Aristotelian causes.

Aristotle now begins his positive account of the relation between demonstration and definition. We have *scientia propter quid* when we know why something is or is the case because we grasp something of its essence, as knowledge that a lunar eclipse is the earth's interposition between moon and sun allows us to infer an eclipse given this interposition:

The interposition of the earth between the sun and the moon is an eclipse of the moon
<u>The moon suffers such an interposition</u>
Therefore, the moon is eclipsed[43]

Or we may have *scientia quia* that the moon is eclipsed simply because it cannot cast a shadow. By way of contrast with the *propter quid* proof that defines the lunar eclipse, this *quia* demonstration cannot explain why one is happening:

Inability to cast a shadow ... is an eclipse of the moon
<u>The moon is unable to cast a shadow</u>
Therefore, the moon is eclipsed

Next, Aquinas discusses Aristotle's *propter quid* demonstration of thunder in the clouds:

The extinguishing of fire in the clouds is thunder
<u>In the clouds, fire is extinguished</u>
Therefore, in the clouds there is thunder

Aquinas' exposition is noteworthy, as he suggests that to explain why it now thunders we may need to look to factors extrinsic to the essences of clouds and thunder (In PA 2.7.8). Scholars question whether Aquinas endorses a natural necessity akin to the necessity that is had in axiomatic sciences, wherein considerations prescind from matter. Longeway (2011) proposes that, for Aquinas, we cannot get at necessity as regards natural bodies, given the contingencies that affect the exercise of their causal powers and points to this passage and its talk of extrinsic phenomena to support of his conclusion. At best, we discern that these powers exist (66–8). Aquinas notes elsewhere (In PA 1.42), 'The necessary ... is not the same in natural things ... as in the disciplines, i.e. in mathematical things. For in the disciplines there is *a priori* necessity, whereas in natural science there is *a posteriori*.' Necessity in natural science is hypothetical. We know that if a certain event is to unfold, other events must precede (Aristotle, *Physics* 2, 200a15-b8). By contrast, in certain disciplines wherein material contingencies do not interfere, we have absolute necessity. Given a finite straight line, we may construct an equilateral triangle, employing various postulates, common notions, and definitions as we find in Euclid. And yet Aquinas attaches comparable necessity to the eclipse.

> These things, insofar as there is demonstration of them, are always. And as in the case of the eclipse of the moon, so in all kindred matters ... It never fails that under given conditions the effect follows, as in the eclipse of the moon. For the moon never fails to be eclipsed when the earth is diametrically interposed between sun and moon. (In PA 1.16.8)

The necessity of the eclipse is set off from the certainty we have of what is true for the most part: 'Others happen not to be always even in respect to their causes, i.e. in those cases where the causes can be impeded. For it is not always that from a human seed a man with two hands is generated' (ibid.). Why carve out this liminal space? The answer exceeds the scope of this chapter. But it may be that there is no such space but, rather, that knowledge of an eclipse of the moon is necessary, because the moon is a heavenly body and, as such, incorruptible (ST 1.66.2). Perhaps the 'kindred matters' pertain to astronomy.

Aristotle then turns to the subject of definition as it relates to demonstration, drawing on what has preceded to characterize the types of definition that pertain to the scientific syllogism. Aquinas detects three[44]: '(1) an indemonstrable notion of a thing's *quod quid* ... (2) that which is, as it were, a demonstrative syllogism of a thing's *quod quid* and differs from a demonstration merely by structure ... (3) the definition which only signifies *quod quid* and is the conclusion of a demonstration' (In PA 2.8.10).[45]

Consider the following *propter quid* demonstration:

A quenching of fire in the clouds produces a noise in the clouds
<u>Thunder is a quenching of fire in the clouds</u>
Thunder is a noise in the clouds

(1) is the middle that designates the essence. (2) expresses the demonstration as a definition: 'Thunder is the noise of fire being extinguished in the clouds.' (3) is the conclusion, an effect now grasped in terms of its cause.

Notes

1   For further reading on these themes, see Dod (1982), Lindberg (1992: ch. 9), Longeway (2007), Pasnau (2009), D'Ancona (2016), and Spade (2016).
2   All translations of Aristotle's *Posterior Analytics* (An. Post.), and of Aquinas' In PA, are taken from Larcher's text (Aquinas 1970), available online: http://dhspriory.org/thomas/PostAnalytica.htm.
3   For Plato, see *Republic* 533c1-8, where he uses the term to distinguish the waking knowledge of one who knows the essences of things from geometers and the like, who merely dream about being.
4   For (1), see In PA 1.4 (on *scientia*, strictly speaking), 1.5 (on axiomatic systems and the shared principles of demonstration, e.g. non-contradiction), 1.13 (on principles of demonstration as necessary), 1.16 (on necessary knowledge of eclipses and the like), and 2.20 (on a grasp of an essence had by induction). For (2), see In PA 1.16, 42; 2, 12.
5   Broadly construed, because, in a somewhat stricter sense, *scientia* is of the conclusion of a scientific syllogism (In PA 1.4.9). (On the scientific syllogism, see Section 3.) Axioms particular to a science and the principles of demonstration are the better known principles from which *scientia* proceeds. On its strictest possible sense, see note 12 and Section 3.3.
6   For the placement of natural phenomena in either (1) or (2), see In PA 1.16, 2.12. Note: thinkers associated with the Radical Orthodoxy movement held that Aquinas (1947–48 (ST): 1.2.3c) allows another, looser sense of '*scientia*' in his natural theology, wherein he seeks to demonstrate the existence of God. (This translation is available online: http://dhspriory.org/thomas/summa/index.html.) Here, *scientia* is presented as somewhat uncertain, akin to the results of investigative logic (see Section 2.2) (Pickstock 2005: 570n4). In general agreement with Pickstock, Milbank (1999: 447) speaks of *scientia* as analogical. Again, Stump (2005) suggests that, for Aquinas, its origin in induction undermines the certainty of *scientia*. Pickstock and

Milbank are motivated by the worry that apodictic knowledge of God erodes the distance between God and creatures (Turner 2004: 26). But their reading seems to misconstrue Aquinas on several key points (Hall 2014; Sirilla 2014). I discuss Stump's claims below.

7   *Republic* X suggests that there are forms for things such as beds. Whether we are meant to take this seriously is unclear. This account is drawn from Plato's middle period (c. 365–c. 347). His later writings may break with the theory of forms: for example, Plato's *Parmenides* is a sustained critique of the doctrine. On the dating of these works, see Kraut (1992: xii).

8   See, for example, Plato's middle-period *Republic* 504e–518c, 596e–597a, *Phaedo* 100b–102a3, and *Phaedrus* 247c3–247e6.

9   Leaving aside Aristotle's belief in the existence of various immaterial entities (*Metaph.* 12.6).

10 This translation is by J. L. Ackrill (Aristotle 1984: 5).

11 For Aristotle's account of the development of the notion of the universal definition and Plato's theory of forms along with a sustained critique of this theory, see *Metaph.* 13, 4–5.

12 The expression 'unqualified' designates the strictest sense of *scientia*, whereby knowledge of a thing's essence accounts for its essential properties. Qualified *scientia* lacks this unmediated grasp of an essence. See Section 3.3.

13 Pasnau (2009: 365–6) notes that the link between *scientia* and certainty is not present in Aristotle but rather is the product of the Arabic translation and commentary tradition.

14 For Aristotle's criticism of Plato's theory of forms, see *Metaph.* 1, 7, 13, 14, and *Nicomachean Ethics* (*NE*) 1.6.

15 'Of course, induction is a notoriously uncertain mode of inference, as Aquinas himself recognizes [In PA 2.4] … Not only is there no guarantee that what a cognizer uses as a proper first principle of *scientia* will be something known with certainty, there is not even a guarantee that what the cognizer starts with as a fist principle will be true, since it is the result of induction' (Stump 2005: 229).

16 See also Section 2.2, and MacDonald (1993: 179).

17 See Pickavé (2011: 311); In PA 2.20; *Commentary on Aristotle's* Nicomachean Ethics (In NE) Book 6; *Commentary on Aristotle's* Metaphysics (In M) 1.1.34. Briefly, wisdom, understanding, and *scientia* are speculative habits whereby knowledge is sought for its own sake, whereas art and prudence are practical. Wisdom is of the most universal and primary causes, and is ultimately of God as first mover (In M 1.2.36, 12.12); understanding grasps the principles of scientific demonstration (In PA 2.20); art concerns production that passes over into external matter, for example, healing (In PA 2.20, In M 1.1.34); whereas the activity of prudence perfects the agent (In NE 6; In M 1.1.34).

18   In PA 2.20.11: 'From the sense and memory of one particular and then of another
     and another, something is finally reached which is the principle of art and science.'
     And 'no knowledge is more certain than the knowledge of these principles'. As
     no knowledge is more certain than principles, principles are more certain than
     unqualified knowledge (*episteme simpliciter*), which Aquinas thinks is necessary.
     Again, '[s]ince we take a knowledge of universals from singulars ... it is obviously
     necessary to acquire the first universal principles by induction' (ibid.). From this, it is
     clear that Aquinas recognizes instances wherein induction grasps necessary truths.

19   Aristotle takes up *scientia quia* at An. Post. 1.13, which I discuss in Section 3.3.

20   I have altered Larcher's translation, replacing 'primary' with 'first' in order to retain
     a consistent reading of this technical term.

21   The doctrine of the transcendentals emerges from the tradition in the *Summa de
     bono* of Philip the Chancellor (composed c. 1225). On this doctrine, we can speak
     of a being as true (to kind) inasmuch as it exists and is good.

22   See also Euclid (1956) and Ross (1949: 511).

23   'Since one may not proceed to infinity in demonstrations, principles immediate and
     indemonstrable must be reached' (In PA 1.4.14).

24   On this sense of 'concomitant', see In PA 1.14.2 and Section 3.2.

25   The third use of 'per se' picks out the mode of existence proper to a subject, which
     is 'through itself'. Aquinas does not think that this use of 'per se' is relevant to the
     premises of the scientific syllogism as here the expression concerns how things
     exist, not how we speak of them.

26   This sentence is a more literal rendition of Aristotle's '*to men di'hauto huparchon
     hekastoi*', replacing Larcher's 'a thing consequentially connected with anything'.

27   Here and throughout, I replace Larcher's rendering of *kath'hauto* as 'essential' with
     the more literal 'per se'.

28   In *Metaph*. 5.2, 1013a24-5, Aristotle defines the material cause in terms of the
     physical matter of a thing, as bronze is a cause of a statue. Aquinas' broader
     statement takes in both sensible matter as well as the intelligible matter of, for
     example, mathematics. See Berquist's translation (Aquinas 2007: 442).

29   *Haec praepositio per designat hatitudinem causae efficientis vel cuiuscunque alterius.
     Et ideo dicit quod quidquid inest unicuique propter seipsum, per se dicitur de eo; quod
     vero non propter seipsum inest alicui, per accidens dicitur* (In PA 1.10.7).

30   In Hall (2011), I argue that Aristotle intends, rather, to place PS1 and PS2 in the
     conclusion of the scientific demonstration, and that Aquinas' selection of PS2 and
     PS4 stems from a mistranslation of Aristotle. James Ross (1949: 521–2) and Hugh
     Tredennick (1960: 44) likewise contend that Aristotle intends to place PS1 and PS2
     in the demonstration's conclusion.

31   Note: Longeway (2011: 1065) has it that the minor is PS4: 'Aquinas argued that
     the middle term of the highest sort of demonstration is the real definition of the

subject. This led him to claim that the minor premise is *per se* in the fourth way listed in *Posterior Analytics* 1.4.' Longeway (2009) repeats the claim:

> The fourth way in which something can be *per se* pertained to demonstration since it indicates an efficient causal connection, and the minor premise will be true in a demonstration because of the efficient causal connection between the essence of the subject, as expressed in its real definition, and the attribute proven of it, making it *per se* in the fourth way.

Here it seems as if the restriction of PS4 to mere efficient causality lies behind Longeway's attribution. By contrast, Longeway (2007: 147) describes the minor as PS1.

32 Other medieval thinkers construe Aristotle differently as regards the structure of the paradigmatic scientific syllogism. See Longeway (2007: 146–7).

33 This line of argument is taken directly from Berquist's excellent commentary (Aquinas 2007: 357–9).

34 'The enunciation is formed in two ways: in one way from a name and a verb without an appositive [in response to the simple question], as when it is stated that man is; in another way [in response to the compound question] when some third item is set adjacent, as when it is stated that man is white' (In PA 2.1.3).

35 Here, and in the previous passage, I have altered Larcher's translation.

36 Strictly speaking, the middle of a *quia* proof can designate either an effect or a cause. In the latter case, the *quia* proof is a defective *propter quid* proof, defective on account of the fact that the major premise is not immediate, that is, indemonstrable. Presumably, Aquinas would rank these defective *propter quid* proofs as answers to type (2) and type (4) questions. I discuss this other type of *quia* proof later in this section.

37 Aquinas notes that Aristotle in fact does not believe that thunder is a quenching of fire in a cloud, but rather is adopting for the sake of convenience the definition of Anaxagoras and Empedocles (In PA 2.7). Aristotle's theory that thunder is the product of a dry exhalation combining with cold air in the cloud is in *Meteorology* 2, 369a10-b4.

38 Aquinas himself is happy to take this approach in setting up his proof for the existence of God at ST 1.2.2c.

39 This scheme omits In PA 1.25, which discusses how knowledge *propter quid* and *quia* differ in different sciences wherein (1) one science is subalternated as harmonics is subalternated to geometry, and (2) one science is not subalternated to another. In the former case, the subalternated science receives its principle from the science under which it is placed. In sciences not thusly related, one may only know *that* something is the case whereas the other knows *why*, as the doctor knows by experience *that* circular wounds heal slowly, whereas the geometer knows that this is *because* a circle is a figure without angles. Note that this shows that knowledge *why* is not always knowledge *that*, that is, one can grasp a principle but not its

application. As this *lectio* tells us more about Aquinas' views on subalternation than on *scientia quia*, I do not introduce it into the scheme that divides types of *quia* with reference to the grasp of first and immediate causes.

40 See Berquist's commentary (Aquinas 2007: 425–33).

41 As Berquist notes, this is not, strictly, a demonstration by the material cause, because wood and stone are not unique to houses. Rather, the example is useful for showing the dependence of the material upon the final cause. Aquinas offers another, more complicated, demonstration regarding virtue that avoids this issue, but this need not occupy us here, provided we grasp the point that it seems as if one definition can be used to demonstrate another, especially given the Aristotelian hierarchy of causes wherein form is the cause of matter, an agent is the cause of form, and the end, the cause of the causes, is the cause of the agent (for which she acts) (In PA 2.8.3). See also Aquinas (2007: 434–8).

42 See Berquist (Aquinas 2007: 436–8).

43 This and the two proofs that follow are adapted from In PA 2.7.

44 Various commentators detect various numbers of definitions at An. Post 2.10. Ross (1949: 634–6) contends that there are two, noting that Alexander of Aphrodisias and Themestius find four.

45 Cf. In PA 1.16.4: 'A definition is either a principle of a demonstration, a conclusion of a demonstration, or a demonstration with a different ordering of its terms.'

References

Aquinas, T. (1947–48), *Summa Theologica*, trans. Fathers of the English Dominican Province, New York: Benziger Bros. (Cited in this chapter as 'ST'.)

Aquinas, T. (1970), *Commentary on the 'Posterior Analytics of Aristotle'*, trans. F. R. Larcher, New York: Magi Books. (Cited in this chapter as 'In PA'.)

Aquinas, T. (1993), *Commentary on Aristotle's* Nicomachean Ethics, trans. C. I. Litzinger, Notre Dame, IN: Dumb Ox Books. (Cited in this chapter as 'In NE'.)

Aquinas, T. (1995), *Commentary on Aristotle's* Metaphysics, trans. J. P. Rowan, Notre Dame, IN: Dumb Ox Books. (Cited in this chapter as 'In M'.)

Aquinas, T. (2004), *Commentary on Aristotle's* On Interpretation, trans. J. Oesterle, Notre Dame, IN: Dumb Ox Books.

Aquinas, T. (2007), *Commentary on Aristotle's* Posterior Analytics, trans. R. Berquist, Notre Dame, IN: Dumb Ox Books.

Aristotle (1984), *The Complete Works of Aristotle*, ed. J. Barnes, vol. 1, Princeton: Princeton University Press.

D'Ancona, C. (2016), 'Greek Sources in Arabic and Islamic Philosophy', in E. N. Zalta (ed.), *The Stanford Encyclopedia of Philosophy* (Spring 2016 Edition): http://plato.stanford.edu/archives/spr2016/entries/arabic-islamic-greek/.

Dod, B. (1982), 'Aristoteles latinus', in N. Kretzmann, A. Kenny, and J. Pinborg (eds), *The Cambridge History of Later Medieval Philosophy*, Cambridge: Cambridge University Press.

Euclid (1956), *The Thirteen Books of Euclid's Elements*, trans. T. L. Heath, vol. 1, New York: Dover Publications.

Hall, A. (2011), 'Aquinas, Scientia and a Medieval Misconstruction of Aristotle's "Posterior Analytics"', in G. Klima and A. Hall (eds), *Knowledge, Mental Language, and Free Will*, Vol. 3, *Proceedings of the Society for Medieval Logic and Metaphysics*, Newcastle upon Tyne: Cambridge Scholars Publishing.

Hall, A. (2014), 'The Burden of Proof: Aquinas and God Science', in G. Klima and A. Hall (eds), *Metaphysical Themes Medieval and Modern*, Vol. 11, *Proceedings of the Society for Medieval Logic and Metaphysics*, Newcastle upon Tyne: Cambridge Scholars Publishing.

Jenkins, J. I. (1997), *Knowledge and Faith in Aquinas*, Cambridge: Cambridge University Press.

Kraut, R. (1992), 'Introduction to the Study of Plato', in R. Kraut (ed.), *The Cambridge Companion to Plato*, Cambridge: Cambridge University Press.

Lindberg, D. (1992), *The Beginnings of Western Science*, Chicago: The University of Chicago Press.

Longeway, J. (2007), *Demonstration and Scientific Knowledge in William of Ockham*, Notre Dame, IN: University of Notre Dame Press.

Longeway, J. (2009), 'Medieval Theories of Demonstration', in E. N. Zalta (ed.), *The Stanford Encyclopedia of Philosophy* (Spring 2009 Edition): http://plato.stanford.edu/archives/spr2009/*entries*/demonstration-medieval/.

Longeway, J. (2011), 'Posterior Analytics, Commentaries on Aristotle's', in H. Lagerlund (ed.), *Encyclopedia of Medieval Philosophy*, vol. 1, Dordrecht: Springer.

MacDonald, S. (1993), 'Theory of Knowledge', in N. Kretzmann and E. Stump (eds), *The Cambridge Companion to Aquinas*, Cambridge: Cambridge University Press.

Milbank J. (1999), 'Intensities', *Modern Theology*, 14: 445–97.

Pasnau, R. (2009), 'Science and Certainty', in R. Pasnau (ed.), *The Cambridge History of Medieval Philosophy*, vol. 1, Cambridge: Cambridge University Press.

Pickavé, M. (2011), 'Human Knowledge', in B. Davies and E. Stump (eds), *The Oxford Handbook of Aquinas*, Oxford: Oxford University Press.

Pickstock, C. (2005), 'Duns Scotus: His Historical and Contemporary Significance', *Modern Theology*, 21: 543–74.

Ross, W. D. (ed.) (1949), *Aristotle's Prior and Posterior Analytics*, Oxford: Clarendon Press.

Sirilla, M. (2014), 'Comments on "The Burden of Proof: Aquinas and God Science"', in G. Klima and A. Hall (eds), *Metaphysical Themes Medieval and Modern*, Vol. 11, *Proceedings of the Society for Medieval Logic and Metaphysics*, Newcastle upon Tyne: Cambridge Scholars Publishing.

Spade, P. V. (2016), 'Medieval Philosophy', in E. N. Zalta (ed.), *The Stanford Encyclopedia of Philosophy* (Spring 2016 Edition): http://plato.stanford.edu/archives/spr2016/entries/medieval-philosophy/.

Stump, E. (2005), *Aquinas*, New York: Routledge.

Tredennick, H. (1960), 'Introduction', in *Aristotle: Posterior Analytics; Topics*, trans., respectively, H. Tredennick and E. S. Forster, Cambridge, MA: Harvard University Press.

Turner, D. (2004), *Faith, Reason and the Existence of God*, Cambridge: Cambridge University Press.

6

John Duns Scotus on Knowledge

Richard Cross

1. Introduction

Scholastic philosophers typically discern three stages in human intellectual cognition. Scotus summarizes: 'The first operation of the intellect ... is the apprehension of simples, which composition and division follow as the second act, and argument as the third.'[1] 'Apprehension of simples' is the apprehension of particulars and of their natures. 'Composition and division' is the formation of affirmative and negative propositions. 'Argument' is syllogistic and inductive reasoning.

Prior to the first operation of the intellect is sensation: 'simple things ... cannot be understood ... unless they are first sensed'.[2] In what follows, I examine each of these activities in turn, focusing first on the mechanisms involved, and second on the extent to which we can be said to *know* the outputs of the various mechanisms – in Scotus' parlance, to be *certain* about them. The closest Latin cognate of 'knowledge' in scholastic philosophy is '*scientia*'. In the strictest sense, what is required for *scientia* is that the relevant propositions are necessary and understood to be such, either because *scientia* is a priori, or because its necessity is discovered inductively, or because it is the conclusion of a syllogistic argument that has such necessary propositions as premises.[3] In some cases falling short of *scientia*, however, it is quite possible to achieve equal *subjective* certainty, and it can be just as reasonable to believe such things as it is in cases of genuine *scientia*. This is what Scotus says about the Christian faith that one might acquire by listening to a human authority:

> On account of the credibility (*credulitatem*) of the revealed articles, it is not necessary to posit infused faith so that a human being might firmly believe all the revealed articles, and be determined to one side without fear of the opposite;

neither can its necessity be deduced on the grounds that acquired faith (*fides acquisita*) is above opinion (*opinio*) (which assents to one side of a contradiction with fear of the opposite) but below knowledge (*scientiam*) (which is from the evidence of a scientific object).[4]

(Acquired faith is something available on the basis of merely human testimony.) As Scotus puts it elsewhere, '[W]e can believe in the testimony of others, and even so firmly that that belief is called ... knowing (*scire*).'[5] But since the content of the proposition does not 'compel (*cogit*)' assent,[6] assent in such cases requires conscious causal input on the part of the agent, and thus requires the *will* as a 'general mover moving [the intellect] (*generalis motor movens*).'[7]

As we shall see, Scotus would not count as an out-and-out internalist on these questions, since he usually treats certainty as simply an objective matter, not a subjective one (we can know things without *feeling* certain about them). For example, in his *ex professo* anti-sceptical discussion (covering sense knowledge, various sorts of abstractive intellectual knowledge, and self-knowledge), his focus is solely on the reliability of the relevant mechanisms. But while he thus does not hold that knowing that we know is necessary for knowing, he certainly holds that, in many cases, we do nevertheless know that we know. After all, the point of showing reliability is precisely to make this reliability internally accessible to us.

2. Sensation

2.1 Mechanisms

Scotus does not hold that there is any innate knowledge: everything we know is, or derives from, sensation. But while Scotus is at times a startling innovator in the domain of intellectual cognition, there is very little original in his account of sensation, which largely follows established patterns deriving from Aristotle and Avicenna, and filtered through what became the *opinio communis* of thirteenth-century scholasticism.[8] The basic idea is that sensible objects generate what were labelled (sensible) 'species' – content-bearing likenesses – first in the medium between the object and the sense organ, and then in the organ itself. This content is in some sense the same (in kind) as the forms of the object of sense, but received in the relevant subject (the medium, the sense organ) 'without the matter', as Aristotle puts it: without making the recipient to be an instance of the relevant kind (*De anima* II, c. 12: 414a18-20). (When I see a horse, neither the intervening air nor my eye literally becomes a horse.) When the species is received in the appropriate kind of subject – a sense organ – the object is sensed.

Scotus more or less agrees with this, but he makes a few tweaks around the edges. Most significantly, he does not believe that actual sensation can be reduced simply to the reception of a species in an organ. His reason is that the reception of the same kind of form in different recipients (e.g. the air, the sense organ) does not seem to be sufficient to explain the fact that one of these recipients – the organ – is cognitive, while the other is not. Cognition must involve something over and above a species, and be different in kind – namely, an *act*.[9] As he puts it, the organ 'receives something of which nothing of the same kind is received in the medium'.[10] Both species and act are caused by the object itself, with the various species being necessary but non-causal conditions for the act.[11] Given that all of these items are in some sense real accidents of their subjects, Scotus spells out what he means by thinking about their correct categorial classification. Species are something like habits or dispositions, and are thus classified in the first of Aristotle's four types of quality.[12] Sensory acts are affections, and are thus classified in the third of Aristotle's four types of quality.[13]

Scotus also has quite a lot to say about Aristotle's notion of the immaterial reception of a form. As I have just noted, he holds that both the sensible species and the sensory act are real accidents. There has been a very long and rather heated debate in Aquinas studies on whether or not sensation intrinsically involves any such accidents. According to one influential line of interpretation, Aquinas holds that sensation fundamentally consists in a 'spiritual' change – the immaterial reception of the form – rather than a 'natural' change – the reception of the form such that the recipient becomes an instance of the relevant kind. Aquinas clearly believes that such a spiritual change is at least necessary for all kinds of sensation; otherwise, as he puts it, 'all natural bodies would sense when they are altered' (*Summa theologiae* I, q. 78, a. 3 c). But Aquinas holds, too, that all sensations 'manifestly occur with some alteration of the body', and he identifies this real alteration as the reception of a species (I, q. 75, a. 3 c).[14] So, the idea would seem to be that these real accidents – sensible species – are somehow such that they are *in addition* content-bearers accounting for the representational function of sensation. What these real accidents do not do is make the recipient an instance of the relevant kind – they are not natural properties *in that sense*.

Whether or not this is Aquinas' view, it is certainly Scotus'. Scotus repeats Aquinas' argument for the necessity of a spiritual change in sensation: if there were no such, it would follow that 'inanimate things, which are naturally changed … could sense'.[15] But this spiritual change is compatible with a real change, and,

I take it, goes along with it. Scotus talks about this dual status of intentional or representational items most clearly in the case of light, which 'is a thing, and can have a real effect; but not … such that it cannot be an intention'.[16] The idea, then, is that sensible species and sensory acts are real categorial items that nevertheless have some natural representational function – as Scotus puts it, 'the species is conformed to the object'.[17]

What is the object of sensation? Peter King (2015: 114) has argued – convincingly, to my mind – that according to Scotus we perceive the individual (e.g. the individual accidents associated with a given substance), but not the individual 'as the very individual that it is': we do not have *de re* cognition of individuals. The reason for this is that *de re* cognition of an individual would require cognizing that individual's individuating principle – its haecceity. And this is not something that can be done by the postlapsarian human mind.[18] Rather, we perceive the individual in virtue of perceiving those features that it has in common with other individuals; but not such that we could distinguish between two qualitatively indiscernible instances of a kind.[19] Aristotle claims that 'sensation apprehends … individuals' and 'knowledge apprehends universals' (*De anima* II, c. 5: 417b22-23). As we shall see, Scotus allows for the intellectual perception of individuals, too (though not *de re* perception). We might think of Scotus' view as a kind of modification of the Aristotelian one. Or we might think of it as something more like a rejection of Aristotle's view. I do not have a strong opinion either way.

2.2 Anti-scepticism

Scotus believes that sensation is for the most part a reliable process, and, importantly for his overall anti-sceptical stance, that this reliability can be shown. Scotus considers two cases. In the first, the deliverances of the senses are all in conformity with each other. In the second, this condition does not obtain. Scotus discusses the first case by appealing to a principle of inductive reasoning that he takes to undergird empirical knowledge in general: 'Whatever comes about (*evenit*), for the most part, from some non-free cause, is the natural effect of that cause'.[20] If such-and-such a visual experience (e.g.) regularly occurs in the apparent presence of such-and-such an object, then the experience is the natural result of the presence of the object (and thus veridical). Uniformity among the different modalities provides (I assume) reason to believe that the object is present – the one sense confirming the other. Scotus holds this inductive principle is sufficient for 'infallible' cognition, and that it is 'known to the intellect' and 'resting in the soul'.[21] As far as I can see, he supposes this inductive principle to be self-evident – in our sense of analytic and a priori – and thus would hold induction to be immune to objections of a Humean kind. (Scotus does not consider scenarios such as Descartes' evil Demon: I suppose that he held himself to have other metaphysical and theological reasons for ruling out this kind of possibility.)

In the second case, Scotus holds that the intellect has (or can get) a principle enabling it to adjudicate between the different deliverances of the various senses.[22] He gives two stock examples. First, we see a semi-submerged stick apparently bent or broken.[23] But we know through various sensory modalities – 'both sight and touch' – that a stick is harder than water, and in any case we have a self-evident principle that harder things are not broken by softer things. ('Self-evident', because it is part of the meaning of 'hardness' to be thus unbreakable.) So we have a way of adjudicating between the different deliverances of the different senses (sight and touch).[24] Second, the sun (and anything far away) looks smaller to us than it really is.[25] But 'a measure applied to an extended object is always equal to itself', and 'both sight and touch attest to the fact that the same measure can be applied to something that is seen, whether the thing is near or far'.[26] So the idea is that we always have the means to discern when we are subject to some kind of illusion – there is always in principle a mechanism to enable us to discern and correct deviant outputs. Scotus does not mean to suggest that it is easy, or that failure to attend sufficiently might not result in error. But sufficient care can enable us to avoid error. (This is an intellectual function, requiring cognition of the relevant principles; animals without intellect are not so fortunate in their ability to detect deception and illusion.)

3. Intellectual cognition of simples

3.1 Mechanisms

Sensation is antecedent to – and presupposed by – intellectual cognition. As we saw above, intellectual cognition can have as its content both syntactically simple objects and syntactically complex ones – propositions. But syntactic simplicity is compatible with both semantic simplicity and semantic complexity. I consider both kinds of objects here, since Scotus holds that cognition of syntactically simple items is antecedent to – and presupposed by – cognition of syntactically complex ones. Simple objects can be either particulars or kinds. And our cognitive acts can be related to such objects in two different ways: as those objects are present to us; or indifferently to the presence or absence of the object. The first of these is Scotus' so-called intuitive cognition; the second is abstractive cognition.[27]

I begin with intuitive cognition. Intuitive cognition is of objects really present to the cognizer. What really exist are individuals and the common natures that are realized in them – and these are the objects present to the intellect, just as for sensation. I take it that, as for sensation, intuitive cognition gets us cognition of an individual in virtue of those features that the individual shares with others of the same kind – that is to say, in virtue of the common nature – but not *de re* cognition of an individual. One reason that Scotus has for supposing that the intellect can cognize these things is that sense can do so, and the intellect is more perfect than sense. But intellectual intuitive cognition has some significant theoretical justification, too:

> The intellect not only cognizes universals (which is true of abstractive cognition, about which the Philosopher speaks, because that alone is scientific), but also intuitively cognizes those things which the sense cognizes (because the more perfect and higher cognitive power in the same thing cognizes those things which the lower power does), and also cognizes sensations: and each of these is proved by this, that it knows contingently true propositions, and syllogizes from them; but forming propositions and syllogizing is proper to the intellect; the truth of those things is about the objects as intuitively cognized, namely as existent – in the same way in which they are known by the sense.[28]

Scotus claims, for example, that it is possible to know that, for example, Peter is sitting down.[29] But the components of propositions are mental items inherent in the intellect. (As Aquinas had earlier put it, '[I]t belongs to the intellect to form a proposition': *Summa theologiae* I, q. 75, a. 3 c.[30] In the next section, I return to the topic of propositional thought.) Scotus presupposes that intuitive intellectual cognition requires both sensible species, and an antecedent act of sensation, as causal intermediaries allowing the intellect to cognize the extra-mental particular. The act itself is caused (mediately) by the object (via the sensible species and sensory act) and the agent intellect (as a power that 'transfers from order to order' – that renders the material intelligible: something to which I return in a moment).[31]

So much for intuitive cognition. Abstractive cognition gets us cognition of a common nature by means of a cognitive intermediary sufficient to allow for cognition of that nature even in its real absence. The basic idea is that the agent intellect, along with what was known as the 'phantasm' – a unified representation of any particular or particulars formed through one or more sense modalities – causes a representation of the common nature as such.[32] This representation is labelled an 'intelligible species', a habitual or dispositional cognition which enables the intellect to think about something absent.[33] The idea is that the object – the common nature – is intentionally present in the species, and it is this that makes the absent object cognitively available, as it were.[34] The species inheres in the intellect considered as a passive power – the possible intellect – and in turn the species along with the intellect causes simple occurrent cognitions: simple thoughts about this or that kind of thing.[35] This representation is that on the basis of which a universal is cognized – something really predicable of many things of the same kind.[36] Unlike some of his contemporaries, Scotus does not believe that this universal is somehow really present in the phantasm, just waiting to be uncovered, as it were, by stripping away non-essential conditions.[37] The agent intellect and the phantasm *produce* an intelligible species, variously identified as a representation of the universal and as the universal itself.[38]

All of these various items are real categorial items – in fact, they are all in the category of quality.[39] The basic idea is that these various mental items are in some sense episodic – they can come and go (or at least come) – and this requires *real* changes in the intellect, not just intentional ones: intentional changes must supervene on real ones.[40] We have, then, a set of categorial items that are themselves representational – that represent the world in different ways – and thus are both real and intentional. The contrast is with a view such as Henry of Ghent's, Scotus' opponent: for Henry, items that represent the universal must be simply and wholly intentional – bare content, as it were, the 'known in the knower', as Henry puts it – and intentional change does not require any real or categorial change in the soul at all (Rombeiro 2011).

Scotus does not believe that the process I have just described is sufficient for knowledge of a *definition* of a kind. As he sees, the basic abstractive move is from more particular to more general. But he does not believe that abstraction from particulars immediately or unproblematically gets knowledge of the *essence* of a thing – knowledge of its defining properties. (Classic case: the definition of 'human' as 'rational animal'. But I will note a restriction on this in a moment.) Scotus makes a distinction between knowing a kind or nature by means of a real definition, and knowing it 'as it is expressed by a name'.[41] As we shall see in the next section, the aim of scientific investigation is to get at the real definition and thence to the necessary features that follow from that definition – the *propria* of a substance, in the Aristotelian jargon. Abstraction – the process from more particular to more general – starts off simply with some knowledge about how to use a specific name successfully. It gets us the most specific kind, 'cognized confusedly' – 'as it is expressed by a name'. We thence abstract more general features by widening the comparison class: 'Whiteness is actually conceived before colour is, in the order of confused cognition, because colour, under the notion of colour, is not cognized other than under the notion of greater abstraction than the abstraction of whiteness from this whiteness. And this greater abstraction is harder, because it is from things that are less similar.'[42] The abstractive process eventually yields a most general concept – namely, *being*. Since *being* is a completely simple concept, it cannot be cognized confusedly, but rather only distinctly. Cognizing distinctly is cognizing a definition – in effect, cognizing a thing 'as it is', so to speak – and a simply simple concept cannot be known other than as it is.[43] None of this abstractive process by itself gets us cognition of – the definition – of a most specific kind. But that is a task for scientific investigation, the subject of my next section.[44]

One aspect of Scotus' thought might generate surprise: he insists that the items that are known abstractively must be accident-natures, not substance-natures. His basic reason is the Aristotelian insight that only sensible accidents are the immediate objects of sensation.[45] Given this, only sensible accidents can be the immediate objects of intellection.[46] Substances can be known, but only inferentially, as the bearers of accidents; and substance-kinds distinguished not by means of distinct definitions but rather as the bearers of distinct congeries of accidents.[47] Not so much scepticism, I suppose, as pessimism about the scope of some natural cognitive capacities.

3.2 Anti-scepticism

Intuitive cognition, I assume, is as reliable and corrigible as sensation. How reliable is abstraction? Scotus does not address this question head-on. But he says some things that make it clear how he would answer. The initial abstractive process is automatic and unconscious,[48] and Scotus simply asserts that it is a reliable process: the causes of abstraction are natural, and they thus 'produce the most perfect concept that they can.'[49]

4. Propositional thought

4.1 Mechanisms

Scotus adopts what, I think, is the standard medieval view, in claiming that the components of propositions are mental items – specifically, items belonging somehow to the intellect. Subject and predicate are said by the medievals to be 'composed' in affirmative propositions and 'divided' in negative propositions. These operations are performed by the intellect, be it agent or possible intellect (see note 36 on the production of occurrent cognitions).

The semantic item that joins subject and predicate is the copula 'is'. Since the copula is itself a mental item, joining two concepts, Scotus holds that the default status of complexes is merely a predication, with semantic content, but of itself no assertive force. Judgement (that such a predication is true or false) is a further mental operation (Pini 2004). For Scotus, the parts of a proposition are really distinct, in the sense that subject and predicate are distinct mental acts combined into one syntactic complex: mental sentences are molecular representations built up from atomic representations by means of an appropriate syntactic structure.[50] Aquinas is a contrast: he maintains that it is not possible for more than one mental act to inhere in the intellect at once – a proposition for him is a single whole, in some sense prior to its parts.[51] In any case, Scotus adopts the standard line of maintaining that propositions are true if and only if subject and predicate 'belong to the same thing'.[52] More specifically, subject and predicate in standard cases have different significations, but the things signified belong to the same object.[53] Truth and falsity are features of non-complex cognitions, too: veridicality in completely simple concepts simply amounts to having the concept; in syntactically unstructured complexes, the complex is true if instantiated in the world, and false otherwise.[54]

4.2 Anti-scepticism

Syntactic complexes are either contingent or not. Contingent complexes are known on the basis of intuitive cognitions and have singulars as their subjects. I discussed above the mechanisms for forming such cognitions on the basis of sensation and intuitive intellectual cognition, and Scotus' conclusions concerning the reliability of such mechanisms. The reliability of the processes forming non-contingent complexes – logically and metaphysically necessary truths, and impossible complexes – is the subject of the later part of the next section.

5. Science and argument

5.1 Mechanisms

When discussing abstraction, I noted two components in the discovery of essences. The first is abstraction, from species confusedly known to being, known distinctly. The second is a process of division, identifying specific differences that divide these genera into ever more specific kinds, from being downwards, until a complete definition is formed, comprising every genus/difference that comprises a kind.[55] How might we do such a thing? The answer has to do with what Scotus takes to be the principal function of Aristotelian science: discovering truths about a thing's *propria* or natural effects. Scotus holds there to be four requirements for Aristotelian science:

> If we take 'science' properly, as it is taken in *Posterior Analytics* I, then there are four conditions required for a science: the first, that the cognition is certain, excluding every doubt and deception; the second condition it is of a necessary object; the third, that it is through a cause evident to the intellect; the fourth, that it is through a necessary cause that is evident and that applies the principles to the conclusion through syllogistic discourse.[56]

The 'evidence' requirement can be satisfied in two different ways: by what we would label logically necessary truths (propositions true in all possible worlds and known a priori by us), and metaphysically necessary truths (propositions true in all possible worlds but not known a priori). The domain of logically necessary truths is largely restricted to certain logical principles – the kinds of thing that generally underwrite, rather than feature in, syllogistic reasoning (Scotus' usual example is 'every whole is greater than its part').[57] Scotus treats self-evidence as a criterion for concept possession: the idea is that *any* intellect, grasping the terms, would intuit the truth of the proposition – and thus that someone not intuiting the truth of the proposition had simply not grasped the terms. Such a person would be committed to affirming an evident contradiction, and such an affirmation is not possible:

> The argument is confirmed … by Aristotle, in *Metaphysics* IV, where he claims that the opposite of the first principle (i.e. 'it is impossible for the same thing to be and not to be') cannot enter into anyone's intellect, 'for then there would be contrary beliefs in the mind': and this is certainly true about contrary beliefs, namely, ones that are formally incompatible, because a belief asserting being of something and one asserting non-being of the same thing are formally incompatible.[58]

By the same token, if it is not possible for one who possesses the relevant concepts to intuit the truth of the proposition, then that proposition is not self-evident.

Not all necessary truths are evident to us in this way. Definitions of substance-kinds, for example, are necessary but a posteriori. But they can still figure in scientific syllogisms. The process of discovering such definitions is inductive, in the sense that what we paradigmatically start with – what allows us to use a word successfully without knowing the essence that the word signifies – is knowledge about a thing's *propria* or effects; what we need to discover is the essence of the thing to which the *propria* or effects belong. Once that discovery is made, we can formulate explanatory scientific syllogisms – demonstrations *propter quid*, in the jargon – taking the essence to explain the *propria* or effects: much as, for example, being a rational animal is what explains something's having a capacity to smile (and not the other way round).[59]

Scotus describes this process as a case of division:

How might we come to the knowledge of a cause from a sensible effect? Answer: by dividing, in the following way. In *a* there are *b*, *c*, and *d*. If you want to know which is the cause of *d* – whether it is *b* or *c*, separate them. Where you find *b* without *c*, if, there, *d* follows *b* and not *c*, then, in *a*, *b* was the cause of *d*. In this way it is possible to know the cause, when many things are joined.[60]

What is to be explained is *d* – which is either a *proprium* or a necessary effect of *a*. By 'follows' here, I think that Scotus means that there is some kind of intrinsic connection between *b* and *d*, and no such connection between *b* and *c*. If there is no connection between *c* and *d*, then *b* is the cause of *d*.

Inductively seeking explanatory hypotheses allows Scotus to give an account of what we would label necessary a posteriori propositions, such as 'water is H_2O' or 'man is a rational animal' (the latter is Scotus' example; clearly, he had no idea that water was H_2O) – propositions that are metaphysically necessary, but not known to be such a priori. The idea is that the subject and predicate do not have exactly the same signification (though they have, of course, the same referent): the subject signifies 'confusedly' – that is to say, it picks out some or all of the substance's *propria* – whereas the predicate signifies the essence itself. Scientific conclusions are thus genuinely informative.[61] One case that Scotus considers is the following:

Every rational animal has a capacity for humour
<u>Man is a rational animal</u>
Man has a capacity for humour

This is the so-called *demonstratio potissima*, in which the major premise predicates a *proprium* or natural effect of an essence, and the minor premise is the definition (or part of the definition) of the essence. We discover that every rational animal has a capacity for humour, and that humans are rational animals – in both cases, I take it, by the hypothetical method outlined above.[62]

In this case, it seems that both premises count as necessary, but not known to be such a priori (indeed, not known to be true a priori). In other cases, the major premise is simply self-evident: a priori, or semantically necessary:

> When an experience of the conclusion is accepted – for example, that the moon is sometimes eclipsed – and we suppose that the conclusion is true, we look for the cause of the conclusion by the way of division. And when we arrive, from the experienced conclusion, to principles known from their terms, then the conclusion can be known more certainly (namely, in the first genus of knowledge, because deduced from a principle that is known *per se*) when derived from the principle known from its terms. For example, this is known *per se*: an opaque body interposed between a visible object and a light source prevents the multiplication of light to the visible object. And if it were found by division that the earth is such a body, interposed between the sun and the moon, then [the conclusion] will be known by a *propter quid* demonstration (because through the cause), and not merely by experience (as the conclusion was known before the discovery of the principle).[63]

Scotus supposes that we discover, by the kind of division just described, that the earth has the requisite properties. The intended explanatory syllogism must look something like this:

> Every opaque body (sometimes) interposed between the moon and the sun is such that it (sometimes) prevents the multiplication of light to the moon.
>   The earth is an opaque body (sometimes) interposed between the moon and the sun.
>   The earth is such that it (sometimes) prevents the multiplication of light to the moon.

The major premise here is just an instance of Scotus' explanatory principle, 'An opaque body interposed between a visible object and a light source prevents the multiplication of light to the visible object', and the conclusion is equivalent to 'the moon is sometimes eclipsed.'[64]

5.2 Anti-scepticism

In the case of the scientific syllogisms just described, the process is epistemically underwritten by a premise that is evident (either self-evident, or such that its necessity can be discovered by the way of division). In such cases, Scotus claims that the conclusion is known 'most certainly' by scientific method,[65] and that as a result of this method the 'expert infallibly knows' such-and-such a conclusion.[66]

So, he holds that once we grasp (e.g.) what water is, 'water is H_2O' is as evident to us as Aristotelian first principles: it is something that we know in the strongest sense, something that we could not deny, given a grasp of the content of the proposition. Scotus provides a helpful summary of the certitude attaching to these propositions that are 'immediate' (necessary) but not a priori.

> [The intellect] forms other propositions, which are immediate but not immediately known, or known to be immediate (since the terms are not known). By inquiring what is said by the terms, the intellect is regulated, by dividing and removing one thing, and by attributing another, by common conceptions. Once it knows what is said by the name, it is known if the proposition is immediate, and immediately assents to it on its own account.[67]

But Scotus considers, too, a case in which the process is underwritten by the inductive principle, outlined above: 'Whatever comes about (*evenit*), for the most part, from some non-free cause, is the natural effect of that cause.' In such a case, in our investigation 'we stop at some one thing whose extremes are known through experience to be frequently united for the most part, for example, that this plant of such-and-such a species is hot' (in the sense of 'spicy').[68] In this case, what we know is not 'the actual union of the extremes, but an aptitudinal [one]', and this constitutes the 'lowest degree of scientific cognition'.[69]

But what about the syllogistic form itself? Scotus, unsurprisingly, agrees with Aristotle that the *dictum de omni* (that whatever is true of all members of a given class is true of the members of any subclass) underwrites all syllogistic reasoning.[70] He notes that the validity of such syllogistic inferences – 'perfect syllogisms' – are 'evident' to the mind.[71] I assume that he means that someone doubting the validity of such syllogisms simply fails to understand what it means for an inference to be valid, and hence that the *dictum de omni* is something akin to an a priori principle.

6. Testimonial evidence

Scotus assigns a surprisingly high degree of warrant to testimonial evidence:

> I believe (*credo*) that the world did not begin at the same time as I did, not because I know (*scio*) that it preceded me (because there is no knowledge (*scientia*) of the past, according to Augustine), or because I opine (*opinor*) that the world preceded me; but I assent to the claim that the world preceded me firmly, by acquired faith (*fidem acquisitam*), on the basis of the testimony of

others (*ex auditu aliorum*), whose veracity I believe firmly; neither do I doubt that the world preceded me, or that there are parts of the world that I have not seen, because I do not entertain doubts about the veracity of those who tell me these things and who assert that these things are true. For this reason, just as I do not hesitate about their veracity (which is as it were the premise (*principium*)), so too neither do I hesitate about what they say (which is as it were the conclusion that follows).[72]

What Scotus is talking about here is subjective certainty – a credence level. And his optimism (ceteris paribus) about testimonial beliefs leads him to treat such beliefs as having a credence level equal to that attaching to knowledge (*scientia*). (See, too, the discussion at the very opening of this chapter.) At various places in his work, Scotus gives some examples of fully credible beliefs based on testimony: here, his belief that the world existed before he did, and that there exist parts of the world that he has not seen; elsewhere, more specifically, that Rome exists (given that Scotus has never been to Rome),[73] and, more generally, beliefs about 'histories and things written about wars and other events, which are written in chronicles'[74]; and 'that there is anywhere in the world that you have not been, [and] that this person is your father and this your mother'.[75] The rest of the quoted passage explains how acquired faith – belief (without doubt) on the basis of merely human testimony – is possible. Basically, in cases where we unhesitatingly accept the veracity of our informants, we unhesitatingly accept their testimony. The examples that he gives show that Scotus holds this to apply to very commonplace beliefs; I assume that there is a presumption in favour of the veracity of our informants: we automatically trust them unless there is a defeater. The belief in testimonial evidence is inferential: what is *basic* is our belief that informers are ceteris paribus reliable.

There seems to be a tension here. Certainty is sometimes taken by Scotus externalistically as requiring infallibility (see above), and on the face of it the account of the (quasi-?) *scientia* that he proposes in the case of testimony must be fallibilist, not infallibilist. I do not know what to say about this.

7. Self-knowledge

7.1 Mechanisms

In his *ex professo* discussion of scepticism, Scotus includes a further class of cognitions that it is not possible to doubt: our own mental acts. In the text, he does not say anything much about the mechanism, preferring to content himself with the view that our having particular mental states is 'evident' to us – that our 'certitude' of them is 'like that of self-evident propositions'.[76] The same goes for our knowledge about the identity of our own souls: not even God could substitute my soul for another and it still be the case that I would have the same self-awareness.[77]

Elsewhere, however, Scotus says more about the mechanism involved. Awareness of our own acts is a kind of second-order or reflex act:

> We experience that we cognize that act by which we cognize these things [viz. the universal, being, relations between objects that cannot be sensed, the distinction between sensory and non-sensory objects, and second intentions], and do so inasmuch as this act is in us: which is by a reflexive act directed to the direct act, and that receives it [viz. the direct act] … By a certain sense (*sensu*), that is, by interior perception (*perceptione interiori*), we experience these acts in ourselves.[78]

So, I take it that Scotus believes consciousness to involve some distinct second-order cognition. Although he is here talking about direct acts that have other concepts as their objects, it is clear that he holds the same thing about acts that have extra-mental objects. Scotus is explicit, too, about indexicality: 'we experience these acts *in ourselves*' – we experience that they are our acts, or we experience them as ours.

7.2 Infallibility

Scotus thinks it obvious that we cannot be mistaken about these things. Curiously enough, it is not obvious that what he says is sufficient to secure knowledge that the relevant acts are *ours*. He is here presupposing (I imagine) that the mental is necessarily private. But Walter Chatton, for example, a few years later, argues that this assumption is illegitimate. Simply being aware of a mental act is not sufficient, since (as Scotus, too, believes) the case of angelic (or divine) mind-reading undermines the privacy of the mental: God, or an angel, could be fully aware of my thoughts, just as I can be; and that awareness is not sufficient to make my thoughts God's thoughts, or the angel's thoughts.[79]

A few years further on, Nicholas of Autrecourt proposes an even more radical objection to the thought found in Scotus. Suppose – with William of Ockham, Peter Auriol, and Nicholas' opponent Bernard of Arezzo – that any mental act that can be produced by a natural agent can be produced by God; and include among the list of possible mental acts intuitive cognitions. God could then deceptively produce an 'intuitive' act that lacks an object.[80] And suppose, too, the reflex or second-order account of our cognition of mental acts, as a second-order intuitive cognition with those first-order acts as its objects. In this case, God could deceptively make me believe that I had such-and-such a mental state, when I did not: 'Intuitive cognition ... does not, within the natural order, yield evident certitude.... And thus it follows evidently that you are not certain of the evidentness of your impression. And, consequently, you are not certain whether anything appears to you at all' (Nicholas of Autrecourt 1994: 53). Still, perhaps Autrecourt was wrong about this, and Scotus need not be troubled.

Notes

1 *Quaestiones super libros Metaphysicorum* I, q. 4, n. 12 (OP: 3:99). (Throughout, references are to Scotus unless otherwise indicated.)

2 *Quaestiones super libros Metaphysicorum* I, q. 4, n. 13 (OP: 3:99).

3 *Ordinatio* I, d. 3, p. 1, q. 4, nn. 230–1, 235 (Vatican: 3:138, 141–2).

4 *Lectura* III, d. 23, q. un., n. 19 (Vatican: 21:103).

5 *Quodlibetum*, q. 14, n. 5 (Wadding: XI, 356).

6 See *Lectura* III, d. 25, q. un., n. 41 (Vatican: 21:172).

7 Scotus, *Lectura* III, d. 25, q. un., n. 45 (Vatican: 21:173–4).

8 For a good summary of the background, see Tachau (1988: ch. 1).

9 *Ordinatio* I, d. 3, p. 3, q. 2, n. 472 (Vatican: 3:283).

10 *Ordinatio* I, d. 3, p. 1, q. 4, n. 241 (Vatican: 3:147).

11 *Ordinatio* II, d. 9, qq. 1–2, n. 61 (Vatican: 8:163).

12 *Ordinatio* I, d. 3, p. 3, q. 2, n. 396 (Vatican: 3:241–2). Note that this passage is about intelligible species. I cannot find a text in which Scotus expressly says the same about sensible species, but I see no reason why he should not have done so. For the types of quality, see Aristotle's *Categoriae*, c. 8 (8a25-10a25).

13 *Quodlibet*, q. 13, n. 25 (Wadding: 12:338). For Scotus, the category of action is restricted to *productive* activity: see *Ordinatio* I, d. 6, q. un., n. 14 (Vatican: 4:92–4).

14 For the controversy in Aquinas interpretation, see Pasnau (1997: 42–7); and, more recently, Burnyeat (2001: 129–53), denying any material change, and Perler (2002: 42–60), affirming a material change.

15 *Quaestiones super libros De anima*, q. 6, n. 7 (OP: 5:45).

16 *Ordinatio* II, d. 13, q. un., n. 39 (Vatican: 8:241).

17 *Quaestiones super libros De anima*, q. 6, n. 7 (OP: 3:44). Scotus also comes to reject the view that there is a sense in which the intentional item is the *same* form as the

form of the external object, at least in anything other than a metaphorical sense. His basic worry is that there is no sense of 'same' available with which to parse the relevant claim. He comes to the view that mental representation – the fact that such-and-such an intentional item is about such-and-such an object – is just a primitive matter. See *Quodlibetum*, q. 13, n. 12 (Wadding: 12:312).

18 See, for example, *Ordinatio* II, d. 3, p. 1, qq. 5–6, n. 191 (Vatican: 7:486); II, d. 3, p. 2, q. 1, n. 294 (Vatican: 7:539–40).

19 See *Quaestiones super libros Metaphysicorum* VII, q. 15, n. 20 (OP: 4:301).

20 *Ordinatio* I, d. 3, p. 1, q. 4, n. 235 (Vatican: 3:142), roughly repeated at n. 241 (Vatican: 3:146).

21 *Ordinatio* I, d. 3, p. 1, q. 4, n. 235 (Vatican: 3:141–2).

22 *Ordinatio* I, d. 3, p. 1, q. 4, n. 242 (Vatican: 3:147).

23 *Ordinatio* I, d. 3, p. 1, q. 4, n. 242 (Vatican: 3:147).

24 *Ordinatio* I, d. 3, p. 1, q, 4, n. 243 (Vatican: 3:147–8).

25 *Ordinatio* I, d. 3, p. 1, q. 4, n. 242 (Vatican: 3:147).

26 *Ordinatio* I, d. 3, p. 1, q. 4, n. 244 (Vatican: 3:148).

27 See *Quodlibetum*, q. 6, nn. 7–8 (Wadding: 12:145).

28 *Ordinatio* IV, d. 45, q. 3 (Vatican: 14:181).

29 *Ordinatio* III, d. 14, q. 3, n. 112 (Vatican: 9:468).

30 Aquinas, in his reply, does not reject the principle; he simply provides a mechanism distinct from intuitive intellectual cognition to get a representation of a particular into the intellect.

31 On the agent intellect, see *Ordinatio* I, d. 3, p. 3, q. 1, n. 359 (Vatican: 3:217). For its role in intuitive cognition, see *Ordinatio* IV, d. 45, q. 2, n. 65 (Vatican: 14:157–8). For a defense of the necessity of sensible species and sensory acts in intuitive intellectual cognition, see Cross (2014: 48–50).

32 Scotus does not seem to suppose, then, that intuitive intellectual cognition is a necessary condition for abstractive cognition.

33 See *Ordinatio* I, d. 3, p. 3, q. 1, nn. 352–63 (Vatican: 3:211–21).

34 See, for example, *Ordinatio* I, d. 3, p. 3, q. 1, n. 386 (Vatican: 3:235); I, d. 3, p. 3, q. 3, nn. 563–4 (Vatican: 3:335).

35 *Ordinatio* I, d. 3, p. 3, q. 2, nn. 486–9, 497–8 (Vatican: 3:289–90, 294); also the second text cited in the previous footnote – that is, nn. 563–4. Scotus is undecided as to whether it is the active or possible intellect that is responsible for producing occurrent acts: see *Quodlibetum*, q. 15, n. 20 (Wadding: 12:431). He prefers to use the Augustinian distinction between memory (as the storehouse of intelligible species and the partial cause of occurrent cognition) and intelligence (as the subject in which occurrent cognitions inhere): see *Ordinatio* I, d. 2, p. 2, qq. 1–4, n. 311 (Vatican: 2:314) for the first of these, and *Ordinatio* I, d. 27, qq. 1–3, n. 46 (Vatican: 6:83) for the second.

36 *Ordinatio* II, d. 3, p. 1, q. 1, n. 33 (Vatican: 7:403–404).

37 *Ordinatio* I, d. 3, p. 3, q. 1, n. 361 (Vatican: 7:219).

38 For the (content of the) species as the universal, see *Ordinatio* I, d. 3, p. 3, q. 1, *text. int.* (Vatican: 3:212.9–20). For the signification of common terms in general (as signifying the content of a mental act or species), see Pini (1999, 2001).

39 For the species, see, for example, *Quodlibetum*, q. 13, n. 32 (Wadding: 12:345); for the act, see *Ordinatio* I, d. 3, p. 3, q. 4, n. 601 (Vatican: 3:354).

40 *Ordinatio* I, d. 3, p. 3, q. 1, n. 339 (Vatican: 3:204–205).

41 *Ordinatio* I, d. 3, p. 1, qq. 1–2, n. 72 (Vatican: 3:50).

42 *Ordinatio* I, d. 3, p. 1, qq. 1–2, n. 86 (Vatican: 3:58).

43 *Ordinatio* I, d. 3, p. 1, qq. 1–2, n. 80 (Vatican: 3:54–5).

44 Scotus' approach to this question is quite distinctive. Aquinas, for example, believes that we first abstract more general features, and then work to more specific ones (see *Summa theologiae* I, q. 85, a. 3 c). But Scotus thinks that this cannot be right: as Scotus notes, forming more general concepts is harder, and presupposes more particular ones. Aquinas wrongly assumes that the only progression from confusion to clarity is from more to less general, and he lacks Scotus' distinction between cognizing confusedly and distinctly.

45 See *Quaestiones super libros Metaphysicorum*, II, qq. 2–3, nn. 76–7, 83, 114–15 (OP: III, 223–5, 232–3).

46 *Ordinatio* I, d. 3, p. 1, q. 3, n. 139 (Vatican: 3:87–8).

47 See *Ordinatio* I, d. 22, q. un., n. 7 (Vatican: 5:344–5). Something similar, incidentally, can be found in Aquinas, too: see *Summa theologiae* I, q. 77, a. 1 ad 7.

48 For automaticity, see *Ordinatio* I, d. 3, p. 3, q. 1, n. 366 (Vatican: 3:223), and for its unconscious nature, see *Ordinatio* I, d. 3, p. 3, q. 1, n. 349 (Vatican: 3:210).

49 *Ordinatio* I, d. 3, p. 3, qq. 1–2, n. 76 (Vatican: 3:52).

50 See *Quaestiones super libros Metaphysicorum* VI, q. 3, n. 65 (OP: 4:80), and *Ordinatio* IV, d. 8, q. 2, nn. 106–109 (Vatican: 12:25–6). See my discussion in Cross (2014: 174–6).

51 See, for example, Aquinas, *Summa theologiae* I, q. 85, a. 4 ad 2.

52 *Quaestiones super libros Metaphysicorum* VI, q. 3, n. 65 (OP: 4:80). On predication, see Malcolm (1979).

53 *Quaestiones super Praedicamenta Aristotelis*, q. 8, nn. 1–9, 14–18 (OP: 1:313–15, 317–18); *Ordinatio* III, d. 7, q. 1, n. 14 (Vatican: 9:265–6); *Quaestiones in duos libros Perihermenias*, I, qq. 5–6, n. 31 (OP: 2:174); *Ordinatio* I, d. 4, p. 2, q. un., n. 9 (Vatican: 4:3).

54 On all of this, see *Quaestiones super libros Metaphysicorum* VI, q. 3, nn. 31–3 (OP: 4:67–8).

55 *Ordinatio* I, d. 3, p. 1, qq. 1–2, nn. 80–2 (Vatican: 3:55–6); *Quaestiones super libros De anima*, q. 16, n. 19 (OP: 5:152).

56 *Lectura* III, d. 24, q. un., n. 50 (Vatican: 21:144).

57 *Ordinatio* I, d. 3, p. 1, q. 4, n. 234 (Vatican: 3:141).

58 *Ordinatio* I, d. 3, p. 1, q. 4, n. 231 (Vatican: 3:139), quoting Aristotle, *Metaphysica* III, c. 3 (1005b29-32). See, too, *Quaestiones super libros Metaphysicorum* I, q. 4, n. 44 (OP: 3:108).

59 For the explanatory nature of scientific syllogisms, see Aristotle, *Analytica posteriora* II, c. 24 (78b1-3).

60 *Quaestiones super libros Metaphysicorum* I, q. 4, n. 70 (OP: 3:116).

61 *Ordinatio* I, d. 2, p. 1, q. 1-2, n. 19 (Vatican: 2:134).

62 *Ordinatio* I, d. 2, p. 1, q. 1-2, n. 17 (Vatican: 2:132).

63 *Ordinatio* I, d. 3, p. 1, q. 4, n. 236 (Vatican: 3:143).

64 For some discussion of this, see Vier (1951: 136-52, esp. 150-2) and Demange (2007: 77-114, 187-95).

65 *Ordinatio* I, d. 3, p. 1, q. 4, n. 236 (Vatican: 3:143).

66 *Ordinatio* I, d. 3, p. 1, q. 4, n. 235 (Vatican: 3:141).

67 *Quaestiones super libros Metaphysicorum* I, q. 4, n. 44 (OP: 3:108-109).

68 *Ordinatio* I, d. 3, p. 1, q. 4, n. 237 (Vatican: 3:143-4).

69 *Ordinatio* I, d. 3, p. 1, q. 4, n. 237 (Vatican: 3:144).

70 See Aristotle, *Analytica priora* I, c. 2 (24b26-30).

71 *Ordinatio* I, d. 3, p. 1, q. 4, n. 233 (Vatican: 3:140).

72 *Lectura* III, d. 23, q. un., n. 19 (Vatican: 21:103-104).

73 *Lectura* III, d. 23, q. un., n. 15 (Vatican:1:102).

74 *Lectura* III, d. 23, q. un., n. 4 (Vatican: 21:97). This list occurs in the context of an objection; but Scotus never rejects the view that we 'firmly adhere' to these things 'by acquired faith'.

75 *Ordinatio* prol., p. 2, q. un., n. 107 (Vatican: 1:68-9).

76 *Ordinatio* I, d. 3, p. 1, q. 4, n. 239 (Vatican: 3:145). On this, see Pich (2010).

77 *Ordinatio* I, d. 3, p. 1, q. 4, n. 239 (Vatican: 3:145). See, too, *Quaestiones super libros Metaphysicorum* VII, q. 13, n. 158 (OP: 4:271).

78 *Ordinatio* IV, d. 43, q. 2, nn. 10-11 (Wadding: 10:25). See, too, for example, *Quodlbetum*, q. 14, n. 25 (Wadding: 12:405).

79 For this debate, see Brower-Toland (2012).

80 Ockham denies that God could do this deceptively, maintaining that any such divinely caused cognition would in turn cause a negative act of judgement in relation to the existence of the object. But Auriol seems to hold the view that Nicholas is attacking here. For all of this, see Tachau (1988: 335-52).

References

Aquinas, T. (1265-74), *Summa Theologiae*, available at http://www.corpusthomisticum. org/iopera.html. (Translations mine.)

Brower-Toland, S. (2012), 'Medieval Approaches to Consciousness: Ockham and
    Chatton', *Philosophers' Imprint*, 12.
Burnyeat, M. (2001), 'Aquinas on the "Spiritual Change" in Perception', in D. Perler
    (ed.), *Ancient and Medieval Theories of Intentionality*, STGM, 76, Leiden and Boston,
    MA: Brill.
Cross, R. (2014), *Duns Scotus's Theory of Cognition*, Oxford: Oxford University Press.
Demange, D. (2007), *Jean Duns Scot: La théorie du savoir*, Sic et Non, Paris: Vrin.
King, P. (2015), 'Thinking About Things: Singular Thought in the Middle Ages', in
    G. Klima (ed.), *Intentionality and Mental Representation in Medieval Philosophy*,
    New York: Fordham University Press.
Malcolm, J. (1979), 'A Reconsideration of the Identity and Inherence Theories of the
    Copula', *Journal of the History of Philosophy*, 17: 383–400.
Nicholas of Autrecourt (1994), *Prima epistola ad Bernardum*, n. 12 (*Nicholas of
    Autrecourt: His Corresepondence with Master Giles and Bernard of Arezzo*), ed. L. M.
    de Rijk, STGM, 42, Leiden, New York, Cologne: Brill.
Pasnau, R. (1997), *Theories of Cognition in the Later Middle Ages*, Cambridge:
    Cambridge University Press.
Perler, D. (2002), *Theorien der Intentionalität im Mittelalter*, Frankfurt am Main:
    Klostermann.
Pich, R. H. (2010), 'Scotus on Contingent Propositions "Known through Themselves"
    (*per se notae*)', in L. Honnefelder, H. Möhle, A. Speer, T. Kobusch, and S. B. del
    Barrio (eds), *Johannes Duns Scotus 1308–2008: Die philosophischen Perspektiven
    seines Werkes*, Archa verbi, Subsidia, 5, Münster: Aschendorff.
Pini, G. (1999), 'Species, Concept and Thing: Theories of Signification in the Second
    Half of the Thirteenth Century', *Medieval Philosophy and Theology*, 8: 21–52.
Pini, G. (2001), 'Signification of Names in Duns Scotus and Some of His
    Contemporaries', *Vivarium*, 39: 20–51.
Pini, G. (2004), 'Scotus on Assertion and the Copula: A Comparison with Aquinas', in
    A. Maierù and L. Valente (eds), *Medieval Theories on Assertive and Non-assertive
    Language: Acts of the 14th European Symposium on Medieval Logic and Semantics,
    Rome, June 11–15, 2002*, Lessico intellettuale europeo, 97, Florence: Olschki.
Rombeiro, M. E. (2011), 'Intelligible Species in the Mature Thought of Henry of Ghent',
    Journal of the History of Philosophy, 49: 181–220.
Scotus, John Duns (1950–2013), *Opera omnia*, ed. C. Balić and P. M. Perantoni, 21 vols,
    Vatican City: Vatican Press. (Cited in this chapter as 'Vatican'.)
Scotus, John Duns (1968–69 [1639]), *Opera omnia*, ed. L. Wadding, 12 vols,
    Hildesheim: G. Olms. (Cited in this chapter as 'Wadding'.)
Scotus, John Duns (1997–2006), *Opera philosophica*, ed. G. J. Etzkorn, R. R. Andrews,
    B. C. Bazàn, and D. Mechthild, 5 vols, St Bonaventure, NY: Franciscan Institute
    Publications. (Cited in this chapter as 'OP'.)
Tachau, K. H. (1988), *Vision and Certitude in the Age of Ockham: Optics, Epistemology
    and the Foundations of Semantics 1250–1345*, Leiden: Brill.
Vier, P. C. (1951), *Evidence and Its Function According to John Duns Scotus*, St
    Bonaventure, NY: Franciscan Institute Publications.

7

William Ockham on Testimonial Knowledge

Jennifer Pelletier

1. Introduction

It is an incontestable fact of human life that much of what we say we know depends on the word of others, whether peers, teachers, experts, and so on. That Robespierre played a decisive role in the French Revolution, that subatomic particles exist, that Syria is in the midst of a civil war, and, more mundanely, that your spouse is happy and that you are suffering from bronchitis are typical instances of knowledge by testimony or 'testimonial knowledge'. Put simplistically, some hearer knows p on the ground that some speaker, who is competent and honest, tells her that p. A description of how we claim to acquire knowledge must concede that we at least sometimes accept testimony as a source of knowledge like perception, memory, and inference (it is an open question whether testimonial knowledge is reducible to inferential knowledge). Nonetheless, testimonial knowledge has been largely neglected in the history of Western epistemology with the much-noted exceptions of David Hume and Thomas Reid. In his pioneering book on the subject, *Testimony: A Philosophical Study*, Coady (1992: 13) suggests that past philosophers tended to ignore the social dimension of epistemology, having been primarily preoccupied with an 'individualistic ideology'. Following the publication of his book, the issue of testimonial knowledge, and social epistemology more generally, has attracted significant contemporary philosophical attention in the English-speaking world.[1] Recently, some work has appeared on medieval views on different forms of knowledge or belief and the function of testimony.[2]

William Ockham (c. 1287–1343) briefly suggests that in some sense we can be said to *know* certain truths on the grounds that someone else tells us that they are true. The truths in question range from the banal (this woman gave birth to me) to the miraculous and exalted (Christ was incarnate; Christ was crucified). The texts are few, various main themes are underdeveloped, and many of the issues that dominate the contemporary debate are absent. However, I hope to show that Ockham does have some notion of testimonial knowledge. Moreover, he addresses what I take to be sources of testimonial knowledge: namely, religious and non-religious authorities (speakers or writers), whose sayings we (hearers or readers) can be said to know under certain conditions. He further provides a detailed account of how and why we would accept the testimony of an authority at all, which amounts to an analysis of the causes of testimonial knowledge.

In Section 2, I present the key text where Ockham advances the claim that one form of knowledge (*scientia*) extends to knowledge that we acquire through the testimony of others. Here, we encounter salient epistemological notions: belief, evidence, certainty, and doubt, all of which play a part in shaping the peculiarities of this form of knowledge. I then argue that knowledge, as thus outlined, includes testimonial knowledge. In Section 3, I turn to two main sources of testimonial knowledge: religious and non-religious authorities. The latter includes the sources both of quotidian testimonial knowledge and of philosophical or scientific testimonial knowledge. In Section 4, I discuss Ockham's causal analysis of how and why we are led to believe the testimony of some authority in the first place. The result, I hope, is a first attempt at exploring this relatively neglected aspect of Ockham's account of knowledge.

2. Knowledge and belief: truth, evidence, certainty, and doubt

Although medieval philosophers adopted Aristotelian demonstrative knowledge as the ideal form of knowledge, they recognized that the term '*scientia*' covered a wide spectrum of less-than-ideal forms of knowledge.[3] The difficulties of uniformly translating '*scientia*' by 'knowledge' become immediately apparent since, as we shall see with Ockham, the Latin term can refer to anything from ordinary true belief to rarefied expert scientific knowledge. In this tradition, Ockham opens the prologue to his commentary on Aristotle's *Physics* with four different and increasingly rigorous ways that the term 'knowledge' is used.[4] The first and weakest is of particular interest for our purposes. He writes:

> In one sense, knowledge is a certain cognition of some truth. In this sense, some truths are known only on trust [*fides*]; for instance when we say we know that Rome is a large city, even though we have not seen it, and similarly I say I know

that this person is my father and this person my mother. And so with many other [truths] that are not cognized evidently. Yet, because we adhere to these truths without a shadow of doubt and they are true, we are said to know them.[5]

Knowledge, understood in this sense (henceforth: K1), refers to any cognition of a truth that we judge to be true with a high degree of certainty. The objects of acts of judgement – what we know, believe, doubt, opine, and so on to be true or false – are typically mental sentences that we have apprehended or formed in the intellect. Ockham distinguishes between the act of apprehending some sentence *p* and the act of judging *p* to be true or false. Judging *p* to be true is an act of assenting to *p*; judging *p* to be false is an act of dissenting from *p*. Both presuppose having first apprehended *p*. We cannot assent to, or dissent from, a sentence that we have not apprehended. What he means, then, by 'cognition of some truth' is the twofold act of forming and then assenting to an apprehended sentence like 'this man is my father' or 'Rome is a large city'.[6]

K1 knowledge-acts extend to sentences that we judge to be true solely on the basis of trust, and in this way we can be said to know a sentence that we believe to be true. Ockham typically appeals to evident cognition to distinguish knowledge (*scientia*) from belief (*fides*), often implying if not explicitly stating that knowledge and belief with respect to the same sentence are mutually exclusive because the former is evident while the latter is non-evident.[7] On occasion, he suggests that what he means is evident knowledge, intimating the possibility of non-evident knowledge.[8] This precision is consistent with the language used in the *Physics* commentary, where some K1 knowledge-acts are indeed belief-acts.

The notion of evident cognition is crucially present in the remaining three senses of 'knowledge'.

K2   A cognition by which a knower evidently assents to *p*, whether *p* is a contingent sentence, which can be true or false if formed ('this wall is white') or a necessary sentence, which is always true if formed ('all human beings are rational').[9]

K3   A cognition by which a knower evidently assents to a necessary sentence ('every animal is a substance').[10]

K4   A cognition by which a knower evidently assents to a necessary sentence resulting from a demonstration ('all human beings can laugh').[11]

Before comparing the different uses of 'knowledge' in more depth, we need to become clear on what evident cognition is and on how one cognizes a sentence *p* evidently. For, with the notable exception of K1, knowing that *p* requires evidently cognizing *p*. An evident cognition is the cognition of a true sentence *p*, the assent to which is either (1) immediately caused by the cognition of its terms or (2) mediately caused by the cognition of the terms of a true sentence *q* from which *p* can be inferred. A knower – the intellect – cognizes *p* evidently when she has formed *p* and cognized its terms in such a way that they cause her to assent to the truth of *p*.[12]

There are different ways in which the knower must cognize *p*'s terms in order to evidently assent to *p* depending on the kind of sentence that *p* is. A knower can only evidently assent to a contingent sentence like 'Socrates is white' if she *intuitively* cognizes Socrates and the whiteness inhering in him. Under normal circumstances, she must perceive white Socrates, existing and present to her, to be able to evidently assent to 'Socrates is white.' By contrast, a knower can evidently assent to a necessary sentence like 'a whole is greater than its parts' regardless of whether she *intuitively* or *abstractively* cognizes a whole and its parts. An intuitive cognition naturally causes an abstractive cognition of the very same object, so that, when the object is non-existent or absent, the knower can still evidently assent to 'a whole is greater than its parts.'[13] She cannot evidently know that Socrates is white when he is absent, since he could have changed colour; but she can evidently know that a whole is greater than its parts when she is not perceiving an existing and present whole. Put otherwise, just by understanding the terms 'whole' and 'part', she can evidently assent to 'a whole is greater than its parts'. For this reason, such a sentence is said to be 'known per se', known simply through its terms.

The causal process of assenting to *p* evidently on the basis of how its terms are cognized is naturalistic and involuntary.[14] Once *p*'s terms have been appropriately cognized, whether intuitively or abstractively, and *p* has been formed or apprehended, the intellect cannot but assent to the truth of *p*. In the same way, once *q*'s terms have been appropriately cognized and *q* has been formed such that *q* is evidently cognized, then, if *p* follows from *q* and *p* is apprehended, the intellect cannot but evidently assent to the truth of *p*. This is how evidence is transmitted from the premises to the conclusion of a demonstration.

While K2 extends to ordinary evident knowledge of contingent truths, K3 is more rigorous, being restricted to the scientific knowledge of the necessary principles and conclusions that make up demonstrations. Most rigorous of all, and consequently the ideal form of knowledge, K4 is limited to the proper scientific knowledge of the necessary conclusions of demonstrations. K3 and K4 are designed to accommodate scientific knowledge conceived of as Aristotelian demonstrative knowledge.

Ockham himself notes that on K2 we are 'said to know something not merely because someone has told us about it [*propter testimonium narrantium*] but we would assent to it even if no-one were to tell us about it'.[15] The idea here is clearly to emphasize that, *in contrast* to some K1 knowledge-acts, all K2 knowledge-acts are evident. Therefore, K2 does not extend to sentences that we can be said to know solely on the basis of trust – that is, because we believe the speaker who tells us that *p*. I know (K1 knowledge-act) that *p* 'Rome is a large city' is true, even though I have never been to Rome and seen that it is large. I know (K1 knowledge-act) that *q* ('this woman is my mother') is true, even though I did not witness my own birth in any way that would allow me to evidently cognize *q*. Had I been to Rome where I would have intuitively cognized Rome and its size, I would be able to know (K2 knowledge-act) that *p*. Had I been able to adequately witness my own birth, I would be able to know (K2 knowledge-act) that *q*, again because of having intuitively cognized this woman – my mother – in the act of giving birth to me. Notice that, although Ockham's K1 examples are contingent, there is no reason to think that the objects of K1 knowledge-acts cannot be necessary.

A subset of K1 knowledge-acts are true beliefs because K1 knowledge-acts can be non-evident. Evident cognition is not required on K1 but nor, conversely, is it excluded. The first and weakest sense of 'knowledge' is in fact broad enough to cover both true beliefs and evident knowledge. K2-K4 knowledge-acts do, however, require evident cognition, and consequently exclude any true belief-acts.

All K1 knowledge-acts are acts of assent to true sentences. If we assent to a false sentence, we do not *know* that sentence in any sense. In this case, we have a false belief that not-*p* when *p* is true, or vice versa. Ockham addresses true and false belief in *Quodlibet* 4, q. 6, where he compares the epistemic state of a Christian who hears a priest preaching the articles of the Catholic faith, and who witnesses miracles that substantiate those articles, with a Muslim who hears an imam preaching Islamic law and who witnesses miracles that supposedly substantiate Koranic law. Ockham holds, of course, that the former articles are true and the miracles real, while the latter law is false and the miracles merely apparent. He concludes, nonetheless, that the Christian and the Muslim are in the same epistemic state. Both believe their respective articles. The witnessing of miracles, real or apparent, just serves to deepen their belief without allowing either the grounds upon which they might be said to know their articles.[16] The main point of the passage is to highlight the evidentness of knowledge-acts as opposed to the non-evidentness of belief-acts. Even the Christian does not evidently know that his articles of faith are true, because he cannot possibly cognize the terms of those articles in the appropriate way in this life. Yet he believes them to be true, and this despite them actually being true. In *Quodlibet* 4, q. 6, belief is consistent with truth or falsity. In the *Physics* prologue, false belief is disqualified as any kind of knowledge.

All K1 knowledge-acts are acts of assent to true sentences characterized by a high degree of certainty in and lack of doubt about their truth-value. Ockham does not explore certainty at much length but states in the *Ordinatio* prologue that 'certainty [*certitudo*] is taken either for adherence or evidence'[17] and, just a bit later, 'theology with respect to what is believable ... is not evident but certain'.[18] We might think of firm adhesion as the believer's subjective certainty, a phenomenological feature of her K1 knowledge-acts that are belief-acts. If I strongly or firmly adhere to the truth of *p*, in the sense that I entertain no doubt as to *p*'s being true, then I know (K1 knowledge-act) that *p*. This is not the same as the objective certainty that would accompany an evident knowledge-act. Because a belief-act is non-evident, the believer has no objective grounds for being certain that *p*. Neither the Christian nor the Muslim has objective certainty about their respective articles of faith or law, even if they have ample subjective certainty.

The language of K1 suggests that if I am subjectively certain enough that *p*, then I can be said to know *p*. This further suggests that if I am less subjectively certain that *p* then I merely believe that *p*. Most people are sufficiently certain that this man and this woman are their parents that they can be said to know who their parents are. Take, however, someone who is less certain who her parents are. She can still be said to believe who her parents are, although we might stop short of saying that she knows who they are. Not all belief-acts, on this reading, are characterized by a high degree of certainty; only those that qualify as K1 knowledge-acts are thus characterized. Ockham notes elsewhere that we frequently believe certain sentences with such conviction, without any doubt whatsoever, that we adhere to them as if they were evidently known (*sicut evidenter notis*).[19] It is not clear if he is referring to belief-acts tout court or just those that are K1 knowledge-acts. The context – our assent to the conclusions of dialectical syllogisms inferred from probable or plausible (*probabilis*) premises – evokes a distinction between belief-acts and opinion-acts. Like certainty, opinion is another relatively undeveloped theme in Ockham's writings, but he appears to uphold the standard view that I opine that *p* when, though I recognize the likelihood that *p*, I still doubt that *p* insofar as I grant that not-*p* is possibly true. I assent to *p* but 'with fear' (*cum formidine*) of its opposite – not-*p* – being true. Like belief-acts, opinion-acts are non-evident,[20] so they would lack the objective certainty accompanying an evident knowledge-act. However, since more doubt remains about the truth of p in opinion-acts, they lack the subjective certainty and adhesion of belief-acts. Perhaps opinion-acts take place when the threshold of subjective certainty is too low to sustain any belief-act at all.

In short, K1 knowledge-acts include true belief-acts but only those that meet a high degree of subjective certainty. Generally, Ockham holds that on

---

K1   A subject can be said to know that p if (i) p is true and (ii) she firmly adheres to p.

---

3. Testimonial knowledge

Why would we believe that 'Rome is a large city' when we have not visited Rome ourselves? Because some speaker tells us that it is. Ockham says as much in K2 where he points out that some K1 knowledge-acts can depend on the testimony of a speaker telling the knower, a hearer, that p. K2-K4 knowledge-acts, by contrast, issue from the knower's own experience and reasoning capacities, which is why they are evident. She does not need to rely on the testimony of a speaker, but has the resources to assent to p by herself. If testimonial knowledge is minimally taken to be a hearer's knowing or believing that p because a speaker says that p, then some K1 knowledge-acts are testimonial knowledge-acts:

$K1^T$ A subject can be said to know that p if (i) p is true and (ii) she firmly adheres to p because (iii) some speaker says that p.

Contemporary accounts of testimonial knowledge include other conditions that $K1^T$ knowledge-acts fail to meet: for example, (1) the speaker invites the hearer to understand and believe his testimony (Adler 2015: sec. 1), (2) the speaker has the competence or authority to state that p (Coady 1992: 42), and (3) the speaker's testimony that p is important for resolving a question and aimed at those who require clarification on the matter (ibid.).

Ockham might well partly agree with (1). On his account of judgement, a hearer cannot assent to p without apprehending it in the first place. Assuming that the speaker wants the hearer to believe that p, the speaker must count on or invite the hearer to understand p. It is less obvious that, for all $K1^T$ knowledge-acts, the speaker utters p in the hope that the hearer will believe that p. A speaker may say that p but without expecting the hearer to believe it. Imagine, for example, that the speaker is doubtful about *p* but ineffectively conveys her doubt, so that the hearer mistakenly thinks that the speaker firmly adheres to *p*, with the consequence that the hearer ends up believing that *p* despite the speaker not having knowingly invited the speaker to believe her.[21]

Ockham might not agree with (3). His example of knowing who our parents are is telling. For most of us, that the people who raised us are our biological parents is not a matter that needs to be resolved. Nevertheless, Ockham thinks that I know (K1^T knowledge-act) 'this woman is my mother'. It does not seem that he would restrict testimonial knowledge to cases where some matter must be resolved for a particular party.

Finally, it is difficult to see that Ockham would disagree with (2). Surely we believe the testimony of a speaker who is competent or reliable in general or in the matter at hand – what *p* is about – and sincere. We tend to find the testimony of a doctor more compelling than the testimony of a friend in medical matters, and similarly we tend to find the testimony of someone who is generally truthful to be more compelling than the testimony of someone we believe to be prone to exaggeration or deception. We trust speakers who meet certain conditions, and consequently we are more legitimately confident in their authority as speakers of testimony.

A key aspect of testimonial knowledge is some notion of the authority or trustworthiness of its source – the speaker's competency and sincerity in saying that *p*.[22] To know that *p* on the basis of some speaker having said so, the hearer must recognize the speaker's authority to some degree or another. By 'authority', I mean, very broadly, something like the reliability or trustworthiness of a speaker who tells a hearer that *p* such that the hearer assents to the speaker's testimony that *p*. Ockham mentions authority (*auctoritas*) infrequently and superficially, without much discussion on what authority is or of how it could be epistemically relevant.[23] However, there are a few texts where authority, in a broad sense, can be connected to testimonial knowledge. In the remainder of this chapter, I look at these texts.

3.1 Religious sources of testimonial knowledge

Two formulations of Ockham's principle of parsimony explicitly refer to religious authority:

1. '[N]othing ought to be posited without a given reason [*ratione assignata*] unless it is cognized per se, or known by experience, or proved by the authority of Sacred Scripture.'[24]

2. '[N]o plurality should be posited except by reason, or experience, or the authority of those who cannot be deceived, nor err, nor be refuted.'[25]

Both counsel us to posit something – typically, a really distinct entity that adds to the ontology – only if compelled to do so by an argument ('reason'), our having had the relevant intuitive cognition ('experience'), or because an authority says so. If some authority says that p '(this thing x is really distinct from that thing y'), then I must assent to p. Furthermore, if p is true and I firmly adhere to p then I know (K1^T knowledge-act) that p.

Ockham would agree that p is true if the authority in question is by definition non-deceivable, unable to err, and unable to be disproved – namely, an infallible religious authority such as Sacred Scripture. My assent to p cannot be caused by having evidently cognized p, since this would obtain in case I were compelled to assent to p on the basis of an argument or experience. A non-believer can have the same experience as the believer and enjoy the same reasoning capacities as the believer and yet deny that the articles of the faith are true. The very existence of non-believers, Ockham thinks, supports his claim that we do not and cannot evidently assent to many or most theological truths in this life. Finally, I should firmly adhere to p if it has been posited by an infallible religious authority.

We find a more detailed analysis of religious authority in Ockham's treatise on quantity, *Tractatus de quantitate*, when he defends Peter John Olivi's novel view that quantity accidents are not really distinct from substances and quality accidents against Richard of Middleton. The larger context here is the Eucharist where, according to orthodox doctrine, in transubstantiation the substance of the bread is absent from the altar while the substance of the body of Christ is present as are the accidents of the bread, accounting for why we continue to perceive a white round object of certain dimensions. Richard alleges that Olivi's view is contrary to the 'common opinion of doctors', implying that such doctors are authorities whose assertions (testimony) about the ontological status of quantity accidents ought to be assented and adhered to.

Ockham retorts by asking: what does Richard mean by 'doctors'? Either (1) doctors approved by the Church, or (2) modern doctors. Ockham does not question the authority of doctors approved by the Church, but without explaining why he does not. Is it because they, too, are infallible? Or institutionally sanctioned, such that their testimony cannot be questioned? In any event, he maintains that no religious authority of this kind in fact asserts that quantity ought to be posited as really distinct from its substance or a quality. There is no reason, then, to be compelled to assent to any assertion that a quantity is so distinct![26] Moreover, he continues, if it seems as though a doctor of the Church does argue that really distinct quantities should be posited to exist, 'this ought to be explained'.[27] So, he urges some hermeneutic latitude even when it comes to religious authorities whose testimony that p ought to be assented to, and therefore ought to be believed, by a hearer.

Ockham extends no such authority to modern doctors who refute one another 'in public, in secret and in their writings', happily conceding that Olivi's view on quantity, which he happens to share, is contrary to the consensus view.[28] He affirms the following general principle for some p that a modern doctor says is true: 'p should only be assented to if it can be proved by (i) evident reason, (ii) the authority of Sacred Scripture, (iii) a determination of the Church, or (iv) doctors approved by the Church'.[29] Unless p is found in the sayings or writings of Sacred Scripture, the determinations of the Church, or doctors approved by the Church, I am free to dissent from p if I am not convinced by the argument(s) put forth by a modern doctor for p, as Ockham and Olivi do on the question of quantity. If I am convinced by their argument(s) for p, then I do not assent to p because some modern doctor says so, but because I have been convinced of p through my own efforts. I would, in short, have evidently cognized p, and in this case I do not believe that p by a $K1^T$ knowledge-act or rely on a modern doctor's testimony that p. Rather, I come to agree independently with him that p. No philosophical – or, better, philosophical-theological – authority or rational argument, Ockham declares,

> that I have ever heard or read, has moved me more to believe that a quantity is a different thing from a substance and a quality than to believe that creation is a different thing from God and creatures. But yet if it could be proved that this was what some saint or doctor approved by the Church meant, which it is not permitted to deny, then because of him, I will that my intellect be convinced [*volo intellectum meum captivare*] and concede that a quantity is different from a substance and a quality.[30]

For a modern doctor's testimony that p, belief, or $K1^T$ is not necessarily the appropriate attitude to adopt. It might be preferable that one endeavour to work out whether p is true for oneself, despite the consensus expert opinion. But Ockham himself qualifies as a philosophical-theological expert who can be reasonably expected to engage in debate with fellow experts on questions about the ontology of the Eucharist. The same expectations may not be applicable to an intelligent lay person, for whom believing that p just because philosophical-theological experts say so may be more acceptable. Everyone, however, experts included, is always compelled to believe the testimony of religious authority.

3.2 Non-religious sources of testimonial knowledge

The two examples from the *Physics* prologue, the size of Rome and the people who are our parents, are banal and very representative of the kind of non-religious testimonial knowledge of ordinary contingent truths that we acquire throughout our daily lives. Other people have the requisite experience to know (K2 knowledge-act) that p and tell us so: for example, my mother who bore me, or my friend who visited Rome. They are eyewitness authorities. Assuming that we believe the speaker in question has actually had the appropriate experience, does not lie or exaggerate, and is certain that p is true, we are in the position to firmly adhere to p ourselves. We can, therefore, be said to know (K1$^\mathrm{T}$ knowledge-act) that p on the basis of our trust in their authority as speakers in general or at least on the size of Rome and our parentage.

Necessary truths that we have not evidently cognized, but that we believe or opine, to be true because they are deemed acceptable to everyone, the many, or the wise are considered plausible (*probabilia*). They can function as the premises of dialectical arguments, the conclusions of which are likewise plausible. Here we seem to have a case of commonly received secular reputable opinion (I hesitate to use this word, for reasons that will become apparent) and philosophical or scientific expert authority. Ockham describes what conditions a sentence must meet to be plausible in the *Summa logicae*, when he introduces his classification of syllogisms. Having defined a demonstrative syllogism as that from which one can acquire the first cognition of a conclusion from necessary premises that are evidently cognized, a dialectical syllogism is 'from plausibles': that is, from premises that are not evidently cognized but are taken to be true by everyone, or by many, or by the wise.[31] Basing himself on Aristotle, Ockham proposes that

[a] sentence p is plausible if and only if p is (i) necessary, i.e. always true if formed, (ii) not known per se, nor inferable from sentences q and r that are known *per se*, nor evidently known through experience, nor from what follows from experience, yet (iii) because of being true, p seems to be true to everyone, to many or to the wise.[32]

Condition (i) excludes any contingent or false sentence from being plausible: for example, 'I was born in Canada', 'It is raining in Brussels', and 'Water boils at 5°C'. Condition (ii) excludes the principles and conclusions of demonstrative syllogisms, which are by definition evidently cognized by the syllogizer and cannot, then, be plausible. Condition (iii) excludes particular sentences that are necessary but that are nonetheless taken to be false by everyone, the many, or the wise.[33] Ockham adds that the articles of faith are not plausible sentences because, despite being necessary, they are considered false by everyone, the many, or the wise. He specifies that, by 'wise', he (or Aristotle) means those who rely exclusively on natural reason.[34] Presumably, in a predominantly Christian society, necessary articles of faith would be plausible since they are accepted as true by everyone, and the many and the wise as well if these include those who do not limit themselves to the findings of natural reason alone.

Ockham further concludes that 'not every dialectical syllogism always and only produces doubt and fear but frequently also produces firm belief [*fides*], without any doubt, since sometimes we adhere to plausible sentences as though they were evidently known'.[35] This suggests that the plausible conclusions of dialectical syllogisms can be the objects of belief as well as opinion. Recall that opinion-acts are those where we assent to p but recognize the possibility that not-p – namely, with some degree of doubt and 'fear' of the contrary being true. If we are subjectively certain that a plausible conclusion is true, then we believe it. If we entertain some doubt as to its opposite being true, then we opine it.

It seems reasonable to think that Ockham would agree that, when a plausible sentence p is believed by some hearer with a sufficiently high degree of certainty, she can be said to know (K1^T knowledge-act) that p. For p is true and, although the hearer has not evidently cognized p, nevertheless she firmly adheres to p because everyone, the many, or the wise say that p. Plausible truths are exactly the sorts of truths that comprise non-religious but not quotidian (contingent) testimonial knowledge, truths that a hearer can be said to know because they are accepted and communicated to a broader community by lay ('everyone or the many') and expert philosophical or scientific authorities ('the wise').

A couple of questions arise. First, if plausible sentences are plausible even to experts and not, therefore, evidently known by them, then in what sense are experts authorities, and on what grounds would their testimony be considered authoritative and trustworthy? Second, even if experts are authorities whose testimony is authoritative and trustworthy, why should the lay testimony of everyone or the many be so as well? Why would I believe that p just because everyone or the many think that p? Ockham could be thinking of expert testimony that filters down to the lay community so that we all or most of us can be said to know what experts say; but there is no justification for this interpretation. Neither question can be adequately answered on the basis of the text.

4. Causes of testimonial knowledge

There is a distinction between assenting to a speaker's testimony and assenting to that speaker as an authority whose testimony is to be believed in the first place. In *Quaestiones variae* 5, Ockham argues against John Duns Scotus' view that the intellect is an active power. At one point, he distinguishes between the causes of belief-acts in two cases:

1. Either an acquired belief-act with respect to p is caused by (i) a belief-act with respect to q, (ii) a cognition of p's terms and (iii) the apprehension of p without any activity of the intellect or the will;
2. Or an acquired belief-act with respect to q is caused by (i) a cognition of q's terms, (ii) the apprehension of q and (iii) an act of willing.[36]

What follows is an extended analysis of two examples, to illustrate each case. For (1), Ockham states that

> if someone were to believe that a man is generally truthful in word and deed, and this by acquired faith, if he were then to say to him assertively and in good faith that something is certainly true that he did not previously believe to be true, then if he indeed believes the first complex, he cannot dissent from the second complex.[37]

Imagine that Elizabeth does not think that Mr. Collins is in the library or simply does not know whether he is. Jane, however, says that p ('Mr. Collins is in the library'). Suppose, further, that Elizabeth believes that Jane is generally truthful. Presumably, she has knowingly and repeatedly experienced Jane's tendency to utter true sentences. She knows that Jane does so sincerely without lying and with a high degree of certainty in their being true. Elizabeth has, in effect, already assented to a sentence like q ('Jane is generally truthful'). If Elizabeth were to persist in believing that Mr. Collins is not in the library or to doubt that he is – if she were to believe that p is false even when Jane tells her that p – then Elizabeth would contradict herself. For believing that Jane is generally truthful while disbelieving Jane's testimony is contradictory.[38] Elizabeth's assent to p is caused by (i) her belief act with respect to q, (ii) her cognition of p's terms, and (iii) her apprehension of p. As long as all three conditions are fulfilled, Elizabeth automatically assents to p and her will is powerless to make her dissent from p, at least on pain of contradiction.[39]

But what causes Elizabeth to assent to q in the first place? For (2), Ockham asks, 'since he thinks him to be truthful in word and deed such that he firmly assents to this complex "this man is truthful in word and deed", I then ask: by what is this act of believing or assenting caused?'[40] Ockham argues by process of elimination:

1. Assent to q is caused by one of the following: (i) a cognition of q's terms and the apprehension of q alone, (ii) some other evident and scientific cognition resulting from a demonstration, (iii) the relevant intuitive cognition(s), (iv) a belief-act with respect to another prior sentence r from which q evidently follows (e.g. 'no one could do as Jane does unless she were truthful'), or (v) an act of the will.[41]
2. Because (i)–(iii) characterize evident cognition, they are disqualified, since q, as the object of a belief-act, is not evidently cognized.[42]
3. The threat of an infinite regress disqualifies (iv). For what causes our assent to r? Not (i)–(iii), for the same reasons given in (2). Not (iv), since then we have to posit another belief-act with respect to another prior sentence s from which r is evident, *ad infinitum*.[43]
4. Therefore, the only viable cause of assent to q is (v) an act of will.[44]

Elizabeth's assent to q ('Jane is generally truthful') is caused by (i) her cognition of q's terms, (ii) her apprehension of q, and (iii) an act of will.

The thrust of (1) is that we believe a sentence like p because we already believe a prior sentence like q. A basic belief in q necessitates the derived belief in p by means of a process of default reasoning: if I accept q then I must accept p on pain of contradiction. The thrust of (2) is that we believe a sentence like q because we will to do so, and not because we believe in any prior sentence like r. A basic belief in q, unlike a derived belief in p, is adhered to by the will alone.

What is at stake is precisely the distinction between believing that p because a speaker says so, and believing that the speaker is an authority whose testimony ought to be believed. The latter is a basic belief in the authority of the speaker, expressed in a sentence like q. The former is a derived belief in a sentence like p that the trusted speaker in question says. We believe what the speaker says – p – because we believe in the authority of the speaker – q. In an earlier passage of *Quaestiones variae* 5, Ockham considers the causes of assent to a particular class of sentences that are contingent, dubitable, and not inferred from previously evidently cognized sentences. Appropriate examples include 'Christ died on the cross', 'Rome is a large city', and indeed 'Mr. Collins is in the library'. What would cause the intellect to assent to such a sentence? Again, we see that Ockham posits two possible causes corresponding to the cases (1) and (2) above. Namely,

A. Either assenting to some authority (*auctoritas*) causes assent to *p*;

B. Or the will, which wills to believe *q* from which p follows, causes assent to *p*.[45]

The sentence *p* ('Mr. Collins is in the library') is contingent (Mr. Collins might not be in the library), dubitable (Elizabeth is uncertain as to whether Mr. Collins is in the library), and not inferred from another sentence that she has evidently cognized. Elizabeth assents to *p* because she has assented to Jane's authority as expressed by *q* ('Jane is generally truthful'). Elizabeth has assented to *q* because her will wills to believe that Jane is an authority, which entails that Jane's testimony that *p* should be believed as well.

The role of the will in causing belief acts, basic and derived, is the subject of much debate in the literature. Whereas the naturalistic process by which the *intellect* evidently assents to a truth is necessitated, the *will* is free to believe, or not, a truth. If belief ultimately originates in a first act of will that causes a first free act of assent to some believed sentence, then, so the argument goes, Ockham is a doxastic voluntarist who holds that basic beliefs are unjustified and inexplicable. We believe a truth just because we want to do so, without any regard to what the intellect tells us we should will. A dissenting interpretation argues that the practical intellect can order the will to assent to a first believed sentence, so that there is a moral justification, evident or not, for believing that sentence, although the will can always ignore the intellect's dictate.[46]

On my reading of the material from *Quaestiones variae* 5, we can have reason(s) for assenting to an authority and her testimony despite the fact that neither belief-act is evident. In his example for (1), Ockham explicitly mentions two conditions that a speaker should meet for her testimony to be believed by a hearer: she must be certain and convinced that *p*, and she must utter *p* in good faith without lying. I added that the hearer ought to have knowingly and repeatedly experienced the trustworthiness of the speaker, and I admit this is an extrapolation (see also Grellard 2014a: 69). These surely constitute reasons for the recognition of a speaker's authority. And it is the hearer's intellect that would grasp when it is that a speaker meets these conditions and, consequently, that there are grounds for believing the speaker generally and her testimony in particular.

I think, somewhat speculatively, that at this point the intellect, which has determined that the speaker's testimony ought to be adhered to, would command the will to assent to the authority of the speaker. The will freely chooses to obey or to ignore the intellect. If it chooses to heed the intellect, then it assents to that authority. If it chooses not to do so, then it rejects that authority. Ultimately, the will causes acts of assent to authority (basic acts of belief) and by extension acts of assent to their testimony (derivative acts of belief). Depending on the authority in question, there is a moral dimension at issue: it would be vicious for the will to disregard the intellect's dictate, but virtuous to follow it. This applies in the case of assenting to religious authority like Sacred Scripture.

If I am right, then Ockham is not an advocate of blind authority for at least some cases (a hearer may not always have reasons for assenting to an authority). More importantly for the epistemological context, he does provide some slight indication of acknowledging that we can identify various factors inclining us towards believing a speaker and her testimony as opposed to not doing so. Taking the Rome example, I will be inclined to believe that Rome is a large city, when the speaker who says that it is large has – so she tells me – been to Rome, has an adequate knowledge of cities so as to be able to appreciate its relative size, is not prone to lying or exaggeration, and so on. Fulfilling these or similar conditions goes some way to explaining why we might assent to a speaker's authority and, therefore, to be said to know what she says.

5. Conclusion

Ockham was not the first scholastic to note the existence of testimonial knowledge (*scientia*). In his *Summa*, Henry of Ghent identifies two sources of human knowledge: exterior testimony that comes from others, and interior testimony that comes from the knower's own sense perception and intellective cognition.[47] Scotus, too, is relatively optimistic about the possibility of testimonial knowledge, and appeals to some of the same examples as Ockham does.[48] My intention was never to make any claims as to Ockham's originality. Rather, I wanted argue that, in the seminal text of the prologue to Ockham's *Physics* commentary, the first sense in which 'knowledge' is used is wide enough to cover testimonial knowledge. This set the background against which I explored various religious and non-religious sources and causes of testimonial knowledge with a focus on the role of authority, broadly conceived of as the reliability and trustworthiness of a speaker.

There is no question that Ockham is not especially interested in testimonial knowledge. He is typically preoccupied with more stringent forms of knowledge. Some themes are fairly underdeveloped – namely, certainty, opinion, and indeed authority itself, which demands significantly more consideration than

I have accorded it here. Other questions suggest themselves as lines of inquiry. What is the importance of belief and trust in the testimony of other people for a political and religious community? Is there a place for the transmission of testimonial knowledge between experts working within related domains of research – for instance, between subalternate and subalternated bodies of scientific knowledge? And what is Ockham's conception of authority? I hope that the present contribution serves to stimulate future work on late medieval discussions of what is now called 'social epistemology' and its attendant issues, including testimony, belief or faith, and trust.[49]

Notes

1 For a selection of recent overviews, see Lackey (2006), Greco (2012), Adler (2015), and Goldman and Blanchard (2015).

2 See Pasnau (2010), on Ockham and Buridan especially, and Siebert (2016). Siebert (2014) examines epistemic testimony in Augustine and Aquinas. See also King and Ballantyne (2009) and Cross (forthcoming) on Aquinas and John Duns Scotus.

3 See MacDonald (1994) and Pasnau (2010: 26). MacDonald refers to 'paradigmatic' and 'non-paradigmatic' *scientiae*.

4 For discussion of Ockham's analysis of 'knowledge', see Perini-Santos (2006: 135–9), Panaccio (2008), and Pelletier (2013: 17–25).

5 *Expositio in libros Physicorum Aristoteles* [*Expos. Phys.*], Prol., OPh. IV, p. 5, ll. 29–34. Translation, with modification, from Boehner (Ockham 1990: 4). Unless otherwise stated, all citations of Ockham in this chapter are from the critical edition of his *Opera Philosophica* [OPh.] and *Theologica* [OTh.]. Translations are my own, except where otherwise specified.

6 I am bypassing a significant nuance here. In earlier texts (e.g. his revised commentary on the first book of the *Sentences*, the *Ordinatio*), Ockham claims that the objects of judgement are apprehended mental sentences. In later texts (e.g. his quodlibetal questions, the *Quodlibeta*), he argues that the objects of some judgements are apprehended sentences while the objects of other judgements are things themselves. How to understand this latter claim has been much discussed. On his changing views on the objects of judgement, see Boler (1976), Karger (1995), Panaccio (2009), and Brower-Toland (2014). Ockham continues to hold that, strictly speaking, sentences are the objects of judgement because only sentences are properly the bearers of truth or falsity.

7 See, for example, *Quodlibeta septem, Quodlibet* [*Quodl.*] 5, q. 3, OTh. IX, pp. 490–1, ll. 80–6; *Quodl.* 5, q. 2, OTh. IX, pp. 484–5, ll. 81–103; and *Scriptum in librum primum Sententiarum* [*Ordinatio*], Prol. q. 7, OTh. I, p. 197, ll. 18–22.

8   For instance, at *Ordinatio* Prol. q. 7, OTh. I, pp. 187–8, ll. 21–9, Ockham argues that most theological truths are believable and, therefore, not *evidently* known.

9   *Expos. Phys.*, Prol. OPh. IV, p. 6, ll. 35–42.

10 *Expos. Phys.*, p. 6, ll. 43–5.

11 *Expos. Phys.*, p. 6, ll. 46–8.

12 *Ordinatio*, Prol. q. 1, OTh. I, pp. 5–6, ll. 18-5. Ockham's concept of evident cognition is extensively discussed in Perini-Santos (2006: c 2). See also Alanen and Yrjönsuuri (1997) and Panaccio (2008: 7).

13 The distinction between intuitive and abstractive cognition, which originates in John Duns Scotus, is pivotal for Ockham's account of knowledge and cognition. The literature on this topic is extensive. For introductory and clear discussion, see Stump (1999) and Maurer (1999: 473–8).

14 With the caveat that the act of forming *p* in the first place is an act of will (the bringing together of subject term, copula, and predicate term) preceding this natural causal chain of assent. See Perini-Santos (2006: 64).

15 See note 9. Translation with modification from Ockham (1990: 5).

16 *Quodl.* 4, q. 6, OTh. IX, p. 323, ll. 13–22.

17 *Ordinatio*, Prol. q. 7, OTh. I, p. 200, ll. 6–7.

18 *Ordinatio*, p. 201, ll. 2–3. See Pasnau (2010: 28–33).

19 See *Summa logicae* III-1, c. 1, OPh. I, p. 360, ll. 40–2. I cite this passage in note 35.

20 *Quodl.* 5, q. 2, OTh. IX, p. 484, ll. 81–4. He goes on to declare that there is a fundamental incompatibility (*repugnantia*) between the act(s) of knowing, opining, and believing the same conclusion (he must mean evidently knowing, since knowing can be non-evident). In this regard he would disagree with Aquinas, for instance, who holds that at least strong opinion acts are a kind of belief- or faith-act. See Siebert (2016: 567–8).

21 This points to a related issue often discussed in the contemporary debate on the transmission of knowledge or belief from speaker to hearer: namely, is it necessary for the speaker to know that *p* in order for the hearer to know that *p*? See Lackey (2006: 434–8) and Greco (2012: 20–1).

22 This issue could be subsumed within the larger question of the reliability of testimony, which surprisingly Greco notes (2012: 21–3) is a newly emerging question.

23 Perini-Santos (2006: 73n2) declines to discuss authority since he thinks that it is an ambiguous concept that Ockham does not treat systematically. The concept of authority plays a much greater role in Ockham's later political works, for instance, in the context of the official or institutional authority of the Pope, as opposed to the doctrinal authority of expert theologians in matters of faith. On this, see Iribarren (2012). It is interesting to note that Ockham everywhere speaks of the expert theologians' knowledge (*scientia*), which is what grounds their authority to probe matters of faith. In view of the *Physics*' prologue classification, even expert

theologians would be largely limited to K1^T knowledge-acts. See also Grellard (2014b: esp. 356–60) for some discussion of authority and heresy.

24 *Ordinatio*, d. 30, q. 1, OTh. IV, p. 290, ll. 1–3.
25 *Tractatus de corpore Christi*, c. 29, OTh. X, pp. 157–8, ll. 11–13.
26 *Tractatus de quantitate*, q. 3, OTh. X, p. 69, ll. 99–102.
27 *Tractatus de quantitate*, p. 69, ll. 103–104.
28 *Tractatus de quantitate*, p. 70, ll. 118–20.
29 *Tractatus de quantitate*, p. 70, ll. 120–3.
30 *Tractatus de quantitate*, p. 70, ll. 137–44.
31 *Summa logicae* III-1, c. 1, OPh. I, p. 359, ll. 14–17. Ockham cites Boethius' translation of Aristotle's *Topics* I, c. 1 (100b 21–3). For the Aristotle in English translation and commentary, see Smith (1997). For introductory treatments of dialectical argumentation in Aristotle, see Reeve (2012: 150–70), and, for the epistemic status of reputable opinion in particular, see Anagnostopoulos (2009: 115–20). Ockham's discussion of dialectical arguments here is cursory.
32 *Summa logicae*, p. 360, ll. 20–4.
33 *Summa logicae*, p. 360, ll. 26–9.
34 *Summa logicae*, p. 360, ll. 29–34.
35 *Summa logicae*, p. 360, ll. 39–42.
36 *Quaestiones variae [Quaes. var.]* 5, OTh. VIII, p. 184, ll. 596–601.
37 *Quaes. var.*, pp. 184–5, ll. 602–606.
38 *Quaes. var.*, p. 185, ll. 606–10.
39 *Quaes. var.*, p. 185, ll. 610–21.
40 *Quaes. var.*, p. 186, ll. 626–9.
41 *Quaes. var.*, pp. 186, ll. 629–35.
42 *Quaes. var.*, pp. 186, ll. 635–6.
43 *Quaes. var.*, pp. 187, ll. 650–8.
44 *Quaes. var.*, pp. 187, ll. 664–7.
45 *Quaes. var.*, p. 173, ll. 364–70.
46 For the view that Ockham is a doxastic voluntarist, see Perini-Santos (2006: 87) and Grellard (2014a: esp. 64–78). For the dissenting interpretation, see Roques and Faucher (2015). I find the second interpretation more convincing, since it allows for a more nuanced reading of the interplay between will and intellect in acts of assent, which renders the will rational or irrational – and so justified and explicable, or not – depending on whether it follows the dictates of the intellect. All three comment on the same passage in *Quaes. var.* 5. See Perini-Santos (2006: 74–6), Grellard (2014a: 67–74), and Roques and Faucher (2015: 10–12). They discuss the companion passage, which I do not, in *Quodl.* 4, q. 6, OTh. IX, pp. 325–6, ll. 50–97.
47 Henry of Ghent, *Summa*, a. 1, q. 1, 10, ll. 94–9.
48 See Cross (forthcoming).

49 I would like to thank Russell Friedman, Jan Opsomer, and Martin Pickavé for their
    comments on an earlier draft of this chapter. I am particularly grateful to Martin
    for having suggested the topic of testimonial knowledge to me in the first place in
    Toronto.

References

Adler, J. (2015), 'Epistemological Problem of Testimony', in E. N. Zalta (ed.), *The Stanford Encyclopedia of Philosophy* (Summer 2015 Edition): http://plato.stanford.edu/archives/sum2015/entries/testimony-episprob/.

Alanen, L. and Yrjönsuuri, M. (1997), 'Intuition, jugement et évidence chez Ockham et Descartes', in J. Biard and R. Rashed (eds), *Descartes et le Moyen Âge*, Paris: Vrin.

Anagnostopoulos, G. (2009), 'Aristotle's Methods', in G. Anagnostopoulos (ed.), *A Companion to Aristotle*, Malden, MA: Wiley-Blackwell.

Boler, J. (1976), 'Ockham on Evident Cognition', *Franciscan Studies*, 36, 85–98.

Brower-Toland, S. (2014), 'How Chatton Changed Ockham's Mind: William Ockham and Walter Chatton on Objects and Acts of Judgment', in G. Klima (ed.), *Intentionality, Cognition and Mental Representation in Medieval Philosophy*, New York: Fordham University Press.

Coady, C. A. J. (1992), *Testimony: A Philosophical Study*, Oxford: Clarendon Press.

Cross, R. (forthcoming), 'Testimony, Error, and Reasonable Belief in Medieval Religious Epistemology', in M. Benton and J. Hawthorne (eds), *Knowledge, Belief, and God: New Insights*, Oxford: Oxford University Press.

Goldman, A. and Blanchard, T. (2015), 'Social Epistemology', in E. N. Zalta (ed.), *The Stanford Encyclopedia of Philosophy* (Summer 2015 Edition): http://plato.stanford.edu/archives/sum2015/entries/epistemology-social/.

Greco, J. (2012), 'Recent Work on Testimonial Knowledge', *American Philosophical Quarterly*, 49: 15–28.

Grellard, C. (2014a), *De la certitude volontaire: débats nominalistes sur la foi à la fin du moyen âge*, Paris: Publications de la Sorbonne.

Grellard, C. (2014b), 'La *fides* chez Guillaume d'Ockham: de la psychologie à l'ecclésiologie', *Archa Verbi, Subsidia*, 12: 335–68.

Henry of Ghent (2005), *Summa, Opera Omnia* vol. XXI, ed. G. Wilson, Leuven: Leuven University Press.

Iribarren, I. (2012), '"The Eyes of the Church": William of Ockham and John XXII on the Theologians Doctrinal Authority', *American Catholic Philosophical Quarterly*, 86: 487–506.

Karger, E. (1995), 'William of Ockham, Walter Chatton and Adam Wodeham on the Objects of Knowledge and Belief', *Vivarium*, 33: 171–96.

King, P. and Ballantyne, N. (2009), 'Augustine on Testimony', *Canadian Journal of Philosophy*, 39: 195–214.

Lackey, J. (2006), 'Knowing from Testimony', *Philosophy Compass,* 1: 432–48.

MacDonald, S. (1994), 'Theory of Knowledge', in N. Kretzmann and E. Stump (eds), *The Cambridge Companion to Aquinas,* Cambridge: Cambridge University Press.

Maurer, A. (1999), *The Philosophy of William of Ockham in Light of Its Principles,* Toronto: PIMS.

Ockham, W. (1967), *Scriptum in librum primum Sententiarum,* in G. Gál and S. Brown (ed.), *Opera Theologica* vol. I, St Bonaventure, NY: Franciscan Institute Publications.

Ockham, W. (1974), *Summa logicae, Opera Philosophica* vol. I, ed. P. Boehner, G. Gál, and S. Brown, St Bonaventure, NY: Franciscan Institute Publications.

Ockham, W. (1980), *Quodlibeta septem, Opera Theologica* vol. IX, ed. J. C. Wey, St Bonaventure, NY: Franciscan Institute Publications.

Ockham, W. (1984), *Quaestiones variae, Opera Theologica* vol. VIII, ed. G. I. Etzkorn, F. E. Kelley, and J. C. Wey, St Bonaventure, NY: Franciscan Institute Publications.

Ockham, W. (1985), *Expositio in libros Physicorum Aristoteles, Opera Philosophica* vol. IV, ed. V. Richter and G. Leibold, St Bonaventure, NY: Franciscan Institute Publications.

Ockham, W. (1986a), *Tractatus de corpore Christi, Opera Theologica* vol. X, ed. C. A. Grassi, St Bonaventure, NY: Franciscan Institute Publications.

Ockham, W. (1986b), *Tractatus de quantitate, Opera Theologica* vol. X, ed. C. A. Grassi, St Bonaventure, NY: Franciscan Institute Publications.

Ockham, W. (1990), *Philosophical Writings: A Selection,* rev. edn, trans. P. Boehner, Indianapolis: Hackett.

Panaccio, C. (2008), 'Le savoir selon Guillaume d'Ockham', in R. Nadeau (ed.), *Philosophies de la connaissance,* Québec/Paris: Presses de l'Université de Laval/Vrin.

Panaccio, C. (2009), 'Le jugement comme acte mental selon Guillaume d'Ockham', in J. Biard (ed.), *Le langage mental du Moyen Âge à l'Âge classique,* Leuven: Peeters.

Pasnau, R. (2010), 'Medieval Social Epistemology: *Scientia* for Mere Mortals', *Episteme,* 7: 23–41.

Pelletier, J. (2013), *William Ockham on Metaphysics: The Science of Being and God,* Leiden: Brill.

Perini-Santos, E. (2006), *La théorie ockhamienne de la conaissance évidente,* Paris: Vrin.

Reeve, C. D. C. (2012), 'Aristotle's Philosophical Method', in C. Shields (ed.), *The Oxford Handbook of Aristotle,* Oxford: Oxford University Press.

Roques, M. and Faucher, N. (2015), 'Les justifications de la foi d'après Guillaune d'Ockham', *Freiburger Zeitschrift für Philosophie und Theologie,* 62: 219–39.

Siebert, M. K. (2014), *The Medieval Social Epistemologies of Augustine and Aquinas,* PhD diss., University of Toronto.

Siebert, M. K. (2016), 'Aquinas on Testimonial Justification: Faith and Opinion', *Review of Metaphysics,* 69: 555–82.

Smith, R. (1997), *Aristotle Topics Books I and VII,* Oxford: Clarendon Press.

Stump, E. (1999), 'The Mechanisms of Cognition: Ockham on Mediating Species', in P. V. Spade (ed.), *The Cambridge Companion to Ockham,* Cambridge: Cambridge University Press.

8

Nicholas of Autrecourt on Knowledge

Christophe Grellard

1. Introduction

Fourteenth-century epistemology is characterized by the attempt to give an account of the fallibility of our knowledge.[1] Such an attempt leads to questioning an epistemology grounded in the certitude, elaborated in the thirteenth century, from Robert Grossesteste onwards, and to paying a greater attention to the contingency of the world and to the diversity of the cognitive methods. When we face the fallibility of our cognitive states, two alternative solutions seem to be offered: first, we can weaken the notion of science in such a way that certitude should not be a necessary property of the science; second, we can weaken the notion of certitude by distinguishing degrees of certitude in such a way that all the sciences need not require the highest degree of certitude, even if certitude remains a necessary condition for science. If we assume that certitude is the warrant of truth, we may understand that the problem, implicitly, is the one of truth: namely, shall we accept a cognitive mental state as a science if its truth is not warranted? Buridan's answer is negative: it's why he chose the latter solution.[2]

On the contrary, his main colleague (and adversary) at the Faculty of Arts in the University of Paris (where he was teaching between 1325 and 1335, roughly),[3] Nicholas of Autrecourt, answers positively, and defends the former solution. This is made evident by the fact that Nicholas very rarely uses the notion of 'scientia', by which he means the Aristotelian episteme – that is, demonstrative knowledge of eternal and necessary truths, or, by extension, evident empirical knowledge.[4] He prefers to use a more neutral term, 'notitia' – that is, any cognitive grasp of an object. For this reason, Autrecourt's epistemology aims to identify the highest degrees of epistemic justification (*certitudo, evidentia*) in order to get a cognitive norm. This norm will then allow us to estimate the cognitive values of our mental states.

Nicholas of Autrecourt defends an internalist and foundationalist epistemology where our cognitive states are warranted by some principles to which the cognitive subject may gain access by reflection on his own mental states. The kind of warrant that we claim admits of degrees, from the certain to the probable. This inclusion of the probable in Autrecourt's epistemology allows him to give an account of our defeasible knowledge. For this reason, his epistemology is characterized by a double concern: first, identifying precisely the degree of epistemic justification of our cognitive state (where 'justification' is to be understood as 'to have a proof', whatever the nature of this proof); second, giving an account of the way that we can transfer our epistemic justification from a cognitive state to another.

We will begin by analysing Autrecourt's definition of certitude and evidentness; then we will examine the question of the transfer of justification; finally, we will consider the status of our defeasible knowledge.

2. Knowledge in a strict sense: certitude and evidentness

According to the standard of medieval Aristotelianism, knowledge in a strict sense – that is, *scientia* – is certain knowledge of an evident truth. Nicholas of Autrecourt agrees with this conception that he considers relevant for the highest degree of knowledge. This kind of knowledge is grounded on the first principle, which plays the role of a paradigm of the certitude in Autrecourt's thought.

2.1 The principles and the demonstrative knowledge

There are two kinds of evident objects, according to Autrecourt (1971: 115): first, the objects of immediate perceptions (internal or external); second, propositions *per se notae* ('known by itself'), and conclusions we may infer: 'The following are evident, properly speaking: sensible objects, and the acts which we experience in ourselves. These refer to what is incomplex. As regards what is complex, there are the principles which are known from their terms, and conclusions depending on them.'[5] The first category will be examined in detail below, but it allows us to understand negatively what a principle is. In chapter 6 of *Exigit ordo*, Nicholas lists the properties of immediate perception (that he calls *apparentia plena*). This perception is always true and evident: 'It is therefore probable that whatever appears is true; that is, what is clear and evident in a full light. For otherwise the intellect would be sure of nothing since the intellect can claim to be sure only of what he experienced directly or is reasoned to as a natural result of experience' (108). This is the point: the complete appearance (which has a necessary relation to his object, perceived by senses) cannot be false, and in this way may play the role of a principle of knowledge. Accordingly, the most general definition of a principle could be the following: a judgement that cannot be false. Hence, any such proposition (a report of direct perceptions) can be used as a principle – that is, as a foundation of knowledge. Second, a principle is a proposition that allows us to correct or rectify our knowledge. Third (and this last point is linked to the question of justification with which we will deal later), if we cannot find any principles, we cannot pretend to find any certitude. We need something that is beyond all doubt, in order to make knowledge possible. We can conclude that evidentness is what cannot be erroneous:

> Therefore, on the basis of the preceding, the conclusion seems probable, that, although acts of judging and assenting may be false, acts of appearing (in the strict sense) are not. It also seems probable why whereas in other matters there is general agreement (because such an appearance is the fundamental principle of all the truth we know so that certainty would be remove if this appearance existed without the reality), yet this is not true of the act of judging; though judgment is sometimes false, it will be able to be set right somehow by this further act. (107)

These properties can be found also in the case of propositions *per se notae*. Nicholas never gave an account of this kind of proposition, but we can collect some remarks. He seems to follow the Aristotelian thesis as presented in the *Posteriors Analytics*.[6] A proposition *per se nota* is a kind of analytical proposition – that is, a proposition whose truth and evidentness is known by analysing the signification of terms. Two consequences follow. First, analytical propositions are first, in the sense that they are immediate: their truth cannot be rejected by the intellect, once one has grasped the signification of the terms that compose the proposition. Second, their truth lies in the fact that the predicate is included in the subject.[7] Hence, the proposition '*homo est animal*' (man is an animal) is an analytical proposition: when we assert the subject, we also assert the predicate which is included in the subject. According to Nicholas, our demonstration shall begin with this kind of propositions. In this way, every proposition that can be the premise of a syllogism is a principle. Once again, a principle is a proposition that cannot be false, and can be used to demonstrate other propositions.

Nevertheless, if these propositions are evident, they lack the highest degree of justification called by Nicholas as the 'certitude of evidentness' (*certitudo evidentiae*), obtained by reduction to the first principle. The purpose here is not to demonstrate these propositions, but rather to exhibit their evidentness, to justify them by means of a meta-principle, the first principle. Before examining this question, later in this chapter, we have to solve another problem. What is the nature of first principle, principle of identity (as the topic of analytical inclusion may suggest it) or principle of contradiction?

We have seen that Nicholas tends to assimilate the first principle with the principle of non-contradiction – for example, in the beginning of the second letter to Bernard, and in his letter to the inquisitorial commission. But we have also the evidence of an anonymous Franciscan who asserts that Nicholas gives primacy to the principle of identity.[8] According to this Franciscan, Nicholas has argued that the principle of non-contradiction relies on the principle of identity, since identity is anterior to contradiction: to have a negation, we already need an affirmation. Did Nicholas defend such a thesis? The condemned articles inform us that he did assert that the first principle is not the principle of contradiction but rather the principle of identity, in his hypothetical formulation: if something exists, something exists.[9] How can we understand such an assertion? We may assume that all the articles 57–62 come from the same context – that is, a commentary on the fourth book of *Metaphysics* (except perhaps the article 57 that could come from the prologue to *Sentences*). Indeed, articles 61 and 62 could belong to a commentary on the end of the eight chapters (from 1012b25), dealing with the possibility of a change. Articles 59 and 60 belong to the commentary on the seventh chapter, where Aristotle introduced briefly the topic of the negation. As evidence, we may have a look on Buridan's (2008: 97) early commentary (called *Lectura erfordiensis*), where he asks whether negations are entities (twelfth question). And Buridan examines precisely the same examples as Autrecourt – that is, 'Deus est' and 'Deus non est', and the question of the *complexe significabile* (the significate of a proposition). If my assumption is correct, we may find a key for the interpretation of the relationship between the first principle and the principle of contradiction. Indeed, in the sixteenth question, Buridan evokes the problem of the first principle's exact formulation and points out a thesis close to Autrecourt's (113).

Hence, if we ignore the hypothetical formulation of the first principle and only consider the formulation given by the anonymous Franciscan, we may assume that Nicholas' thesis is close to the one presented by Buridan. Indeed, we find the same progression: anteriority of the categorical propositions *de inesse*, first affirmative and second negative. From this point, we can formulate the principle of contradiction as Aristotle did. So, what is the relationship between the principle of identity and the principle of contradiction? Autrecourt would probably accept the Buridanian distinction between 'priority of simplicity' and 'priority of evidentness', especially because he rejects degrees of evidentness. Consequently, the first principle, from the point of view of the evidentness, is indifferently the principle of contradiction and the principle of identity. As we will see, the principle has mostly a function in the theory of demonstration, but it seems to be a specification of a principle, such that priority relies on its simplicity – that is, the principle of identity, whatever its formulation. Accordingly, we may suppose that the anonymous Franciscan has exaggerated the Ultricurian thesis when he says that evidentness of the principle of contradiction depends on the evidentness of the principle of identity. Probably, Nicholas never required something else than an anteriority of simplicity, since evidentness is the same for the principle of identity and for the principle of contradiction.

2.2 Empirical knowledge

As we have seen, Nicholas claims that some kind of immediate perception can work as a principle for empirical knowledge – that is, as an instance of evident knowledge from which we can transfer the evidentness. His theory of empirical certainty is synthesized in a principle: 'all that appears is true, namely what is clear and evident in full light'.[10] There is a kind of perception (*apparentia*) whose properties (clearness, evidentness, full light) warrant the truth. What is the meaning of these properties? A thing appears in full light if the cognitive subject has a relation (*habitudo*) with the object.[11] And this relation must be a necessary one, not a contingent one, in such a way that the existence of the object may be immediately assumed:

> For if the light itself did not have some relationship to what he says he is sure of, it would be, as it were, completely in darkness in regard to it; and then, like a blind man, he would not be sure of it. If it has a relationship, which one ought to admit, this relationship might be a contingent one, indifferent to whether the relationship exists or not. But then he will not be able to say that he is certain through that light or appearance, because he could not say he was surer of its existence than of its nonexistence. Thus it must have a necessary relationship. (Autrecourt 1971: 108)

The conditions of clarity are therefore the actual existence of the object and a necessary relation between the known and the knower. We may synthesize these conditions in the following way:

S has a clear appearance of X = $_{df}$(a) x actually exists, and (b) the cognitive relation between S and X is necessary.

Condition (b) is the more important, and determines condition (a): the contingent relation between S and X is equivalent to the abstractive cognition (even if Nicholas rarely uses this vocabulary): that is, the thing could be otherwise than it is, or not exist. Therefore, it is required to grasp the thing as existing and present. In this way, the conformity between the appearance and the object may be warranted. Besides this appearance in full light, Nicholas introduces the proper and ultimate appearance (*apparentia proprie et ultimate*). This appearance is a clear appearance in full light, where the object is known by the senses (107). From this, it results that the evident appearance, also called complete appearance (*apparentia plena*), requires that the object actually exists and is grasped by the external senses, in such a way that there is a necessary relation of conformity between the appearance and the object. If these conditions are satisfied, the perception is true and evident.

Nevertheless, Nicholas needs to explain how some of our empirical perceptions, which seem to fulfil all of these conditions, are false. He introduces the distinction between the own light of the thing and the light of its image (109). This distinction between appearance and image permits to explain the errors of perception. An image is an incomplete appearance. Therefore, when I perceive a thing in its image, I do not perceive the external thing, but instead only one of the modes of appearing of the thing. The incomplete perception has only an objective being (*esse objectivum*) as its term. On the contrary, the complete perception has a subjective being (*esse subjectivum*) as its term (110).[12] Strictly speaking, the incomplete perception is not incorrect in itself: the error is located in the judgement or assent that follows from it. When I judge that the sun's size is lesser than the earth's size, or when I judge that the stick in the water is broken, my judgement is correct if its object is the image of the thing and is not the thing itself. I can claim that I see the image of the broken stick, not that I see a broken stick. In other words, the judgement must be proportioned to the appearance. Only a complete appearance may produce an evident judgement on the thing as such.

Nicholas assumes that most of our direct perceptions are complete appearances (Autrecourt 1994: 55). And these direct perceptions fulfil a normative function, since they play the role of a principle of empirical knowledge. Indeed, the complete appearance has all the properties of a principle: it cannot be false, and can be used to rectify or correct other incomplete appearances. When the appearance is complete, its strength is enough to compel an evident judgement on the thing. The appearance is the rule of the judgement:

> According to this teaching, then, it can with probability be said that, if a man can say he is certain of something, what appears (properly speaking and in the final analysis) is true. Let us express this rule in other words: every act of affirmation which is formulated in a full light, in so far as man can have a full light, is true. For every act measuring up to its true norm is true. (Autrecourt 1971: 109)

If the judgement follows from a complete appearance, it will always be true. But if there is some confusion between the thing and its image, and if the incomplete appearance is not known as such, the judgement that follows may be false. Therefore, the complete appearance functions as a norm of empirical knowledge and individuates the optimal conditions of this kind of knowledge.

2.3 On certitude

Most often, Nicholas seems to speak indifferently of evidence, clarity, and certitude. But he actually appears to distinguish and hierarchize these three notions. He gives the following definition of certitude:

> Therefore from above we can easily see what certitude means. For, as concerns certain knowledge with regard to some propositions – for it is its literal meaning – men use this word thus: when someone has clear and evident knowledge of the truth of a proposition and also perceives that he has such clear and evident knowledge, he then says that he is certain. (Autrecourt 1971: 115)

Certitude concerns clear and evident knowledge. It is a higher degree of epistemic justification and it adds something to the evidentness. On this point, the expression 'certitudo evidentiae' used in the letters to Bernard d'Arezzo is meaningful. Moreover, and even if Nichols is not very precise on this point, we could probably distinguish between evidentness and clarity. On the one hand, Nicholas seems to consider that, in a broader sense, clarity is knowledge that compels assent (116, 119). On the other hand, as we have seen, Nicholas expressly individuates the categories of evident knowledge: the objects of the five senses (i.e. the complete appearances) and our own inner mental states on the one hand, and the principles known per se, and the conclusion we may infer on the other. This kind of object compels assent, as clarity, but also adds something else – namely, the exclusion of error: such knowledge cannot be false. But where is the difference between evidentness and certitude? Nicholas' answer is clear, it is the reflexivity: 'The twelfth conclusion is that one would have full certitude if, in addition to something being evident to him, the reasoning 'this is evident to me and therefore is true' was also evident to him' (119).[13] In order to be certain, we may perceive that we do have some evident knowledge: that is, we have grasped an object that compels assent, and such that error is excluded.

Finally, it is possible to distinguish between three main degrees of epistemic justification:

S is certain that $p =_{df}$ (a) S has evident knowledge that p, and (b) S knows that he knows that p.

S has evident knowledge that $p =_{df}$ (a) S has clear knowledge that p, and (b) it is impossible that p.

S has clear knowledge that $p =_{df}$ (a) S has a clear appearance of the subject and the predicate of p, and (b) S is justified in believing p (that is, p compels assent).

3. Transfer of justification

Having identified the degrees of epistemic justification, the problem is to determine how it is possible to transfer such a justification to other cognitive states in order to make them evident or certain. This is the purpose of the reduction to the first principle on the one hand, and of the theory of the evident inferences on the other hand.

3.1 The reduction to first principle

Nicholas emphasizes that the first principle is a foundation of knowledge, since it is the condition of possibility of all speech, and is presupposed by all philosophical debate:

> The first thing that presents itself for discussion is this principle: 'Contradictories cannot be simultaneously true.' Concerning which, two things suggest themselves. The first is that this is the first principle, expounding 'first' negatively as 'than which nothing is prior'. The second is that this principle is first in the affirmative or positive sense as 'that which is prior to any other'. (Autrecourt 1994: 59)

There is a twofold primacy of the first principle. Negatively, nothing is anterior to it: that is, it cannot be the conclusion of a syllogism; it cannot be demonstrated or reduced to another principle. On this point, Nicholas agrees with Aristotle: the first principle is required by all demonstration. The primacy of the first principle is also positive: any conclusion of a demonstration shall be reduced to the evidentness of the first principle. This idea of reduction is equivalent to the idea of epistemic justification.[14] Nicholas introduces this idea of reduction in order to justify propositional knowledge. This question is examined mostly in the second letter to Bernard of Arezzo. Our knowledge is justified because founded – that is, reducible to first principle. Nicholas proves, first, that all certitude is reduced to the certitude of the first principle. Indeed, no other principle can be absolutely certain:

> These two statements are proved by means of one argument, as follows: every certitude we possess is resolved into this principle. And it is itself not resolved into any other in the way a conclusion would into its premises. It therefore follows that the principle in question is first by a twofold primacy. This implication is well known as following from the meaning of the term 'first' according to either of the exposition given. First, as to its first part (to wit, that all our certitude falling short of this certitude is resolved into this principle): regarding anything proven whatsoever, which falls short of the evidentness of this principle, and which you assert you are certain of, I propose this inference: 'It is possible, without any contradiction following therefrom, that it will appear to you to be the case, and yet will not be so. Therefore you will not be evidently certain that it is the case.' (Ibid.)

The argument asserts that if we accept that a principle, which is not reducible to first principle, is certain, this principle will seem certain, and nevertheless could be contradictory. It is therefore necessary that any principle be regulated by the first principle – that is, potentially reducible to it. Thus, the idea of reduction to first principle functions as a rule, allowing us to verify the certitude and evidentness of our principles. Only the first principle warrants that what we assume to be certain is indeed certain. In this way, Autrecourt introduces an ultimate warrant to our knowledge.

3.2 First principle and theory of demonstration

Nicholas' theory of demonstration is mostly a theory of transfer of evidentness. He intends to give rules that will warrant that the evidentness of the premises will be conserved in the conclusion. For this purpose, it is necessary to show a dependence between premises and conclusions. This relationship will be warranted if, and only if, our inferences observe two principles that seem to be an application of the first principle. In one sense, the reduction appears to be a mean to verify this relationship. In the second letter to Bernard, Nicholas introduces two necessary and sufficient rules for the evidentness of an inference. We have to emphasize that Nicholas is looking for evidentness, and not only for validity.

The two conditions are the following:

P1. A consequence is evident if and only if the significate of the consequent is included in or identical to the significate of the antecedent.
P2. A consequence is evident if and only if it is impossible that the antecedent and the contradictory of the consequent are true in the same time. (65, 61)

P1 requires a connection of signification between antecedent and consequent, in order to warrant the dependence of the conclusion on the premises. The aim of such a condition is to exclude all kinds of paradoxal inference, as *ex falso quodlibet*, or *ad necessarium quodlibet*. But, above all, Nicholas assumes that analycity – that is, partial or total inclusion of a significate in another – is necessary to preserve evidentness and necessity. P2 is more frequent in medieval logic, but is of special importance to Nicholas since it is a direct application of the first principle and allows him to exclude the question of God's absolute power (God can't do what is contradictory).

From this point, Nicholas introduces a rule about what we may call 'existential inferences' – that is, inference where the existence of one thing is deduced from the existence of another. Since P1 establishes a relation of inclusion between the significations of the antecedent and the consequent, and P2 forbids all contradiction between them, and since he claims a jointed application of P1 and P2, we can deduce the following rule:

R1. The consequence 'if a exists, then b exists' is not evident if and only if (1) a and b are absolute terms, and (2) a ≠ b. (65)

To this rule of exclusion corresponds a rule of acceptance, never explicitly formulated by Nicholas:

R2. The consequence 'if a exists, then b exists' is evident if and only if (1) b is a term relative to a, or (2) if a and b are two absolute terms, b ⊆ a.

R2 is equivalent to P1, and it allows Nicholas to accept inferences such as 'the house exists, therefore the wall exists' as perfectly evident, since the signification of 'wall' is included in the signification of 'house'. Conversely, R1 (as Nicholas explains it to Master Giles: sec. 8) concerns the different things that could exist without each other (*alia res*). For example, deduction of the substance from accidents, or of the effect from the cause, are prohibited by R1. Such a deduction is not logically evident. This well-known problem is, however, beyond the scope of this study (see Robert 2006).

4. The limits of certitude and the introduction of the probable

When he identifies the highest degrees of epistemic justification and the properties of knowledge in a strict sense, Nicholas is aware of the limited scope of this kind of knowledge and of the necessity to introduce some weaker degrees of justification in order to give an account of all our cognitive states. A theory of evident knowledge must be completed by a theory of probable knowledge.

4.1 The limits of empirical certainty

When he develops his theory of the complete appearance, Nicholas cannot avoid facing the sceptical challenge.[15] He examines two kinds of traditional argument against the reliability of sense perception: first, there are relativist arguments concerning taste and, to a lesser extent, the perception of colour; second, there are the properly sceptical arguments – that is, errors of senses, illusions, and hallucinations (Nicholas mentions the sun appearing to be a foot across, the stick that appears broken in water, and trees that seem to move when seen from a boat). There are also two other sceptical arguments that he considers: the dream argument, and the existence of disagreement between men.[16] The first level of Autrecourt's answer is traditional. It consists in distinguishing appearance from judgement. Relativist and sceptical objections arise from the fact that the considered appearance is not totally clear and seen in full light, although it is judged as if it were. So, there is a gap between appearance and assent:

> First, it will seem to follow that all things are true and that all things are false.
> I hold that this undesirable consequence does not follow. To prove this I say
> by way of preface that not every act of a knowing faculty is the appearance of
> an object. Thus, as has been said elsewhere previously, the intellect judges and

assents concerning things which are not present to it as appearance, even if
'appearances' be taken in the wide sense. For example, a man gives judgment
and assent to the proposition that 'Rome is a large city' even though he has not
seen Rome. Thus it is true that your conclusion would follow if we were saying
that everything judged to be true is true, or that everything to which the intellect
assents is true. But this is not what we say; our statement concerns only an act
involving an appearance. (Autrecourt 1971: 106)

Since truth and falsehood are a matter of judgement, we have to correct this
first appearance by means of other appearances. The Ultricurian answer to
scepticism about sense perception relies on the power of epistemic faculties to
correct each other. In this respect, Nicholas gives a special weight to the sense of
touch, which gives us access to the *res fixa*, especially in the case of the broken
stick. More generally, the situations mentioned by the sceptic call for correction
by means of other concepts, either mathematical concepts in the case of the sun's
size, or reference to a stable point of view in the case of the moving trees (110).
So, the answer appeals to a posteriori cognitive activity: we do have rational
and sensible means to correct deceptive appearances. Actually, in situations of
sensory illusion, appearance does not aim at the thing in itself, but only at the
image of the thing: 'that appearance terminates at the image of the thing and
not at something subjectively existing in the thing outside' (ibid.). Nicholas
compares this situation with what we see in a mirror: we have only indirect
access to the thing. But when the appearance is complete, there is an identity
between the thing and the image we have of it, and we do have direct access to it.

Nevertheless, once again we may ask: how are we able to discriminate
complete from partial appearances, and to explain the incompleteness of some
appearances? Indeed, in situations involving dreams or illusions, we do think
that we have a complete appearance, and this appearance often compels the will
to assent to it as strongly as a complete appearance (106–107). The sceptical
dreaming argument, for example, assumes a qualitative identity between
wakefulness and sleep.

On this point, Nicholas is much more embarrassed. He admits that if our
dreams, and more generally our illusions, were as clear as complete appearances,
we could never distinguish between them and reality, and we could not have any
certitude. We would be reduced to complete scepticism or absolute relativism:

It is evident that in sleep the appearance is not clear. For, no matter how vividly
it appears to someone in sleep that he has seen a camp, the light of heaven, etc.,
nevertheless everyone experiences when awake that appearance he gets through

sight is clearer and is different in kind, and so he is more attracted by this. For, if they were equally clear, he would have either to say nothing is certain for him or to admit that in both appearances what appears to be true is true. (107)

Of course, this is an important concession from Nicholas since the sceptical dream argument makes two assumptions: the qualitative identity of true and of false appearance, and slippery-slope reasoning of the form 'If I am once deceived, I could be always deceived'. But Nicholas tries to block the first assumption by a dogmatic assertion: since the complete appearances allow us to judge which appearances are incomplete, complete appearances must be immediately recognizable as such. So these appearances are justified by themselves and play the role of principles of sense perception:

> Therefore, on the basis of the preceding, the conclusion proposed seems probable, that, although acts of judging and assenting may be false, acts of appearing (in the strict sense) are not. It also seems probable why, whereas in other matters there is a general agreement (because such an appearance is the fundamental principle of all the truth we know, so that certainty would be removed if this appearance existed without the reality), yet this is not true of the act of judging; though judgment is sometimes false, it will be able to be set right somehow by this further act. (Ibid.; see also 109)

The call to probable principles is the key of Autrecourt's answer to scepticism. It must be conceded, from a theoretical point of view, that the sceptical challenge can hardly be totally answered. But it must also be conceded that, from a practical point of view, our perception usually is correct, and in everyday life we are not systematically deceived. It is the reason why it is more reasonable – that is, probable – to admit that our appearances are true. This probable principle can be understood as a kind of reliabilist answer to the sceptical challenge: our perception is correct most of the time; moreover, we have the capacity to correct a posteriori our perceptual errors with the help of other perceptions or of reason. Nevertheless, this principle that grounds the theory of empirical knowledge is only probable and not evident, since it always remains theoretically possible that our appearances could be false. We cannot totally rule out the fallibility of our perceptual knowledge.

4.2 The limit of demonstrative certainty

Nicholas never tries to escape the problem of the justification of first principle, and he does not look for a dialectical and indirect proof, or for a special intuitive apprehension of it, as is the case for Aristotle. Nicholas claims that it is impossible to state logically the first principle, which is a kind of blind spot for any system of justification.

For Nicholas, all certitude comes from the first principle, by reduction to it. This principle is a kind of meta-principle for analytical propositions that can then be assumed as principles – that is, as premises for a syllogism. Nicholas makes use of the infinite regress argument to show that all principles of demonstration must be reduced to the first principle[17]:

> Accordingly, I shall lay down as a first conclusion that if the intellect can say of something 'this is true', there cannot coexist the opposite of what is known clearly and evidently. Hence what is clear and evident to the intellect is true – a statement universally valid, and convertible. This conclusion is proven: when something is known with clear and evident knowledge, if it were possible for its opposite to be true, it would follow that the intellect could be sure of nothing. But the opposite was maintained in our hypothesis. The reasoning is proven because we have no certitude concerning first principles or anything else knowable except because we know them clearly and evidently. Accordingly we experiment that we have only one kind of act concerning principles: clear knowledge ... I say that a person will be sure when, after the meaning of the terms is grasped, something is so clear and evident to him that he is drawn to assent entirely and cannot backtrack, and especially that that is precisely what has come to his knowledge ... From what has been said a second conclusion is inferred: namely, that that conclusion, which was proved hypothetically (on the supposition that something is true), ought to be accepted as principle. For if it were proven to be true, the premises would be assumed as either evident or true. If as evident only, then though they would make the conclusion evident, they would not prove it to be true. If as true, I have a question: it would be either in virtue of themselves as being evident (and then it would be begging the question), or because they are true (and then it would be necessary that their truth be shown from other premises and so on into infinite. (Ibid.: 116–18)

The conclusion of a syllogism must be reduced immediately or mediately to the first principle, such that the principle of that conclusion is the conclusion of another syllogism. But this *sorite* must stop somewhere if we want to escape the infinite regress. Hence, all proof contains virtually the first principle, and regress in the order of the proof actualizes this foundation. Only the first principle satisfies the criterion of indemonstrability (i.e. the primacy of justification).

At the same time (as appears in the text quoted above), Nicholas claims that, despite this primacy, the first principle cannot warrant the truth of our principles or conclusion. Such a truth is only a useless hypothesis. He first shows that we have an indirect proof of the truth of evident knowledge. Second, he shows that there is no direct proof of the truth of a proposition. If we want to demonstrate the truth of p by the means of premises q and r, we have to show that q and r are either true or evident. To show the first point, we need other premises whose truth has to be demonstrated, and so on, and so we have an infinite regress. If we say that p is true because q and r are evident, we have a petition of principle. The combination of sceptical modes allows Nicholas to say that truth is only an hypothesis.

At the end of his chapter 6, dedicated to the problem of evidence, Nicholas offers eighteen conclusions as a summary of his position. The first set (conclusions 1–7) explains the context of validity of the first principle. Nicholas at this moment concedes that it is impossible to prove that the first principle is evident, since such a proof would require another principle more evident than the first principle. Nevertheless, we shall assume, as a hypothesis, that this first principle is evident, if we want to be able to prove that something else is true and evident (conclusions 1, 2, 3, and 7). In the same way, we cannot prove that the first principle is true, but we have to assume it as true in order to quiet the soul (conclusions 4 and 5). The second set of conclusions examines the relationship between truth, evidentness, and certitude (conclusions 9, 10, 12, 14, 15, 17). Then a last set (conclusions 8, 11, 13, 16, 18) underlines the limits of the first principle. Some propositions are beyond all criteria of evidentness without being false. Indeed, it's not the case that any proposition is demonstrable, if we assume, as Nicholas did, that the conclusion should be included in the premises. Conclusion 8 is close to the analyses of the second letter: any proposition that we cannot reduce to the first principle (i.e. that do not satisfy P1 and P2) cannot be proved to be evident, but can still be knowledge (as justified true belief): 'The eighth conclusion is that not all propositions can be shown to be evident through the first principle. For, along with the first principle, it is necessary to assume something which contains the conclusion actually. The minor premise does not contain the conclusion as do the major premise and the first principle, that is, potentially' (119). Indeed, we must distinguish between propositions whose reduction can be proved to be impossible, from propositions we cannot reduce now, because of a lack of knowledge. When we can show that the reduction is impossible, the proposition is false; but when we cannot show that the reduction is impossible without being able to do this reduction, we leave open the possibility of such a reduction, and give a place to probable knowledge:

> The sixteenth conclusion is that, just as not every proposition can be proven evident by what is called the first principle, as has been said, and we call a proposition impossible only if it cannot become evident to us, so there are some impossible things which cannot be resolved into the first principle in such a way that it shows evidence of their impossibility. (120)

Impossibility is defined by contradiction, such that a proposition is impossible when we can show that it cannot be reduced to first principle. However, we must assume that the reduction of some propositions cannot be shown to be neither possible nor impossible. Some propositions cannot be made evident, but we shall not reject them as irrational or non-scientific.

4.3 Probable knowledge

Autrecourt's epistemology is a foundationalist one: some beliefs are evident by themselves, and these beliefs are the basis for the justification of our other beliefs. But a question remains: what about beliefs that cannot attain the highest degree of justification – that is, evidentness? To answer this question, Nicholas develops a probabilistic account of knowledge that is really a necessary consequence of his conception of epistemic justification. In fact, he claims that many beliefs are known, although, for some of them, the conditions of evidentness cannot apply, as in the case of sentences that cannot be reduced to first principle, or perceptions that are not direct and complete. We may be tempted to introduce degrees of evidentness (as did Buridan and most scholastic philosophers), but Nicholas resists this temptation. Since the first principle is the guarantee of evidentness, we have to conserve its status. In other words, evidentness is the highest degree of justification and it cannot be made relative to anything else: 'The second corollary I infer on this score is 'The certitude of evidentness has no degrees'. For example, if there are two conclusions of each of which we are evidently certain, we are not more certain of one than of the other. For (as has been said) all certitude is resolved into the same first principle' (Autrecourt 1994: 61). In this respect, if we don't want to reduce excessively the scope of knowledge, we have to claim that evidentness and truth are not necessary conditions of knowledge. For knowledge, there are other lesser but still sufficient degrees of justification: for example, clarity and probability. When we cannot demonstrate the certitude and evidentness of a belief, we must try to demonstrate its probability. But probability is a relative property, and to show that a belief is probable is to show that it is more justified than its opposite.[18] Nicholas is clear on this point: what cannot be demonstrated, but remains capable of being defended by rational (but not apodictic) arguments, is probable.

In sum, in all situations where assent can be resisted – that is, in all situations where justification is not absolutely evident and necessary – we must obtain assent by means of other kinds of argumentation that are less restrictive. The goal is to reach conviction through persuasion rather than demonstration. Therefore, what is probable is not absolute, but depends on the quantity and quality of arguments. A proposition is probable if it cannot be demonstrated (i.e. reduced to the first principle) but can nevertheless be defended by means of rational proofs. The probability is a relative notion: a belief is not probable in itself, but is more or less probable than its opposite. We can define the probable in the following way:

$$p \text{ is probable for } S =_{df} S \text{ is more justified in believing p than not-p.}$$

Nicholas does not explicitly present a theory of probability, but he seems to be influenced by the model of the scholastic dispute or by the model of trial, where each parts has to present his proofs and a judge must determine which one is the more convincing. This ideal judge in the realm of epistemology is the 'friend of the truth' in Autrecourt's (1971: 66) philosophy:

> If these arguments should not be found altogether conclusive, yet the position taken is probable, and more probable than the arguments for the opposite conclusion. For, if those who hold opposite conclusions have arguments, let them declare them; and let the lovers of truth make a comparison between the two positions; and I believe that to anyone no inclined in favour of one side rather than the other the degree of probability will appear higher in the arguments to which I would not know how to five probable replies.

Besides this juridical model, the other source of Autrecourt's probabilism naturally is Aristotle's *Topics*. In particular, Autrecourt explicitly quotes Aristotelian's thesis that some falsity may be more probable than the truth: 'I say that even if your conclusion is true, the possibility of my teaching's being true is not thereby eliminated, because even according to Aristotle nothing prevents some false assertions from being more probable than some true assertions' (36–7).

Here, the main goal of Autrecourt's probabilism is made clear: when the evidentness is lacking, it is necessary to give up on the question of the truth and to define knowledge in another way, as a justified belief that can be made more and more justified and approximate to the truth; or, on the contrary, that can be refuted. The degree of probability of a proposition is determined both by the quantity and the quality of the arguments that can prove it. The result is that probable knowledge is defeasible knowledge. Indeed, Autrecourt has an evolutionary conception of knowledge: the accumulation of knowledge allows us to rule out the old theory, as he does Aristotelianism; but it may happen that someone will later rule out Autrecourt's theory, no matter that it now seems more probable than Aristotle's: 'For although in my opinion they appear far more probable than what Aristotle said, yet, just as for a long time Aristotle's statements seemed to be probable, though now perhaps their probability will be lessened, so someone will come along and undermine the probability of these statements of mine' (41). Finally, we may illustrate this theory of probable knowledge by examining the status of inductive proofs.[19] The problem of induction is a meaningful case-study for Autrecourt's epistemology. Indeed, according to his theory of evident perception, the direct report of an experiment (e.g. 'this fire is hot', when I put the hand in a fire) is true and evident. Nevertheless, I cannot deduce from this evident perception the truth and the evidentness, either of the proposition 'Every fire is hot', or of the proposition 'this fire is hot' before I put the hand in the fire (Autrecourt 1994: 73). The problem here is classic: the incompleteness of my experiments, and the possibility that I am not aware of a counterexample to rule out the legitimacy of the generalization. Nicholas rejects the solution that grounds the induction in a common nature,[20] since we cannot be certain that a predicate of the same nature could be attributed to a subject that we have not yet perceived but that we assume would be similar to another that we have experienced. We would be led to a *petitio principia*, since the common nature that grounds the inductive process is discovered by induction. Therefore, we only have evident perceptions of some singular events; any generalization cannot but be probable. Once he has excluded the justification of induction by a common nature, Autrecourt goes even farther by excluding the justification by the principle of causality. He rules out the idea that a mere repetition of an event would be enough to warrant the certitude of its manifestation in the future. If I observed several times that rhubarb purges bile, may I conclude that the proposition 'every rhubarb purges bile' is a scientific principle whose validity is universal? Autrecourt's (1971) answer is negative. Such a principle is a probable conjecture but not a certainty:

> The thirteenth conclusion is that only an habit to the conjecture, not certainty,
> is had concerning things known by experience, in the way in which it is said to

be known that rhubarb cures cholera, or that a magnet attracts iron. When it is proven that certitude comes from the proposition existing in the mind which states that what is usually produced by a non-free cause is a natural effect, I ask what you call a natural cause. A cause which has produced what has happened usually, and which will still produce in the future if the cause lasts and is applied? The minor premise is no known. Even if something has been produced usually, it is still not certain whether it must be produced in the future. (119; translation modified)

Here, the solution criticized is Scotus': in order to make the inductive prediction certain, we need to add as a premise a principle known by itself, like the principle of causality that warrants the evidentness of the repetition. First, Nicholas criticizes the use of the principle of causality from an empirical point of view: we have no evident perception of the fact of the causality as a relation between a cause and an effect. We only perceive a contiguity and a succession of events. Moreover, we cannot identify with certitude all the causes, in such a way we could be sure that no cause remains unknown. Second, he offers a logical criticism of the causality: the proposition 'the cause A exists, therefore the effect B exists or will exist' is not an evident inference since it does not fulfil the conditions of R1. A and B are absolute different things, and the signification of B is not included in the signification of A. It appears that, for Nicholas, any necessity is analytic and the mere contiguity, which is synthetic, cannot be necessary.

But what is the epistemic value of the induction? When we observe several times the conjunction between two events, the frequency and the repetition produce an *habitus conjecturativus*, a habit or a disposition to make a conjecture. Unfortunately, Nicholas does not develop this notion. We may assume that we have a natural tendency to practice inductive generalizations. Since a habit is produced in the intellect by the repetition of a similar act, Autrecourt probably wants to suggest that a *habitus* is produced by the evident perception of an event, and in its turn the habit will make easier the assent to such an event in the future, even if I do not perceive it directly. Therefore, the induction is very close to the probable argumentation by accumulation: the repetition allows us to produce judgement that is more and more probable. The natural causality is nothing else than the extension to the future of a relation of production observed in the past. This extension has no certitude, but can be made probable and confer some trust to the intellect in its capacity to understand the world, even in a weak way.

5. Conclusion

Autrecourt's epistemology aims at making a place for belief, in the sense that any cognitive state is a belief (as an assent) whose epistemic justification can vary from the certitude and evidentness of the science, in the strict sense, to mere probability. For this reason, Nicholas is led to defend an evolutionary conception of knowledge in a cumulative and historical perspective. Knowledge is not exactly a justified true belief, but a belief seeking justification. The truth of the belief can only be warranted at the highest level of epistemic justification. But, finally, it seems that, for Autrecourt, truth is a useless hypothesis in the scientific practice. Truth is not a necessary condition for knowledge: every justified true belief is a knowledge, but not every instance of knowledge is a justified true belief, since many justified beliefs can be labelled as 'knowledge' even if their truth is not warranted. As a consequence of this position, Nicholas departs from the classical model of science in the Middle Ages where truth and evidentness are necessary conditions of knowledge. For Nicholas, evidentness is undoubtedly a sufficient condition for knowledge but not a necessary one: evident knowledge is the ideal goal of epistemology, but in everyday practice the philosopher more often deals with probable beliefs, for which he tries to find better and better justification.

Notes

1   On this topic, see Pasnau (2009) and Pasnau (2017).
2   See Klima's chapter in this book, along with Zupko (2003), Grellard (2005, 2015a), and Biard (2012).
3   On Autrecourt's life, see Kaluza (1995).
4   On this problem, see Byrne (1968) and Grellard (2015a).
5   See also Autrecourt (1994: 57): 'And, therefore, in order to avoid such absurdities, I have upheld in disputations in the Aula of the Sorbonne that I am evidently certain of the objects of the five senses and of my own acts.'
6   Aristotle, *Posterior Analytics*, 71 b 20–23, Barnes (2002), pp. 2–3.
7   See Autrecourt (1971: 102):
    And we must keep in mind that these concepts, as being signs of things, or as being things thus conceived, sometimes are mutually related in a certain way, as container and contained, or part and whole, so that, when one is presented to the intellect, in some way the other is presented also, and when one is removed the other is removed also ... If we posit that some being is a man, we posit

implicitly that it is an animal. Then the intellect abstracts concept from concept until it arrives at a simple concept. By so abstracting it finds ten simple concepts which are included in all others. These concepts, and the things in which they are included are the means for all scientific investigation.

8 Vat. lat. 983: 'Against this, N. of Autrecourt claims and wants to prove that this principle is the first: "being is being", or "nothing is not something", since by this principle all the other have evidence, even the following: "of anything etc."'. <Contra predicta arguit N. de Altricuria et vult probare quod hec est prima: 'Ens est ens', vel 'Nihil <non> est aliquid', quia virtute huius omnis alia habet evidentiam, etiam ista: 'De quolibet etc.'» et si quaeritur quare idem non potest simul esse et non esse, ratio est quia idem maxime sibi idem> (qtd in Kaluza 1995: 206).

9 See Autrecourt (1994: 201–203):

57. That in the natural light, the wayfarer's intellect cannot have evident knowledge of the existence of things, with the evidentness reduced, or reducible, to the evidentness or the certitude of first principle – I deem and assert this article be false and erroneous. 58. That this is the first principle, and no other, 'if something is, it is' – I deem and assert this article to be false. 59. That God and creature are not some thing. – I deem and assert this article to be false and scandalous as it stands. 60. That the complexly signifiable conveyed by the complex expression 'God is distinct from what is created' is nothing. I deem this article false and scandalous. 61. That there is a transition from one state to the contradictory one without there being a real intrinsic change of any of the terms. – I deem this article false. 62. That whatever is distinct both in the highest degree and essentially. – I deem this article false.

10 On this principle and its link with Protagoras, see Denery (2009).

11 On this question, see Denery (2005) and Perler (2006).

12 On this point, see Grellard (2015b). Of course, Autrecourt's theory heavily but implicitly depends on Peter of Aureol's position. This aspect is clearly pointed out by Denery (1998, 2005).

13 See also Autrecourt (1971: 115), quoted above.

14 On this idea of reduction, see Grellard (2005: 77–83) and Krause (2009).

15 See Thijssen (2000) and Grellard (2007, 2010).

16 On the relativist arguments (Autrecourt 1971: 105–107); on the dream argument (107, 110); on the errors of the senses (110); on the disagreement between men (112–14).

17 On this text, see Grellard (2007).

18 Autrecourt mostly uses his probabilism to defend his atomism. The schema is the following: first, to show that Aristotelian physics is not evident, and, even worse, that it is badly justified; second, to show that atomist physics is better

justified – that is, is a better explanation of natural phenomenon. On this point, see Grellard (2002; 2005: 191–226; 2009) and Kaluza (2004).

19 See Thijssen (1987).

20 See Autrecourt (1971: 115):

For instance, someone states a universal proposition which he has accepted only by induction from some individual cases. Sometimes he proposes it by saying 'this is evident to me;' and yet nothing is evident to him except those singular propositions on which he based the induction; nor is it even evident for him that those singulars are of the same nature as far as the predicate is concerned.

References

Autrecourt, N. (1971), *The Universal Treatise*, trans. L. A. Kennedy, R. E. Arnold, and A. E. Millward, Milwaukee: Marquette University Press.

Autrecourt, N. (1994), *His Correspondence with Master Giles and Bernard of Arezzo: A Critical Edition and English Translation*, ed. and trans. L. M. de Rijk, Leiden: Brill.

Biard, J. (2012), *Science et nature: La théorie buridanienne du savoir*, Paris: Vrin.

Buridan, J. (2008), *Lectura Erfordiensis in I-VI Metaphysicam Together with 15th-Century Abbreviatio Caminensis*, Introduction, Critical Edition, and Indexes by L. M. de Rijk, Turnhout: Brepols.

Byrne, E. (1968), *Probability and Opinion: A Study in the Medieval Presuppositions of Post-Medieval Theories of Probability*, The Hague: Martin Nijhoff.

Denery, D. G. II (1998), 'Nicholas of Autrecourt on Saving the Appearances', in S. Caroti and C. Grellard (eds), *Nicolas d'Autrécourt et la Faculté des Arts de Paris (1317–1340). Actes du colloque de Paris, 19–21 mai 2005*, Cesena: Stilgraf.

Denery, D. G. II (2005), *Seeing and Being Seen: Vision, Visual Analogy and Visual Error in Late Medieval Optics, Theology and Religious Life*, Cambridge: Cambridge University Press.

Denery, D. G. II (2009), 'Protagoras and the Fourteenth-Century Invention of Epistemological Relativism', *Visual Resources*, 25: 29–51.

Grellard, C. (2002), 'Le statut de la causalité chez Nicolas d'Autrécourt', *Quaestio*, 2: 267–89.

Grellard, C. (2005), *Croire et savoir. Les principes de la connaissance selon Nicolas d'Autrécourt*, Paris: Vrin.

Grellard, C. (2007), 'Scepticism, Demonstration and the Infinite Regress Argument (Nicholas of Autrecourt and John Buridan)', *Vivarium*, 42: 328–42.

Grellard, C. (2009), 'Nicholas of Autrecourt's Atomistic Physics', in Ch. Grellard and A. Robert (eds), *Atomism in Late Medieval Philosophy and Theology*, Leiden: Brill.

Grellard , C. (2010), 'Nicholas of Autrecourt's Skepticism: The Ambivalence of Medieval Epistemology', in H. Lagerlund (ed.), *Rethinking the History of Skepticism: The Missing Medieval Background*, Leiden: Brill.

Grellard, C. (2015a), 'Science et opinion dans les *Questions sur les seconds analytiques de* Jean Buridan', in J. Biard (ed.), *La tradition médiévale des Seconds Analytiques*, Turnhout: Brepols.

Grellard, C. (2015b), 'The Nature of Intentional Objects in Nicholas of Autrecourt's Theory of Knowledge', in G. Klima (ed.), *Intentionality, Cognition and Mental Representation in Medieval Philosophy*, New York: Fordham University Press.

Kaluza, Z. (1995), 'Nicolas d'Autrécourt. Ami de la vérité', *Histoire Littéraire de la France*, 42-1.

Kaluza, Z. (2004), 'La convenance et son rôle dans la pensée de Nicolas d'Autrécourt', in Ch. Grellard (ed.), *Méthodes et statut des sciences au Moyen Âge et à la Renaissance*, Lille: Presse Universitaire du Septentrion.

Krause, A. (2009), 'Nikolaus von Autrecourt über das erste Prinzip und die Gewißheit von Sätzen', *Vivarium*, 47: 407–20.

Pasnau, R. (2009), 'Medieval Social Epistemology: *Scientia* for Mere Mortals', *Episteme*, 7: 23–41.

Perler, D. (2006), 'Relations nécessaires ou contingentes? Nicolas d'Autrécourt et la controverse sur la nature des relations cognitives', in S. Caroti and Ch. Grellard (eds), *Nicolas d'Autrécourt et la Faculté des Arts de Paris (1317–1340): Actes du colloque de Paris, 19–21 mai 2005*, Cesena: Stilfgraf.

Robert, A. (2006), '*Jamais Aristote n'a eu de connaissance d'une substance*: Nicolas d'Autrécourt en contexte', in S. Caroti and Ch. Grellard (eds), *Nicolas d'Autrécourt et la Faculté des Arts de Paris (1317–1340): Actes du colloque de Paris, 19–21 mai 2005*, Cesena: Stilfgraf.

Thijssen, H. J. M. M. (1987), 'John Buridan and Nicholas of Autrecourt on Causality and Induction', *Traditio*, 43: 237–55.

Thijssen, H. J. M. M. (2000), 'The Quest for Certain Knowledge in the Fourteenth Century: Nicolas of Autrecourt against the Academics', in J. Sihvola (ed.), *Ancient Scepticism and the Sceptical Tradition*, Helsinki: Societas Philosophica Fennica.

Zupko, J. (2003), *John Buridan: Portrait of a Fourteenth-Century Arts Master*, Notre Dame, IN: University of Notre Dame Press.

9

John Buridan on Knowledge

Gyula Klima

1. Introduction: Buridan's essentialist nominalism

In modern philosophy, nominalism is often associated with anti-essentialism, and hence with scepticism.[1] John Buridan, however, despite being a thoroughgoing nominalist, was both an essentialist and a credible reliabilist epistemologist. Of course, after listing so many 'isms', I owe the reader some explanation. So, in this section, I begin by explaining in what sense Buridan is both a nominalist and an essentialist. In the second section, I will explain how Buridan's essentialism grounds his scientific realism, and generally his reliabilist epistemology. In the third section, I will show how Buridan's reliabilist epistemology satisfactorily handles some sceptical challenges coming from his contemporaries. However, in the closing section, I will argue that his epistemology would not be able to cope with an extreme form of scepticism, which would be avoidable in a different, 'moderate realist', conceptual framework, such as that of Thomas Aquinas.

When modern readers hear the term 'essentialism', they tend to think of a realist doctrine that would assign essential properties to individuals sorted into natural kinds on the basis of shared, universal essences. Clearly, this idea of essentialism is incompatible with the idea of nominalism, which, by definition, is committed to denying the existence of anything like 'shared, universal essences'. But then how can Buridan be a nominalist *and* an essentialist, if at all? To understand how this is possible, I need to outline here the relevant parts of his nominalist semantic theory.

What do we mean, precisely, when we say that Buridan was an essentialist? When we call someone an essentialist, we usually mean at least one of two things: (1) the person is committed to attributing *essential predicates* to things, and/or (2) the person is committed to attributing some common, *shared essences* to things. Let me call the first version of essentialism *predicate essentialism*, and the second *realist essentialism*. Clearly, with this distinction in hand, we should be able to provide a coherent interpretation of calling someone a 'nominalist essentialist', in the sense that the person in question is a *predicate essentialist* while not a *realist essentialist*, since his nominalism consists in the denial of there being shared essences but not in the denial of there being essential predicates.

However, obviously, this simple 'word magic' can do the job only if we are able to show that what I call here *predicate essentialism* is compatible with the denial of *realist essentialism*. In any case, my first contention is that this is precisely what Buridan is trying to accomplish: one of the basic aims of his philosophy of language and metaphysics is to show that he can be a staunch nominalist in denying real, shared essences to things in the way that realists conceive of them,[2] yet at the same time he can attribute scientifically knowable essential predicates to things.

To see exactly how Buridan attempts to achieve this, we have to take a closer look at his semantic conception – in particular, his theory of predication.

Buridan does not feel the need to argue for a distinction between essential and non-essential predicates. As he sees it, that distinction is part and parcel of Porphyry's traditional distinctions of the five predicables. As Buridan writes:

> [S]ince something is called a predicable because it is apt to be predicated of many things, it is reasonable to distinguish the species or modes contained under the term 'predicable' according to the different modes of predication. Therefore, everything that is predicated of something is either predicated essentially, so that neither term adds some extraneous connotation to the signification of the other; or it is predicated denominatively, so that one term does add some extrinsic connotation to the signification of the other. This division is clearly exhaustive, for it is given in terms of opposites. (*SD*: 2.1.3: 106)[3]

Obviously, the important thing here is not that Buridan draws the distinction at all, but *how* he draws it. To understand his characterization of essential predication as that in which the terms do not add extraneous connotation over the signification of each other, we should take a quick look at his semantics of terms and propositions.

For Buridan, the simplest form of proposition is a categorical proposition, consisting of a subject and a predicate joined by a copula. To be sure, this need not mean that the terms of such a proposition should be simple; indeed, they may be of any complexity, as long as they can suitably flank the copula to form a proposition. Accordingly, in the Buridanian 'canonical form' of a categorical proposition, both terms are regarded as noun phrases, and so verbal predicates are always to be analyzed into a copula and the corresponding participle. For example, 'Socrates walks on the beach with Plato' is to be analyzed as 'Socrates is walking on the beach with Plato'; or, indeed, to bring out the nominal character of the predicate term, it should even be analyzed as 'Socrates is someone walking on the beach with Plato'.

As this example may already suggest, for Buridan, the copula is a sign of identity: for him, an affirmative categorical proposition is true if and only if its terms refer to the same thing or things at the time connoted by its copula, as required by the quantity of the proposition.

There are a number of things that we should clarify in connection with this apparently simple claim, which expresses what historians of medieval logic dubbed *the identity theory of predication*.

In the first place, when I used the phrase 'refer to' in the previous formulation, it was a somewhat loose rendering of Buridan's technical phrase '*supponit pro*', which indicates what a term does in the context of a proposition in its semantic function – namely, standing for the things the proposition is about. Still, we nowadays tend to transcribe, rather than translate, this phrase in the historical literature as 'supposit for', to avoid confusion with contemporary notions of reference. For, in contrast to most modern conceptions of reference, supposition is an essentially context-dependent property of all simple and complex terms that can grammatically flank the copula, whether they are singular or common. Accordingly, one and the same term may supposit for very different things or for nothing at all, and in very different ways, on different occasions of its use. It is precisely these different ways in which a term may stand for some thing or things, or for nothing, in a proposition that the medieval theory of supposition is designed to describe.

The easiest way to explain the idea is by using some examples. If I say ' "Man" is a noun', then this proposition is true, according to Buridan, insofar as its subject term is used non-significatively (i.e. not to supposit for what it was imposed to signify, but to supposit for itself or for any other token term of the same type); and the reason why the proposition is true is that at least one of these token terms is indeed identical with a noun. This is a case that Buridan would classify as an instance of a term's having *material supposition*. However, if I say 'Every man is an animal', then the subject term of this proposition stands for individual humans (the things that this term is imposed to signify), and the proposition is true because every human is identical with some animal. In this case, Buridan would say that the term has *personal supposition*.[4]

Accordingly, his notion of personal supposition, required for understanding his conception of true predication, presupposes his notion of signification, insofar as a term in personal supposition supposits for things that it signifies.

Now, with regard to their signification, Buridan classifies terms into two kinds: *absolute* or *connotative*.[5] An absolute term is one that signifies absolutely whatever it signifies – that is, not in relation to anything. A connotative term is one that signifies something in relation to something or some things, called the *connotatum* or *connotata* of the term. Accordingly, the *personal supposita* of an absolute term in the context of a proposition are those of its *significata* that are actual with respect to the time connoted by the copula. The *supposita* of a connotative term, however, are those of its significata that are actual with respect to the time connoted by the copula, and are also actually related to the *connotata* of the term in the way that the term signifies them to be related.[6]

A quick example may again be helpful here. If I say 'Socrates is wealthy', then this proposition is true, according to Buridan, if and only if its terms both supposit for the same thing – namely, Socrates. However, the term 'wealthy' is obviously a connotative term, because it signifies human beings in relation to their wealth – namely, as the possessors of wealth. So, this term supposits only for human beings who possess wealth. Therefore, this term will supposit for Socrates only if he actually possesses wealth at the time connoted by the copula (cf. *SD*: 880).

In fact, this example also illustrates two further important points. The first is that, even if all explicitly relative terms are connotative, not all connotative terms are explicitly relative, although they do have to involve some relative concept in their definition.[7] The second point is that a connotative term can become false of a thing that it actually supposits for (and so it can cease to supposit for it), while the thing continues to exist, simply on account of the term's connotata ceasing to be related to its *supposita* in the way required by the signification of the term. If Socrates loses his wealth, he ceases to be supposited for by the term 'wealthy' (in the context of a present-tense sentence). Perhaps I should note here that this holds for every connotative term, unless it connotes something intrinsic to its *supposita* without which these *supposita* cannot exist (an example might be the term 'animate'), or, if the term's *connotata* are the same as its *supposita*, as is the case with terms expressing self-identity, such as the term 'identical with itself' – which, not surprisingly, Buridan treats as equivalent to the terms 'one' and 'being' (Klima 2013). But in all other cases – namely, when their *connotata* are extrinsic to their *significata* – connotative terms can cease to supposit for their actual *significata*: that is, they may become false of their actual *significata* without the destruction of these *significata*, which is precisely the idea expressed in the Porphyrian definition of accident. For example, if Socrates actually has wealth, then he is one of the actual *significata* of the term 'wealthy'. Accordingly, in the proposition 'Socrates is wealthy' the term supposits for Socrates, whence the proposition is true. But if he loses his wealth, he ceases to be one of the actual *significata* of this term, whence it will no longer supposit for him, even if he stays in existence. Therefore, it is no wonder that, for Buridan, all such connotative terms are non-essential, accidental predicates of their *significata*.

By contrast, absolute terms are essential predicates of their *significata*. For example, if we take 'man' to be an absolute term, as Buridan certainly does, then the only way that this term can cease to supposit for Socrates in the proposition 'Socrates is a man' is if Socrates ceases to exist. For the term signifies everything that the concept to which it is subordinated represents: that is, every past, present, future, and possible human being, indifferently. But the actual *significata* of this term are only actual human beings, who are therefore also the *supposita* of the term 'man' in a present-tense proposition. So, the only way that the term 'man' in 'Socrates is a man' can cease to supposit for Socrates is if he ceases to be a human being, that is, if he ceases to exist. Miraculous transformations of Socrates, say, into a rock or some brute animal, while staying in existence, are excluded by the structure of the Porphyrian Tree, as Buridan conceives of it. Since, by that structure, overlaps between non-subaltern species and genera are not allowed (cf. *SD* 3.1.7: 150), if Socrates is once among the *significata* of 'man', then he cannot be driven over into the range of *significata* of 'pig' even by Circe's wand. Therefore, Socrates cannot cease to be one of the *significata* of 'man', although he can cease to be one of its *actual significata*, and hence one of its *supposita*, by ceasing to exist (since, being a man, he is not a necessary being).

In this way, therefore, it may seem that Buridan can maintain a credible essentialist stance without ever having even to mention shared essences, as long as he can establish that at least some of our common terms are in fact absolute terms – in particular, absolute terms that are essential predicates of things falling into the category of substance.

As we could see, whether a term is absolute or connotative depends on the term's signification. But a term's signification, according to Buridan, depends on the sort of concept to which it is subordinated. For a term has signification only insofar as it is subordinated to some cognitive act of our minds, a concept. If I utter the articulate sound 'biltrix', then someone hearing me literally has no idea of what I have just said. And this is how it should be, because this utterance was precisely one of the examples used by several medieval logicians to illustrate a meaningless utterance – that is, one that does not have signification, because it is not imposed to signify anything of which we can think. However, as soon as this utterance is made to signify something of which we are intellectually aware, it will signify precisely what we are aware of and precisely in the way we are aware of it. The intellective cognitive act on account of which we are aware of something is what Buridan calls a concept. And since terms have their significations by virtue of being subordinated to such concepts, the differences between the significations and types of signification of different terms are dependent on the types of concepts to which they are subordinated. Therefore, the abovementioned difference between absolute and connotative terms, which grounds the difference between essential and non-essential predicates of substances, boils down to the difference between the kinds of concepts to which they are subordinated. Absolute terms are those subordinated to absolute concepts – that is, concepts whereby we conceive of things absolutely, not in relation to anything – whereas connotative terms are those subordinated to connotative concepts, whereby we conceive of things in relation to something. Therefore, the distinction between essential and non-essential predicates of substances boils down to the distinction between absolute and connotative concepts, and thus Buridan's essentialism ultimately hinges on the claim that we are actually able to form such absolute concepts of substances.

2. Buridan's reliabilism

Buridan was perfectly aware of these epistemological and cognitive psychological implications of his semantics. Accordingly, he argued that it is indeed possible for us to acquire such concepts, and that these concepts can function as the basis of valid scientific generalizations – that is, the induction of scientific principles, which in turn can reliably serve as the premises of scientific demonstrations.[8]

In his *Questions on Aristotle's Metaphysics* (1964 [1518]: II, 1), raising the question of *whether it is possible for us to comprehend the truth about things*, Buridan lays out the conditions for knowledge, which he characterizes here as 'assent to the truth with certitude' by first stipulating its *objective* conditions, consisting in the *firmness of truth* itself:

> [W]e should note that assent to the truth with certitude requires the *firmness of truth* and the *firmness of assent*. Now the *firmness of truth* is possible; in one

way absolutely, as in the case of the proposition 'God exists', which can in no situation [*in nullo casu*] be falsified. But there is also firmness of truth with the assumption of the common course of nature [*ex suppositione communis cursus naturae*], and in this way it is a firm truth that the heavens are moving and that fire is hot, and so on for other scientific conclusions, notwithstanding the fact that God would be able to make cold fire, which would falsify the proposition that every fire is hot. Thus it is clear that the *firmness of truth is possible.* (Klima 2007: 145; emphases added)

That is to say, reality has certain stable features, either absolutely, as is the existence of God, or conditionally, as are the observable regularities of nature (which are conditioned upon God's will), that allow certitude about them simply because they are necessary, either absolutely or conditionally. But this is only the objective requirement for certitude of apprehension, which in itself would not suffice, were it not accompanied by the *subjective* requirement – namely, the *firmness of assent*, which, however, is not always scientific, as is clear from the continuation of this passage:

But the *firmness of assent* is that whereby we adhere and assent to a proposition without fear of the opposite [*absque formidine ad oppositum*] and this can take place *in three ways.*

In one way, [it proceeds] *from the will*, and in this way Christians assent and adhere firmly to the articles of Catholic faith, and even some heretics adhere to their false opinions, so much so that they would rather die than deny them, and such is the experience of the saints who were willing to die for the faith of Christ. And so it is clear that in this way the firmness of assent is possible for us. (Ibid.; emphases added)

This type of firm assent is clearly not the requirement of scientific certitude, as it is dependent on free acts of will. For the will can certainly provide very strong subjective firmness of assent; nevertheless, this strong subjective assent can attach to complete untruths as well. There is, however, the second type of firmness of assent, which is closer to scientific certitude, but it is still not infallible:

In the second way, firmness proceeds in us *from natural appearances* by means of reasoning, and in this way, it is still possible for us to assent not only to truth but also to falsity. For many people believing and holding false opinions take themselves to have firm scientific knowledge, just as Aristotle says in bk. 7 of the *Ethics* that many people adhere to what they opine no less firmly than to what they know. (Ibid.; emphases added)

Clearly, this sort of firm assent can be the certitude of opinion of strongly opinionated people. It is only the third type of firm assent that can complete the requirements for scientific knowledge, in accordance with the requisite standards appropriate for each science:

> In the third way, firmness proceeds in us *from evidentness*. And it is called the evidentness of a proposition absolutely, when because of the nature of the senses or the intellect man is compelled, though without necessity, to assent to a proposition so that he cannot dissent from it. And this is the sort of evidentness that the first complex principle [the principle of non-contradiction] has according to Aristotle in the fourth book of this work [the *Metaphysics*]. Evidentness is taken in another way not absolutely, but with the assumption that things obey the common course of nature, as was said earlier. It is in this way that it is evident to us that every fire is hot or that the heavens are moving, although the opposite is possible by God's power. And this sort of evidentness is sufficient for the principles and conclusions of natural science. Indeed, there is an even weaker kind of evidentness that suffices for acting morally well, namely, when someone, having seen and investigated all relevant facts and circumstances that man can diligently investigate, makes a judgment in accordance with these circumstances, then his judgment will be evident with the sort of evidentness that suffices for acting morally well, even if the judgment is false, because of some insurmountable ignorance of some circumstance. For example, it would be possible for a magistrate to act well and meritoriously in hanging a holy man because from testimonies and other legal evidence it sufficiently appeared to him concerning this good man that he was an evil murderer. (145–6; emphases added)

Here, Buridan very clearly lays out the foundations for three basic types or degrees of certainty, based on the three types of evidentness between which he distinguished: absolute, physical, and moral. Indeed, it is this gradation of the requisite types of certitude in different fields of inquiry that is his main conceptual weapon in fighting some contemporary sceptical challenges.

3. Buridan's anti-scepticism

In his question-commentary on Aristotle's *Physics*, Buridan raises the question of 'whether in every science the knowledge and understanding of things arises from the preexisting cognition of their causes, principles, and elements' (*QPhys*: I, 4).

In this question, after advancing a number of arguments supporting the negative reply, Buridan begins his discussion by expounding an opinion on the issue, which he is about to refute:

> This question and the arguments brought up in connection with it raise several difficulties. One such difficulty is whether from the cognition (*notitia*) of one thing one can obtain the cognition of another. For there are two sorts of cognition, namely, complex and incomplex. About the incomplex sort some people say that no incomplex cognition can be obtained from another, since no cognition can be obtained from another, except by means of a consequence, but a consequence can only lead from a complex [cognition] to a complex one; therefore, etc. Second, they infer as a corollary that we have no cognition of any substance in terms of incomplex cognition, for we can arrive at the cognition of substances only by means of the cognition of accidents; and so by means of some consequence, which can obtain only between complex [cognitions]. But I do not agree with this opinion, and I posit two conclusions against it. (*QPhys*: I, 4)

Buridan's first conclusion directly attacks the first claim of his opponents, whoever they were[9] – namely, that no simple cognition can be obtained from a simple cognition. He points out that the claim is self-defeating, insofar as the simple intellectual cognitions it involves had to come from some simple sensory cognitions; and so, some *simple intellectual cognition* had to come from some *simple sensory cognition*, whence some simple cognition had to be obtained from some simple cognition, contrary to the original claim. As he writes:

> The first [conclusion] is that some incomplex cognition can be obtained by means of another. For there are incomplex intellectual cognitions, and all intellectual cognitions are obtained by means of another act of cognition; therefore, some incomplex cognition is obtained by means of another [act of cognition]. The major premise has to be accepted, for if a caviler were to deny it, then [by virtue of this denial] he would have to concede at least the existence of some complex intellectual cognition; but that complex [cognition] would have to be composed of simple ones, for it is not divided to infinity as the continuum, and an intellectual cognition is not composed of sensory cognitions; therefore, it is composed of incomplex intellectual ones. But the minor of the principal argument is also clear, for at least the first intellectual cognition has to be obtained from a sensory one, and, in general, every intellectual cognition must be obtained from sensory cognition either directly or indirectly, since one who understands has to attend to [*speculari*] the phantasms, as is stated in book 3 of *On the Soul*; and for this reason it is also claimed in book 1 of the *Posterior*

Analytics that if we lose one of our senses, we also lose the knowledge of the
proper object of that sense. (Ibid.)

So, simple intellectual cognition must somehow come from simple sensory
cognition. But how is this possible? And even if we can provide an explanation
of the derivation of simple intellectual cognition from simple sensory cognition
in general, how do we know that we have such a simple cognition *of substance*
obtainable from sense experience? Indeed, why would the intellectual cognition
of substance have to be simple?

Buridan's second conclusion addresses this issue as follows:

> The second conclusion is that we have simple concepts of substances, for the
> concept of man from which we take the substantial term 'man' is a concept of
> substance, if man is a substance. And that concept supposits only for a substance,
> for if it supposited for an accident or for something composed from substance
> and accident, then it would not be true that man is a substance, for neither an
> accident nor something composed from substance and accident is a substance;
> but precisely a substance is a substance, and that concept, while it supposits for a
> substance, does not even connote an accident other than that substance, for then
> it would not belong to the category of substance, but to that of an accident, as
> do the terms 'white' or 'big' or 'small', etc. For these terms supposit for substance
> and not for anything else, just as the term 'man' does, but they leave the category
> of substance because of their connotation; therefore, a concept from which a
> term in the category of substance is taken is not a concept of any accident, or of
> something composed from substance and accident, but only of a substance or
> substances.
>
> And if anyone were to say that they are complex, then the complex ones are
> combined from simple ones, for in the analysis of concepts one cannot go to
> infinity; and then those simple ones and the ones composed from them are only
> of substances; therefore, there are simple concepts of substances. (Ibid.)

The important thing to note about Buridan's argumentation here is his insistence
on the Aristotelian distinction between substance and accident, and his
combination of this Aristotelian doctrine with his own semantic analysis of the
terms and the corresponding concepts belonging to the Aristotelian categories.
The point of the argument is that even if substances had complex concepts, those
complex concepts would have to be made of simple concepts. But those simple
concepts cannot be concepts of accidents, so those simple concepts would have
to be simple substantial concepts, so we would still have to have some simple
substantial concepts, which was the point to be proved. However, the claim that

complex substantial concepts cannot be made up from accidental concepts is proved here with reference to Buridan's doctrine of the semantics of substantial versus accidental terms and concepts, as being absolute versus connotative terms and concepts.

What Buridan's argument shows is that the assumption that substantial concepts are collections of connotative concepts would lead to the absurd conclusion that a substantial term would not be a substantial term, for then it would be subordinated to a non-substantial concept. As he writes further on:

> Again, if the substantial concept of man were complex, then let us posit that it consists of three simple ones, namely, **a**, **b**, and **c**. Then, if no concept of substance is simple, **a** can only be a concept of accident, and the same goes for **b** and **c**; therefore, the whole combined from them would also be only a concept of accident, and not one of substance, for a whole is nothing over and above its parts. But this is absurd, namely, that the substantial concept of man should be nothing but a concept of accidents; therefore, etc. (Ibid.)

To be sure, centuries later the British empiricists, who provided precisely this sort of analysis for substantial terms, happily embraced this conclusion, and did not regard it as absurd at all. But Buridan's previous argument, combined with his semantic considerations, also shows that this conclusion directly entails the impossibility of the *essential* predication of these 'phony' substantial terms. This, however, entails further that they cannot serve as the basis for valid scientific generalizations: an implication that was to be worked out in the fullest detail by David Hume. But then, unless Humean scepticism is the inevitable consequence of empiricism in general, an empiricist who wants to save the possibility of scientific knowledge in the traditional sense has to be able to find a way to account for the derivation of our *genuine* substantial concepts from experience, without turning the terms associated with these concepts into non-essential predicates of their significata.

This is precisely what Buridan offers in his subsequent considerations in this passage, as well as in a more detailed discussion in his questions on Aristotle's *De Anima* (*QDA*: I, 6).

In that discussion, Buridan argues that it is reasonable to claim that the sensory data provided by the senses about accidents also carries information about the substances to which these accidents belong, and that this information is extractible by the intellect, even if it is not so extractible by the senses. As I have argued elsewhere (2004), Buridan's discussion rests on two fundamental principles.

The principle of the activity of the intellect. The intellect is not just a passive receiver of sensory information, but a cognitive faculty actively processing this information, extracting from it content that is not so extractible from it by the senses.

The principle of the substantial content of sensory information. The sensory information received by the senses, besides its primary, *per se* content concerning the sensible qualities of sensory objects, also carries some further content about the substances bearing these sensible qualities.

Once these two principles are acknowledged, *any* empiricist should be able to provide a plausible account of our ability to acquire *genuine* substantial concepts from sensory information. For in view of the first principle, the intellect is obviously able to extract content from sensory information which the senses could not so extract even though they may carry it, in the way, for instance, light received by a telescope carries not only visible information about the stars, but also information about their material constitution, which, however, is extractible only by means of spectral analysis. But in view of the second principle, the information about sensible accidents also carries such extractible information about the substances to which these accidents belong, for the accidents appear in our experience *as belonging to things* that are changeable in respect of their accidents. Therefore, the intellect should be able to form genuine substantial concepts from this sensory information. But then, these genuine substantial concepts will be denoted by genuine essential predicates of the things conceived by means of these concepts, which will always necessarily apply to these things as long as these things exist. And so, these predicates will be scientifically knowable characteristics of these things.

Therefore, endorsing these two epistemic principles allows Buridan to adhere to an empiricist nominalism while securing the validity of scientific generalizations in the sense that since it is possible to get to know essential features of a potentially infinite class of things based on acquaintance with only a limited number of individuals of that class, we can know that these features, being essential to *any* member of the class in question, will apply to *all*. But these two principles themselves only secure the mere theoretical possibility of such valid scientific generalizations. For securing the actual reliability of particular generalizations, which are, after all, the particular principles of actual scientific demonstrations, we need a further account of the epistemic status of these scientific principles themselves.

In his *Summulae,*[10] Buridan advances two important epistemic principles about the status of such scientific principles that he also alludes to in the question of his *Physics*-commentary discussed above.

The first, which may be termed *the principle of primacy and multiplicity of scientific principles*, is that these scientific principles are not arrived at by demonstration, but as a result of the exercise of the human mind's natural faculties of senses, memory, and experience, and so there are infinitely many such principles. Since these principles serve as the first principles of scientific demonstrations, they cannot possibly be arrived at as conclusions of such demonstrations, because that would lead to circularity. But since they are the premises of all scientific conclusions, which are demonstrably infinite in number, and in any demonstration there are at least as many premises as there are conclusions, indeed, many more, there are infinitely many scientific principles as well.

The second epistemic principle about scientific principles, which may be termed *the principle of gradation of certainty of scientific principles*, is that the certainty and evidentness of these principles come in degrees. Buridan argues that contrary to the opinion of contemporary sceptics, there is not just one absolutely certain first principle to which all principles need to be reduced – namely, the principle of contradiction, as is clear already from the previously mentioned principle regarding the multitude of scientific principles, but there have to be infinitely many principles of varying degrees of certainty, depending on their subject matter, generality, and confirmation in experience. Accordingly, for example, there are scientific principles which are certain naturally, but not logically, insofar as their validity might be overruled by divine omnipotence, yet such principles are absolutely certain with the assumption of the common course of nature. Furthermore, there are principles of prudence that are certain with the degree appropriate to their subject matter, namely, they are certain with *moral* certainty (even though Buridan does not use the actual phrase). These principles are certain enough to serve as the principles of prudential arguments and conclusions, and they are more certain than mere opinions in the same sphere, even if they cannot be proved in terms of some stronger certainty, but they are acquired in a non-demonstrative natural process.

All in all, the upshot of all this is that for Buridan, scientific knowledge is reliably attainable, with the requisite degree of certainty appropriate to the kind of knowledge in the kind of science we are talking about. Clearly, we cannot expect to attain mathematical certainty in a court case, but *can* attain the requisite *moral* certainty using the kind of common sense and scientific certainty available on the basis of observations and scientific demonstrations (as in justifying or falsifying certain test methods). By the same token, it would seem that we cannot expect absolute certainty even in science or metaphysics, even though there can be certain metaphysical or theological doubt about the validity of the principles of these sciences, such as the principle of causality, based on considerations of divine omnipotence and the possibility that God can at any time suspend or alter the ordinary course of nature. However, just as it would be absurd to base a legal defense of a murderer on the slim chance that at the moment of the murder God altered the course of nature, so it would be absurd to suspend all scientific inquiry on the basis of the slim chance that God would do so not just once, in a haphazard manner, but all the time, systematically deceiving us about all our scientific principles and conclusions.

4. Conclusion: some problems with Buridan's account

As we could see, Buridan's reliabilist account of the possibility of scientific knowledge ultimately hinges on his essentialism, which in turn depends on his semantics of absolute terms and the corresponding concepts. This doctrine is well-worked out and is consistent with Buridan's nominalist ontology: he provides a perfectly working semantics of essential predication without a need for anything like the (moderate) realists' shared essences. However, the consistency of Buridan's ontology and semantics in itself does not save his overall epistemology from certain further problems.

In the first place, as I will argue, the semantics of Buridan's absolute terms and the corresponding absolute concepts is inconsistent with his abstractionist cognitive psychology accounting for the acquisition of these concepts.

In the second place, Buridan's cognitive psychology combined with his epistemology leaves wide open the door for the possibility of Cartesian 'Demon scepticism', which, in turn, combined with Descartes' quest for absolute certainty in metaphysics and the foundations of science, quite directly led to the subjectivist trends of early modern philosophy, although, in fact, these could have been avoided on the basis of an earlier paradigm of cognitive psychology exemplified by Thomas Aquinas.

As for the first problem, consider the following passage from Buridan's *Questions on Aristotle's 'De Anima'* (*QDA*: III, 8; Jack Zupko's translation):

> I assume further that if there are some things similar to each other, then whatever is similar to one of them *in that respect in which the two are similar to each other* has to be similar to each of them. For example, if A, B, and C are similar with respect to whiteness because they are white, just as D is similar to A in

whiteness, it must also be similar to both B and C. From this, it follows – given that representation occurs by means of likeness – that what was representative of one thing will be indifferently representative of the others ... And from this it is finally inferred that once the species and likeness of Socrates existed in the intellect and was abstracted from the species of external features, it will no more be a representation of Socrates than of Plato and other humans; nor does the intellect understand Socrates by it any more than other humans. On the contrary, the intellect understands all humans by it indifferently, in a single concept, namely, the concept from which the name 'man' is taken. And this is to understand universally. (Emphasis added)

Buridan is apparently arguing here from the transitivity of similarity. Since a concept D of a thing A is similar to A, and A is similar to things B and C, the concept D will be similar to, and hence equally representative of, things B and C. However, this otherwise valid scheme is vitiated by the equivocation of the notion of similarity. For, whereas concept D is *representationally* similar to A, things A, B, and C are *qualitatively* or *essentially* similar to one another. (In fact, to simplify things, I may add here that qualitative similarity is reducible to essential similarity, for two things are qualitatively similar if and only if each has a quality such that those qualities are essentially similar. So, in what follows let me deal only with essential similarity.) The question, then, is that of why Buridan thinks that his reasoning works in this passage, given that he cannot appeal to the transitivity of similarity, because the representational similarity of D to A along with the essential similarity of A, B, and C in and of itself does not directly imply the representational similarity of D to B and C. I think that the reason why Buridan thinks his reasoning works is his (tacit) appeal to the idea of what might be termed the *aspectuality of abstraction*. The idea is that D can represent B and C on the basis of representing A, because D represents A precisely insofar as A is essentially similar to B and C: in other words, D represents A precisely in that respect in which A is similar to B and C. For if D is a representation of A precisely *in that respect* in which A is essentially similar to B and C, then D is equally a representation of B and C *in the same respect* as well. However, as I have argued elsewhere in more detail (2009: 89–103), this aspectuality is inconsistent with the representative function that Buridan attributes to absolute concepts. After all, an absolute concept is called absolute, precisely because it represents its objects *not* in respect of anything, but absolutely.

As for the second problem, in several earlier papers I have argued that what opened up the conceptual possibility of demon-scepticism (familiar to most of us from Descartes) in the mid-fourteenth century was the emergence of a new conception of concept-identity, tying the identity-conditions of concepts to the internal properties of the mental qualities that realize them (see Klima and Hall 2011). Buridan in the above-quoted passages clearly concedes the (however remote) possibility of our being systematically deceived by divine omnipotence; however, he simply seeks to deflate it as practically irrelevant, by claiming that seeking absolute certainty concerning what is possible by absolute divine power is inappropriate, asking for an unjustifiably high degree of certainty concerning matters about which we cannot have that degree of certainty. However, this answer may just not suffice.

To see why, we first need to understand how the theoretical possibility of demon-scepticism arises out of the new, nominalist, conception of concept-identity; so, we first need to have a proper understanding of the gist of the idea of demon-scepticism itself. The gist of the idea, I take it, is the possibility of having a cognitive subject with exactly the same mental contents as, say, you or I have right now, regardless of the ways that things are or even can be in extra-mental reality (if there is such a reality at all). This idea obviously entails that the conditions of identity of any cognitive acts of this kind of cognitive subjects are totally independent from their veridicality: any and all cognitive acts of such a subject can be exactly the same, whether they are veridical or not (i.e. whether or not they represent extra-mental reality as it is). That is to say, on this conception, the conditions of identity of any cognitive act are dependent entirely on the act's internal properties, logically independently from what things there are and how things there are in external reality, if anything at all. The *phenomenal* content of each such cognitive act (i.e. what and how these acts appear to represent to the cognitive subject) is thus independent from any *real* content that it may have. So, the subject may exist in a completely inaccessible reality: to put the point in Kantian terms, the world of *phenomena* (whatever the subject's cognitive acts *appear to represent* to the subject) constitutes an impenetrable wall between the subject and the world of *noumena* (whatever there *really* is or can be in external reality), not only on the level of sensory cognition (as in the 1999 movie *The Matrix*), but also on the level of intellectual cognition (as in 'an empiricist *Matrix*', in which all intellectual contents derive from sensory contents, just as Buridan laid it out in the passages quoted earlier).

Well, what is *new* in all this, one might ask; indeed, what does it have to do with medieval nominalism? After all, isn't this just the way that all basic problems of modern epistemology emerge in the first place?

To this, I would respond that it is indeed this allegedly possible scenario that lies at the bottom of modern epistemologies, but that conceding this possibility was a radically new phenomenon (see Lagerlund 2010), which historically first emerged in late medieval thought, especially in Ockhamist nominalism, of which Buridan was the foremost promoter in his time at the University of Paris.

Clearly, if the identity conditions of cognitive acts are tied to the internal properties of these acts, which in turn determine the phenomenal content of each, then it clearly should be possible that the same subject has the same cognitive acts, while the same subject is supernaturally placed into a creation in which *all* these cognitive acts are non-veridical.

Perhaps the easiest way to illustrate the novelty of this conception is by contrasting it with the older conception, as this was most clearly articulated by Thomas Aquinas. According to Aquinas, cognition takes place through the cognitive subject's taking on the form of its proper object. In the case of sensation, the senses take on the sensible forms of sensible objects; in the case of intellectual cognition, the understanding takes on the intelligible forms of intelligible objects. The rest of the cognitive processes, such as memory, recollection, recognition, imagination, dreaming, judging, reasoning, and so on, are taking place through storing, retrieving, comparing, recombining, sorting, further processing, and so on of the information thus received. Now, the significance of the idea that cognition takes place through receiving the form of its proper object by the corresponding cognitive power of the subject is that it establishes a *logically necessary* connection between the power and its proper object: hence Aquinas' repeated assertion of the Aristotelian claim that a cognitive power is never deceived about its proper object.

To be sure, this does not render these cognitive powers either absolutely infallible or omniscient. Clearly, they do not – indeed, cannot – cognize everything (sight cannot cognize sounds, and a finite intellect cannot comprehend everything that is intelligible to an infinite intellect, as this is precisely what distinguishes the two from each other), and they are fallible with regard to objects other than their proper object and in their operations other than simple reception or apprehension. However, in their simple receptive operations they are infallible, in the sense that if they receive the form of their proper objects at all then the receptive act unmistakably latches on to those objects – because a receptive act is identified precisely as the form of that sort of object informing the subject about that sort of object. Thus, on this conception, it would involve a contradiction to say that I could have the exact same concept of, say, donkeys in the virtual reality of *The Matrix*, as I have now in this actual, real world, in which my concept informs my mind about the real, intelligible essence of real donkeys. Clearly, whatever cognitive acts a brain-in-a-vat (for short: a BIV) can have cannot be using the same concept, given that, by definition, no cognitive act of a BIV can have the same object (i.e. the real essence of real donkeys).

By contrast, on Buridan's conception, the concept of donkeys is just a quality of the mind that indifferently represents donkeys. As a result, what connects this act of cognition to donkeys is the merely naturally necessary, but logically contingent, causal connection that can easily be overridden by divine power, and not the logically necessary relation of *formal identity*. The important point to note here, though, is that the difference between Buridan's and Aquinas' positions is not in the strength they attribute to divine power, but rather in the strength of the connection between a cognitive act and its proper object; and this difference comes from the difference in how they would take the same cognitive act to be identifiable and re-identifiable in different possible scenarios. In the end, this is what accounts for the apparent possibility of a solipsistic demon-scenario based on the conception of Buridan, which is not a possibility for Aquinas. Indeed, as a matter of fact, it should not be regarded as a possibility.

This can be seen from the following argument. Assume that there is a solipsistic subject S – namely, a BIV – that has exactly the same phenomenal mental contents as we do. According to the nominalist conception, this is possible. However, by hypothesis, S can form the exact same thoughts that we can. So, S can form the judgement 'S is a BIV'. Since according to our hypothesis, S is a BIV, this judgement is true. However, since S is a BIV, S has no veridical concepts; so, none of the judgements that S forms can be true. Thus, the judgement formed by S that S is a BIV is not true. Therefore, we have arrived at the contradiction that the judgement formed by S is both true and not true; so, the assumption (from which it followed) cannot be true. But the assumption was that it is possible that S is a BIV. However, since this assumption leads to a contradiction, it is not possible. Therefore, the conception that entails its possibility is false, and the alternative conception, which excludes its possibility, is true.

To be sure, there are several further considerations that one has to deal with concerning this argument (see Klima and Hall 2011 and Klima 2017), yet I believe that it puts into a sharper focus just exactly where the nominalist semantics and ontology espoused by Buridan, combined with his corresponding nominalist cognitive psychology and epistemology, branched off from an earlier conception, pointing the way to the problems of early modern epistemology and the corresponding problems in modern philosophies of mind.

Notes

1 Cf. Oderberg (2003: 9):
Buridan was a committed Nominalist. He was, in other words, on the
philosophically wrong side of the major metaphysical controversy of the Middle
Ages. Like Ockham, he believed there were no universals: strictly speaking, no
colours, only coloured things; no virtue, only virtuous people; no circularity,
only individual circles. The rest was all just hot air (*flatus vocis*). The Nominalists
ended up poisoning the well of sound philosophy with scepticism, relativism,
agnosticism and even atheism. Fortunately, Realism was not sent to rout and has
many exponents in present-day analytic philosophy.

2 Note that Buridan's opposition to what I call 'realism' here also covers various
forms of what might, more properly, be called 'moderate realism': that is, the
view endorsing individualized essences, inherent in, yet distinct from, particular
substances. For a more detailed account of this issue in connection with Buridan,
see Klima (1999). For my general take on the issue of the medieval problem of
universals, contrasting 'realism' and 'nominalism' in terms of semantics rather than
ontology, see Klima (2001b). For an excellent discussion of Buridan's rejection of
universal entities, see King (2001).

3 Cf. (*SD* 2.5.2: 127):
We call the predication of a term of another 'essential' if neither of these two
terms adds some extrinsic connotation to the things they supposit for. Therefore,
although the term 'animal' signifies more [things] than the term 'man', nevertheless,
it does not appellate over and above the signification of the term 'man' anything
having to do with man, i.e. as something pertaining to man [*per modum adiacentis
homini* – cf. *SD*: 4.5]. A predication is called 'non-essential', or 'denominative', if one
term of it adds some extrinsic connotation over the signification of the other, as for
example 'white' supposits for a man and appellates whiteness as pertaining to him.

4 For more detail on medieval supposition theory, as part of the medieval semantic
theories of the properties of terms, see Read (2015).

5 The distinction drawn in these terms was introduced by Ockham. Buridan usually
makes the distinction in terms of talking about absolute versus appellative terms.
But, in Buridan's interpretation, appellation is just oblique reference to a term's
connotation; so, in the context of supposition theory, his distinction amounts to the
same as Ockham's. Cf. (*SD*: xlix–l, 291–4, 880, 890). Furthermore, Buridan is also
talking about connotative terms, contrasting them with absolute terms in the same
way as Ockham did. Cf. (*SD*: 147, 639, 642, 644–6, 729, 735).

6 To be more precise, I should add that the proposition should not provide an
ampliative context for its terms; but such considerations are irrelevant here (cf.
Klima 2001a).

7   Or, at least, they should involve an 'unsaturated' syncategorematic concept with at least two 'arguments' – as, for example, does the concept to which the preposition 'of' is subordinated, in the construction 'a donkey of a man'. It is an open question whether we should assume such syncategorematic concepts, as this English construction suggests, or whether we should rather assume simple connotative concepts corresponding to the genitive form of a noun, as the Latin construction 'asinus hominis' would suggest. For some more discussion of this issue, see Klima (1993: esp. 47–50; 2009: 103–107).

8   For a detailed discussion of Buridan's account of exactly *how* this is possible, see Klima (2004).

9   Hans Thijssen (1987) has plausibly argued that, since some of the theses and arguments that Buridan opposes here do not reflect Nicholas of Autrecourt's doctrine as we know it, Buridan may well have had other opponents in mind. However, since the theses and arguments in question are at least not incompatible with Autrecourt's known doctrines, it is still possible that Buridan had in mind some further works, or even just oral presentations of Autrecourt's that we simply do not know of from other sources. Indeed, this latter alternative has the advantage of explaining the phenomena *per pauciora*.

10   For Buridan's detailed discussion, see (*SD*: 8.4.4–8.5.4).

References

Buridan, J. (1964 [1518]), *Quaestiones in Aristotelis Metaphysicam: Kommentar zur Aristotelischen Metaphysik*, Frankfurt am Main: Minerva. (Translations in this chapter are from Klima 2007.)

Buridan, J. (2001), *Summulae de Dialectica*, trans. and intro. G. Klima, New Haven: Yale University Press. (Cited in this chapter as '*SD*'.)

Buridan, J. (2015), *Quaestiones super octo libros Physicorum Aristotelis (secundum ultimam lecturam)* Libri I–II, ed. M. Streijger and P. J. J. M. Bakker, Leiden: Brill. (Cited in this chapter as '*QPhys*'.)

Buridan, J. (forthcoming, 2018), *Quaestiones in Aristotelis De Anima*, I, 6., ed. P. Hartman, G. Klima, P. Sobol, and J. Zupko, Dordrecht: Springer. (Cited in this chapter as '*QDA*'.)

King, P. (2001), 'John Buridan's Solution to the Problem of Universals', in H. Thijssen and J. Zupko (eds), *The Metaphysics and Natural Philosophy of John Buridan*, Leiden: Brill.

Klima, G. (1993), 'The Changing Role of *Entia Rationis* in Medieval Philosophy: A Comparative Study with a Reconstruction', *Synthese*, 96: 25–59.

Klima, G. (1999), 'Buridan's Logic and the Ontology of Modes', in S. Ebbesen and R. L. Friedman (eds), *Medieval Analyses in Language and Cognition*, Copenhagen: The Royal Danish Academy of Sciences and Letters.

Klima, G. (2001a), 'Existence and Reference in Medieval Logic', in A. Hieke and E. Morscher (eds), *New Essays in Free Logic*, Dordrecht: Kluwer Academic.

Klima, G. (2001b), 'The Medieval Problem of Universals', in E. N. Zalta (ed.), *The Stanford Encyclopedia of Philosophy* (Winter 2001 Edition): http://plato.stanford.edu/ archives/win2001/entries/universals-medieval/.

Klima, G. (2004), 'John Buridan on the Acquisition of Simple Substantial Concepts', in R.L. Friedmann and S. Ebbesen (eds), *John Buridan and Beyond: Topics in the Language Sciences 1300–1700*, Copenhagen: The Royal Danish Academy of Sciences and Letters.

Klima, G. (ed.) (2007), *Medieval Philosophy: Essential Readings with Commentary*, Malden, MA: Wiley Blackwell.

Klima, G. (2009), *John Buridan*, New York: Oxford University Press.

Klima, G. (2012), 'Ontological Reduction by Logical Analysis and the Primitive Vocabulary of Mentalese', *American Catholic Philosophical Quarterly*, 86: 303–414.

Klima, G. (2013), 'Being, Unity, and Identity in the Fregean and Aristotelian Traditions', in E. Feser (ed.) *Aristotle on Method and Metaphysics*, Basingstoke: Palgrave Macmillan.

Klima, G. (2017), 'Thought-Transplants, Demons, and Modalities', in J. Pelletier and M. Roques (eds), *The Language of Thought in Late Medieval Philosophy*, Springer: Cham, Switzerland, pp. 369–82.

Klima, G. and Hall, A. (eds) (2011), *The Demonic Temptations of Medieval Nominalism*, Proceedings of the Society for Medieval Logic and Metaphysics, Vol. 9, Newcastle upon Tyne: Cambridge Scholars Publishing.

Lagerlund, H. (ed.) (2010), *Rethinking the History of Skepticism: The Missing Medieval Background*, Brill: Leiden.

Oderberg, D. S. (2003), 'Review of John Buridan: *Summulae de Dialectica*', *Times Literary Supplement*, June 6.

Read, S. (2015), 'Medieval Theories: Properties of Terms', in E. N. Zalta (ed.), *The Stanford Encyclopedia of Philosophy* (Spring 2015 Edition): http://plato.stanford.edu/ archives/spr2015/entries/medieval-terms/.

Thijssen, H. (1987), 'John Buridan and Nicholas of Autrecourt on Causality and Induction', *Traditio*, 43: 237–55.

10

Knowledge and *Scientia* in Two *Posterior Analytics* Commentaries after Buridan: Albert of Saxony and John Mair

Henrik Lagerlund

1. Introduction

In the late thirteenth and early fourteenth centuries, medieval philosophy became gradually more concerned with the justification of scientific knowledge and as a result epistemological scepticism became part of philosophy and sceptical arguments were used in various discussions of knowledge.[1] This is evident from Henry of Ghent's treatment of what we can know, and the source of certain knowledge, in the beginning of the *Summa*, art 1, q. 1–2. The first question is 'Whether humans can know anything', and it begins with references to Cicero's *Academica* and Augustine's *Contra academicos*, which was unusual for the time, but set the stage for the fourteenth century and also made Cicero's work on academic scepticism more known. Henry is the first to show a renewed interest in ancient scepticism. Another example of this new interest in epistemology and scepticism can be found in commentaries of Aristotle's *Posterior Analytics* from the same time. After Henry, these commentaries changed somewhat, and questions such as the ones that he had posed started to be included in the beginning of the commentaries.

An early example of this is Walter Burley's commentary on the *Posterior Analytics* from abound 1300. Burley sets out to answer these kinds of questions in the beginning of his commentary. He begins by pointing out two sceptical positions about knowledge – namely, the Academic, which, according to Burley, claims that we cannot know anything, and the Platonic, which claims that we cannot know anything new. The question Burley (2000: 64) then poses to himself is that of whether it is possible to acquire new knowledge.[2] A positive answer would obviously reject both sceptical positions.

The Academic position is outlined with explicit references to Cicero's *Academica*, and Plato's position is presented with references to *Meno*. An interesting thing to note is Burley's attitude regarding the general unreliability of sense perception. Even though he seems to adhere to Aristotle's view that each sense's grasp of its proper sensible is reliable, there is still the possibility of doubt due to sensory illusion, like the stick appearing bent when seen in water or honey appearing bitter when placed on a sick man's tongue – that is, well-known sceptical arguments from Cicero (Burley 2000: 71). The way in which Burley takes on the questions about knowledge is very different from the earlier treatments of this by Aristotle and Thomas Aquinas. For Burley, scepticism is part of the discussion of knowledge, and sceptical arguments have to be addressed, which was never so for Aristotle and Aquinas. This will be further emphasized in later commentaries, such as those by John Buridan, Albert of Saxony, and John Mair.

Burley's response to the question at hand is, however, very cautious, and it is greatly indebted to Augustine and Henry of Ghent and their respective defences of divine illumination. Burley begins by stating that it is a contingent fact that humans have knowledge and that it is certainly not impossible for humans to acquire new knowledge by natural means, as Cicero, for example, has argued. Burley writes:

> It is contingent that humans know something new, because something is in this way true that previously was not true, for example, that you in this way know this to be true, 'that I am sitting'. For, hence, nothing is known unless it is true, and this is a new truth, it must then be the case that something new is known. (69)

This common-sense rejection of scepticism only establishes that we can indeed know something new. A more elaborate discussion is needed to establish that the process of acquiring the first principles of science is justified. Burley turns to this in the fourth question of his commentary, by asking whether humans can know demonstratively with their natural capacities and without the aid of a supernatural agent.

On this question, Burley is considerably less clear, however, and he outlines Aristotle's, Henry of Ghent's, and what he calls the theologian's positions on knowledge-acquisition. Aristotle, of course, argues that humans can know first principles with only their natural capacities. Burley presents, more or less, Aquinas' position as Aristotle's. The theological position is the most extreme, and argues that all knowledge is dependent on divine illumination. Henry of Ghent's view is presented as a middle position. However, on this view, knowledge of first principles is still dependent to a certain extent on divine illumination. It seems that Burley ultimately follows Henry.

The discussion of cognition and the worry of scepticism, visible in Burley's commentary, is representative of commentaries on the *Posterior Analytics* after Henry of Ghent and John Duns Scotus in the fourteenth century. Earlier in the thirteenth century, these kinds of commentary looked quite different. Something had dramatically changed, and by the mid-fourteenth century the kinds of questions visible in Burley's commentary had become standard and even more radical, since one of the main issues for both John Buridan and Albert of Saxony is that of whether it is possible for us to know anything.

In this chapter, I will look at how the notions of *scientia* and knowledge in a more general sense were treated in two *Posterior Analytics* commentaries after Buridan. The first one is Albert of Saxony's (1320–90) commentary. He is a close contemporary of Buridan and was greatly influenced by him. His commentary was written after Buridan's and exerted a great influence on the following tradition. It was also printed in Venice in 1497, as well as several times after that in the sixteenth century. The second commentary is by John Mair (1467–1550). It is not, strictly speaking, a commentary on Aristotle's work, but the part on demonstration or, roughly, *Posterior Analytics*, from Mair's commentary, published in 1505, on Peter of Spain's *Summaries of Logic*.[3] Both of these thinkers belong to the same tradition developed by Buridan, and their views of knowledge are similar for the same reason. They belong to what came to be known as *via moderna*.

2. Albert of Saxony on knowledge and scepticism

An interesting feature of Albert of Saxony's commentary is that he seems to think that epistemological scepticism is a central problem for Aristotelian science. Just like Burley, Albert starts his treatment of knowledge with references to the Academics and Plato. He understands their positions in the same way as Burley did, and divides his discussion into two parts, dealing first with the question of whether it is possible for us to know anything and, next, of whether it is possible to know anything new (1497: I, q. 3, fol. 3vb).[4]

Surprisingly, he begins by presenting a negative answer to the first question. It is not possible for us to know anything, because *scientia* is supposed to be evident without any threat of the opposite being the case, and a notion (*notitia*) or concept, which is the object of knowledge, cannot be evident in this way. The evidentness of a notion is derived from either the senses or the intellect, and neither can ground evidentness, Albert thinks. He shows this by giving ten different arguments. One of these is the following:

> Is it possible for us to know something? It is argued that this is not the case, because we cannot have evidentness about something without fear of the opposite. Hence, it is not possible for us to know something. The consequence holds, from this that *scientia* is evident without fear of the opposite, therefore, it is not possible for us to know something. And the antecedent is proved, because we cannot have a notion of something, that is neither evident by the sense nor the intellect, hence, in no way. The consequence holds. And the antecedent is proved, first, since this is not the case through the senses. For as much as it is apparent to me by the senses that fire is hot, nevertheless, it is at hand that I do not have the judgment or the evidentness about this, that is, that fire is hot, without fear for [the opposite]. For it is possible that some power, for instance a divine, produced in my senses a species representing hot, and that cold has been destroyed and hot introduced [in its stead], and that the action of the cold [thing] is suspended in the senses. If this is posited, then it is apparent to me that fire is hot, but in truth it is cold. By positing this case, which is possible, by the first cause acting freely, it follows that as much as I see the fire, I have to be in doubt about the hotness of the fire, namely, that the coldness has been corrupted and a hotness introduced. Hence, a species of hotness is represented in the senses, and the action of a cold [thing] is suspended in the senses by the first cause. Therefore, as much as something appears to me to be hot, I have nevertheless to be in doubt about [this]. Hence, by the sense of touch, it is not possible to hold a certain judgment about something. (Ibid.)

He continues, a little further down, on the same question:

> By the same reasoning, it is proved that it is not evident to me that you are a human, but that it is [in fact] rational for me to doubt [this and] that you are [perhaps] a donkey or a goat. For, a visible species, which is in my [sense] organ, represents to me a visible nature of you as a human, however, it is possible that in my soul a transformation of your donkey nature has been performed by the power of the first cause. And since this first cause can do whatever it wants, it follows that as much as it is apparent to me that you are a human, I have to doubt [this]. (Ibid.)

This kind of sceptical argument had begun to be well known at the time when Albert writes, but it seems to me that the version of the argument that he uses is not quite the ordinary one. It was thought, according to the dogma of God's omnipotence or his absolute power generally, that God could prevent any secondary cause from achieving its effect and furthermore could bring about with a first cause any effect that a secondary cause could bring about. Albert, however, appeals to the contingency or freedom of the first cause, and argues that the world as we know it could have been radically different from how it now appears to us, so that fires could be cold, which usually was thought to be naturally impossible. I think that this pushes the argument to a level that was not usually acknowledged at the time, and makes his version more in line with Descartes' evil demon argument.[5] Our very constitution as human beings could have been different, and hence we cannot even trust our purely conceptual truths either – that is, necessary truths like '3+2=5' and the principle of non-contradiction.[6]

After having presented this general argument, Albert systematically goes through all the senses and shows that none of them can be the basis for evidentness and, hence, certain knowledge. The intellect cannot be a source of knowledge either, since whatever is in the intellect is derived from the senses. In the same way, Albert argues that we cannot have certain knowledge of the first principles of science. As Aristotle had argued, knowledge of the first principles is based on sense perception, and, according to Albert, we cannot have certain knowledge based on the senses.

Albert, like Buridan before him was, however, not a sceptic. He ultimately wants to save scientific knowledge, and argues that the answers to both of the two initial questions stated above should be 'yes'. We can indeed know something and we can also attain new knowledge. Albert (1497: I, q. 3, fol. 4ra.) therefore begins his answers to the questions at hand by saying that we can know something with evidentness because of (i) scientific demonstrations, (ii) a natural inclination in us humans towards knowledge and truth, and (iii) we know that we exist – that is, I know that I exist (*'ego scio me esse'*).[7] (i) and (iii) are known with certainty, according to Albert, and the reason for this is that (i) is based on the theory of syllogisms and (iii) is due to our first-person privileged perspective. Neither of these can be doubted, hence they are able to ground evidentness. It is important to stress that (ii) is not meant to be some supernatural ability that is similar to the doctrine of divine illumination, but is rather an innate ability (capacity or power) to assent to truth. Buridan (2001: 399) suggests a similar capacity, and he writes the following about it in his commentary on Peter of Spain's *Summaries of Logic* – that is, what is known in Latin as *Summulae de dialectica*: 'For just as the vegetative soul is naturally inclined to generate something similar to itself but does not generate unless the appropriate dispositions preexist, so the intellect is naturally inclined to assent to the universal truth of the indemonstrable principles but does not give its assent until it is disposed to do so by the consideration of many singulars.' It is through the process of induction that we come to realize the truth of the first, undemonstrated, principles.

With the assertion that having knowledge is possible, Albert goes on to explain what he means by *scientia* and demonstration. First of all, he points out that what is known is always a mental proposition or a complex notion (i.e. knowledge is assent of a certain kind to a true mental proposition),[8] and such a mental proposition is *scientia* – that is certain knowledge – if (1) it is firmly assented to, (2) is true, and (3) has necessarily evidentness.[9] *Scientia* differs from an opinion, in that an opinion is not firmly assented to. Belief also differs from *scientia*, but not because of the firmness of the assent to such mental propositions. Instead, they are simply not evident. Albert says that if you assent to the articles of faith because of the evidentness grounded by the sacred scriptures you deserve less credit than if you assent to the proposition: 'Fire is hot' based on the evidence of the senses. The sacred scriptures are much weaker authorities than the senses, he asserts.

Before stating his conclusions and overall answers to the question whether we can know something, Albert presents three suppositions. First, he says that it seems natural to claim that our intellects are naturally inclined to understand an object, provided that the object is sufficiently presented to it. It is natural in the same way as it is natural for a heavy object to fall downward when dropped, he thinks. Second, there are some truths to which the intellect cannot but firmly assent – for example, the principle of non-contradiction ('*de quolibet esse vel non esse, et de nullo simul*'). It is impossible in this life or in this nature not to accept it.[10] Third, there are some inferences that we cannot but accept as well. For example, the first figure syllogisms (Barbara, Celarent, Darii, and Ferio) and also, so-called, expository syllogisms (i.e. syllogisms in the third figure with singular terms as subject terms).[11]

Having said this, Albert states his main conclusion, which is that we can know something, that is, it is possible for us to firmly assent with evidentness to true mental propositions. It is possible because, according to the first supposition, our intellects can be sufficiently presented with an object and come to understand it in such a way that it grounds evidentness. Second, we can know first principles like the law of non-contradiction. Third, we can know evidently some inferences (see the examples given above). The things that we can know simply are, hence, truths of logic or reason, and this does not include anything based on sense experience.

Before starting to answer all the arguments formulated in the beginning against the possibility of knowledge, he ends by clarifying his conception of 'evidentness'. He does so by formulating a distinction between two kinds of evidentness. This distinction is generally credited to Buridan, but Albert's terminology is somewhat different and more in line with the terminology that became the more established one later on, which is usually credited to John Mirecourt and Peter of Ailly writing a few decades after Albert (see Lagerlund 2017). Albert distinguishes between what he calls maximal (*summa*) and natural (*naturalis*) evidentness. Maximal evidentness is the highest form of evidentness and it is impossible not to assent to something with such a high degree of evidentness. The examples he gives are again the principle of non-contradiction as well as the sentence 'I exist' (*Ego sum*). Natural evidentness is a lower degree of evidentness, which is the evidentness mental propositions have that cannot be falsified by other means than reverting to a supernatural agent. It is in this way that 'Fire is hot' is evident.

All knowledge based on our senses can be doubted if we take into account arguments using a supernatural being and causes. No such knowledge, in other words, have maximal evidentness. It is possible, however, to have knowledge based on our senses, but only to a lower degree. For natural science this is enough, Albert claims in Buridan's footsteps. If something is presented to the intellect sufficiently by the senses, the intellect will by its nature understand and form a true mental proposition that it can also firmly assent to with evidentness. By sufficiently presenting something he, of course, means that the intellect has time to ponder the information presented and also check it against other observations and principles. In this way, we can know that the stick is not bent in the water because we can determine by, for example, touch that it is not. Albert would agree with Buridan that natural evidentness is enough for natural philosophy and so the Aristotelian project in the *Posterior Analytics* can be saved. However, the consequence of this is that knowledge comes in degrees and natural philosophical knowledge is fallible.[12]

3. John Mair on knowledge

John Mair's discussion of *scientia* and other kinds of knowledge can be found in his commentary on Peter of Spain's *Summaries of Logic*. After having dealt with syllogisms and what belongs to Aristotle's *Prior Analytics*, he turns to demonstrations and the *Posterior Analytics*. His discussion of this topic covers about thirty folio pages of the 1505 printed edition, and it is an extremely interesting work. It certainly needs a more careful study than I can provide here, particularly since it has never been studied before, as far as I can tell.[13] It contains many interesting points of view, as well as references to, for example, both Ockham and Buridan in the earlier *via moderna* tradition. As we shall see, the overall project and final view is very similar to Buridan's and Albert's, but there are some differences as well.

As Burley does, Mair begins his commentary with references to the two positions mentioned above that are sceptical towards knowledge (i.e. they deny that we can attain knowledge): namely, the positions of the Academics and Plato. Mair, like Albert, argues against both of these and hold that we can indeed attain knowledge. Here, I will give an outline of some of the main aspects of his treatment of knowledge.

The structure of Mair's work is close to Buridan's own commentary on Peter of Spain,[14] but the content, at least of this part on demonstrations, is quite different. His discussion is divided into nine chapters (although it lists eleven, two are missing), and some of the chapters are divided into several *dubitationes*, which are problems or questions (see the Appendix below, for an overview of the book). The first chapter divides into ten. The first of these are about what a sensitive cognition (*notitia*) is, and how is it distinguished from an intellective cognition; the second is about the reliability of sense cognition; several others are also about further details of cognition. The second chapter is divided into nine questions. The first one asks what it is to know and what a known proposition is like, and the fifth, for example, is about the object of *scientia*. In the third chapter, there are three questions. The third of those is about *per se nota* propositions. These are just examples of some of the ones at which I will look more closely here.

The first chapter begins with an account of cognition. He first introduces sensitive and intellective notions (or cognitions: '*notitiae*' in Latin). The reason for separating notions into sensitive and intellective goes back to a distinction between two souls – a sensitive and an intellective – in humans. A cognition is called sensitive because it inheres in the sensitive soul, and vice versa. Mair here follows Ockham, as well as Adam Wodeham's presentation of the distinction between these two cognitions (see Lagerlund 2004). Mair (1505) next notes that we never have an intellective cognition without a sensitive, unless it is about God (or perhaps if it is caused by God). The rest of the second question is about sensory deception and their explanations. Most of these explanations have to do with the reflection and movements of sensory species. A species is something extended and physical that interacts causally with the sense organs. The first conclusion of the second question states that species representing white and black are not in different parts of the medium, but are throughout the medium, and hence are not contrary, since, if they were, they would not be able to occupy the same part of the medium at the same time (139a). Species are only representations of qualities, not the qualities themselves. He states six more propositions or conclusions about species and how they interact with the medium between the sensed object and the organ to cause sensations of external things. This process is essential to the acquisition of any knowledge.

Similarly to both Buridan and Albert, Mair defends a species theory of cognition. As he explains, the species is a representation of a sensible quality. It becomes the content of the sensitive notions, which in turn becomes the content, or object, of intellective cognitions. It is essential for knowledge that this process can happen in such a way that it does not in any way distort the quality sensed. This is the reason why Mair spends several questions of the first chapter on discussing sensory cognition.[15] At the very end of the book, he returns to the question of cognition.[16]

In the fourth question, he introduces a distinction between apprehensive and adhesive or judicative cognitions. An apprehensive cognition (*notitia*) is a simple or complex cognition of the intellect, and an adhesive cognition is a cognition by which we assent to or dissent from a complex cognition (139b). Like the tradition before him, following in the footsteps of Ockham and Buridan, Mair works with a lot of terminology. An apprehensive cognition can be divided into an intuitive and abstractive cognition (*notitiae*). This terminology derives from Scotus as well as Ockham, but Mair uses it in the same way as Peter of Ailly does (Lagerlund 2004; 2009): namely, an intuitive cognition is of a present object, while an abstractive cognition is of a non-present object.

The fifth question asks if knowledge is propositional (Mair 1505: 140a). Mair notes that this is the case, but he does not mean primarily that knowledge is in Greek or Latin. He means that it is in mental language. Knowledge expressed by a spoken or written Latin sentence is merely the expression of a metal proposition. Mental language is not in any spoken language: that is, it is not the mental version of Latin or anything similar. This is a theoretical postulate about the linguistic structure of thought. Any knowledge that I have is at the level of mental language: hence, a true mental proposition can, given certain other conditions, be knowledge. As Mair puts it, knowledge is a complex apprehension, which is what a mental preposition is for him. This is also in line with the general Buridanian tradition, although Mair's terminology is not quite the same. Buridan and Albert hold a similar view, which they all derive from Ockham.

In the sixth question, Mair distinguishes belief (*fides*) from opinion (140b). A belief is a firm assent to a true mental preposition. It is the firmness of the assent as well as truth that distinguishes belief from opinion. An opinion is simply assent to a mental sentence. As we saw above, this is also Albert's view. What distinguishes belief from an expression of knowledge is 'evidentness' (*evidentia*). What Mair says here goes together with a distinctions between six kinds of cognitions (*notitiae*) that were formulated earlier, in question four of chapter 1 – namely, that a cognition or complex notion can be (i) wisdom (*sapientia*), (ii) intellection (*intellectio*), (iii) *scientia*, (iv) belief (*fides*), (v) opinion (*opinio*), and (vi) error (*errore*). The first three are knowledge, he goes on to claim. Wisdom is the combination of (ii) and (iii) – that is, the set of propositions that make up our system of knowledge. With intellection, he seems to mean the premises of a demonstration – that is, the, indemonstrable, first premises – and, with *scientia*, he has in mind the conclusions of demonstrations.

Knowledge is analysed by Mair in very much the same way as it was by Buridan and Albert, but in more detail. For him knowledge is a true mental proposition that is assented to firmly with evidentness. In the first question to chapter 2, he lists four ways we can be said to have knowledge:

> 1. The first way in which we know something is through propositions that are either contingent but obviously true, or necessary and assented to firmly with evidentness. Mair says that, according to this mode of knowledge, 'I know the temple of the mount to be beautiful.'
> 2. The second way in which we know something is through necessary propositions firmly assented to with evidentness. The assent to such propositions derives either from demonstrations or not, and this is the way, Aristotle claims, in which we know the first principles better than we know the conclusions.
> 3. The third way in which we know something by firm assent with evidentness to a necessary propositions is by demonstration, and this holds for both *quia* and *propter quid* demonstrations – that is, demonstrations that look to the causes (facts) or the account of something (reasons).
> 4. The fourth way in which we know a necessary proposition by firm assent with evidentness is by a demonstration as a piece of discursive reasoning – that is, the way that the premises cause the conclusions. (143b)

The definition of knowledge is the same in all four of those ways of knowing, but the objects of knowledge are different. In the first way, the object of knowledge is not related to *scientia* and demonstration, as Aristotle understood these, and it involves knowledge of contingent thing as well as knowledge of the world through sensation. The examples that Mair gives of contingent propositions that we know are familiar ones – namely, such propositions as 'I am (exist)', 'I am alive', 'my head exists', 'my soul exists', and 'my intellect exists'. Mair also refers to Augustine's treatment of this kind of knowledge in *The City of God* where he uses 'I am mistaken' (*ego fallor*) (144vb). Augustine uses the proposition 'I am mistaken, hence, I exist' (*si fallor, sum*) in the same way as Descartes uses 'I think, therefore, I am' (*cogito, ergo, sum*). These are, however, all contingent propositions, but they are also first-person reports or knowledge of my own state of mind or body. Mair uses other examples of contingent propositions that we know through our senses. One such example is given above in (1) – namely, that 'the temple of the mount is beautiful'. Another example is 'the ball is round' (*pilare est rotundum*). This is something that I know, based on my senses: I see or feel the ball to be round. In relation to this example, Mair brings up a general problem for knowledge based on our senses – namely, that God can deceive us. Mair writes: 'God can annihilate the ball without me knowing it while conserving in my soul the assent that I have. In this way, I have assented to [the proposition] that 'the ball is round' and in this I am mistaken' (ibid.). The example used by Mair is a version of an example used by Ockham that became well known in the discussions of intuitive cognition after him. According to Ockham, I can have an intuitive cognition of a star, which God subsequently annihilates while preserving my cognition of the star.[17] Even though Ockham refused to accept this, most later philosophers took this as an example of how an intuitive cognition can, through God's absolute power, be about something that does not exist. It became a standard example of how God can deceive us.[18] Mair has changed the example, but it aims to prove the same thing – namely, that a judgement based on sensation can always be doubted. Hence, knowledge based on the senses, as used in (1)'s way, might be mistaken, given divine deception.

Mair notes in his presentation of (2) that Aristotle thought that knowledge of this kind would be knowledge of the first principles. Mair does not have such a rigid account of what can serve as a first principle. He is much more in line with Buridan, who thinks any kind of true proposition can serve as a premise in a demonstration. Hence, knowledge in the sense of (1) can function as first principles as well. Mair thinks that knowledge of the third kind, (3), is about the conclusions of a demonstration – that is, strictly speaking about *scientia*. The fourth, (4), is about the way in which we know logical truths. Mair sets (3) and (4) apart from (1) and (2), in the sense that the propositions involved in these are *per se nota* – that is, self-evident propositions. However, he thinks that the propositions that are the object of our knowledge in the sense of (2) are *per se*, but not *per se nota*. A proposition like 'all humans are animals' is *per se*, but not *per se nota*. Mair (1505: 149va) explains in chapter 3, question 3, that 'a proposition is called *per se* because there is a natural relationship of one extreme to the other extreme'. The account that he gives of a *per se* proposition is the same as Aristotle's:

I.   A proposition is *per se* in the first sense if and only if the definition of the subject term includes the predicate term. An example of this is 'humans are animals'.
II. A proposition is *per se* in the second sense if and only if the definition of the predicate term includes the subject term. An example of this is 'humans are able to laugh'.

These are not examples of *per se nota* (or self-evident) propositions. Mair defines a *per se nota* proposition in the following way in chapter 3: 'A proposition is said to be *per se nota* on account of its evidentness by the agreement in relation of the terms in that they both are part affirmative and part negative, like in "everything is or is not", or in a disjunction by two contradictory parts' (143rb). As is clear from this quote, *per se nota* propositions are logical truths, like the principle of non-contradiction and the principle of bivalence. This also explains why (4) above is knowledge of *per se nota* propositions. It is less clear why Mair thinks that (3) involves *per se nota* propositions. It seems likely that he has in mind the demonstrative process itself (knowledge in the fourth sense), which is of course based on valid syllogisms, and obviously the knowledge that we have of the process of demonstration is *per se nota*, since the syllogisms are self-evident. The content of a conclusion might not be *per se nota*, since it might be knowledge in the sense of (1) or (2) and the conclusion will only be as strong as the premises.

In his discussion of *per se nota* propositions, Mair discusses another example as well – namely, 'heat is heating' (*calor est calefactium*). He says that it is not *per se nota*, since it can be doubted. As we saw above, Albert of Saxony uses heat as an example of something that God can make us doubt, and hence it is not necessary that heat heats. The same seems to holds for *per se* propositions like (I) and (II) – that is, they can be doubted. The reason for this is that they are not truths of reason or they are not *per se nota*. (1)–(2) and (3)–(4) seem to distinguish knowledge into two categories – namely, knowledge of propositions or truths that are not self-evident and those that are self-evident. It might come as a surprise to some that the kind of first-person reports that he gives as examples of (1) above are not self-evident. The reason he gives for this is that they are contingent, and a contingent proposition cannot be *per se nota*. The distinction between these two groups is based largely on whether knowledge statements can be doubted. To explain this, Mair draws the same distinction as did Albert of Saxony and John Buridan before him – namely, between different kinds of evidentness. Mair acknowledges that the terminology has varied slightly in the tradition before him, and he makes an effort to streamline it. He distinguished between, on the one hand, absolute, maximal (*summa*), or simple (*simpliciter*) evidentness and, on the other hand, natural, conditional, or *secundum quid* evidentness (143va). He writes the following about absolute evidentness: 'Absolute evidentness is true assent without the fear of some natural cause by which it would not be possible for the intellect to assent and to be deceived in its assent without fear of the opinion being rejected' (143vb). Hence, absolute evidentness is assent made without any fear that what we assent to is doubtful in any way and can be rejected. The only propositions that cannot be doubted are *per se nota*, and they all fall under logic or are logical principles of the kind already mentioned. Another similar account that Mair gives is the following: '[Absolute] evidentness [is such that] in accordance with it, assent is given without the fear of some natural cause by which it would not be possible for the intellect to assent [and which would not] stand up to the general influence of God [and by which someone is] deceived in that assent' (ibid.). Absolute evidentness is such that we do not have to fear a natural cause, which can be manipulated by God. However, all natural causes can be manipulated by God through his absolute power, since God (as the first cause) can do everything that can be done by a secondary cause. Hence, the point here is simply that absolute evidentness does not apply to natural causes, and this explains consequently why such evidentness only applies to truths of reason or necessary truths (i.e. *per se nota* propositions).

Natural evidentness is, for Mair, exactly what it was for the tradition before him – namely, the evidentness that can be achieved when you put God aside. Mair says that 'something is said to be a natural cause by the exclusion of faith' (ibid.). If we exclude the possibility of divine deception, then we can have knowledge based on the senses, as well as knowledge of contingent propositions. Everything that he has said in the beginning of his treatment of the *Posterior Analytics* about species and cognition here comes back into play: that is, once the possibility of divine deception is excluded and a full global scepticism is overcome, Mair thinks we can also overcome a more local scepticism. Hence, the distinction between (1)–(2) and (3)–(4) can also be drawn by the distinction between natural and absolute evidentness. Anything based on the senses is still knowledge, but it is knowledge by a lower or weaker kind of evidentness.

In question 10 of chapter 1, Mair addresses the issue of whether it is contingent that we can know something new (fol. 142). He says that this question derives from Plato, who argues that we cannot know anything new. Plato, however, does not think we cannot have knowledge, which is the position that the medieval tradition attributed to the Academics. Plato's view, as Mair presents it, is that God created the human soul with all knowledge in it from the beginning, hence that any knowledge-acquisition becomes a matter of recollection, and as a result we cannot gain any new knowledge. Mair obviously does not accept this view. He is an Aristotelian empiricist, which means that he thinks that knowledge can be gained through sense experience and induction, but he also thinks that *scientia*, and ultimately science, is demonstrative.

4. Conclusions

The *via moderna* commentaries on Aristotle's *Posterior Analytics* present a unified tradition on knowledge and demonstration. They all follow the view set out by Buridan in his commentary from the mid-fourteenth century. It is a surprisingly unified tradition. There are a few common features, as follows, to which I would like to draw the reader's attention:

1. External world scepticism, in the form of possible divine deception, is a precondition for the entire tradition.
2. Knowledge is fallible.
3. Knowledge about logic and logical principles is more certain than knowledge based on sense experience.
4. There are levels of evidentness (*evidentia*).
5. Knowledge is of true mental propositions.
6. *Scientia* is one kind of knowledge – namely, the conclusions of demonstrations.
7. Any piece of knowledge can serve as a first principle.
8. General first principles that are based on sense experience are acquired through induction.
9. Knowledge based on sense experience can always be doubted, given the possibility of divine deception.

10. There is no veridical access to things in the world – only to sensory representations.
11. Science is demonstrative.

All of these, taken together, define a distinctive approach to knowledge that runs for at least 200 years from Buridan to Mair, but there are striking parallels with this tradition and the position of Thomas Hobbes.

Appendix: Table of contents for the part on the *Posterior Analytics*, of Mair's commentary on Peter of Spain's *Summaries of Logic*, fols 137vb–160rb

Caput 1 (fols 138ra–143rb):

Dubitatio 1: Circa litteram dubitatur quid est noticia sensitiva et quo ab intellectiva discrimen habent.
Dubitatio 2: Secundo dubitatur de veritate huius omnis doctrina et disciplina et cetera.
Dubitatio 3: Tertio dubitatur de veritate huis propositionis cognitis maiore et minore simul tempore cognoscitur conclusio.
Dubitatio 4: Quarto dubitatur de idemptitate vel discrimine noticie apprehensive et abhesive et de membris noticie abhesive.
Dubitatio 5: Quinto an noticia adhesiva vel scientia sit propositio.
Dubitatio 6: Sexto quomodo generatur fides.
Dubitatio 7: Septimo de precognitionibus et an bruta syllogizant.
Dubitatio 8: Octo an assensus unius propositionis sit dissensus suis contrii vel contradictorii.
Dubitatio 9: Nono dubitatur an propositio mentalis componatur ex pluribus partialibus noticiis.
Dubitatio 10: Decimo dubitatur an contingit aliquid sciri de novo.

Caput 2 (fols 143rb–148rb):

Dubitatio 1: Primo dubitatur quod est scire et quod propositio scibilis.
Dubitatio 2: Secundo quom se habent actus et habitus, et an sit una qualitas et quom sese intendunt.
Dubitatio 3: Tertio posito quod quis habuerit sciam actualem universalis conclusionis ex qua generabitur habitus antecedenti actuali noticia

praemissarum, sed solo habitur remanente ille habitus posset producer sciam actualem.

Dubitatio 4: Quarto dubitatur an si unus rusticus audiat unum argumentum at assentiat maiori et minori et bonitati conclusione.

Dubitatio 5: Quinto de obiecto scientie.

Dubitatio 6: Sexto an ad hoc quod aliquid cognoscatur omnes eius causas dinoscere opereprecium sit.

Dubitatio 7: Septimo an premisse sine cause conclusionis.

Dubitatio 8: Octavo an non ens potest sciri.

Dubitatio 9: Nono an plus oportet assentire premissis quam conclusioni.

Caput 3 (fols 148rb–150rb):

Dubitatio 1: Primo an sit possibile circulariter demonstrare.

Dubitatio 2: Secundo de modis perfeitatis.

Dubitatio 3: Tertio quid est proposition per se nota.

Caput 4 (fol. 150rb–150rb):

Quartum caput est clarum. Aliqua sunt ibi exempla philosophis dicit ut triangulo per se inest linea et punctum linee.

Caput 5 (fols 150rb–150va):

Quintum caput est clarum pro ita linee dicuntur paralelle que equaliter semper distant, et si sic impossibiliter concurrunt, non concurrere est passio linearum paralellarum.

Caput 6 (fol. 150va–150va):

Sextum caput est clarum et parvis logicalibus deserviens que huic materie sunt sophistice quare transeo.

Caput 7 (fols 150va–152vb):

Dubitatio 1: Circa istud caput dubitatur primo an demonstratio est ex necessariis.

Dubitatio 2: Secundo an contingit demonstrationem de genere in genus.

Dubitatio 3: Tertio quom intelligitur illa propositio medium debet esse eiusdem generis cum extremis.

Dubitatio 4: Quarto quot modis scientia dicitur subalternata alteri scie.

Dubitatio 5: Quinto an scientia propter quod et quia est specie differant.

Dubitatio 6: Sexto utrum sit possibile demonstrationem augeri per diversa media.

Caput 8 (fol. 152vb–152vb):

Circa octavum caput point philosophis discrimen inter dignitatem, suppositionem, et petitionem.

Caput 11 (fols 152vb–155ra):

Dubitatio 1: Primo an eadem conclusio possit in diversis scientiis que non concludunt propter quid et quia est demonstrari et an erit eadem scientia.
Dubitatio 2: Secundo an scientie mathematice sunt certissime.
Dubitatio 3: Tertio quid requiritur et sufficit ad unitatem scientie collective capto terio.
Dubitatio 4: Quarto an sit dabilis unus assensus simplex quo assentitur toti demonstrationi et conclusioni propter premissas.

Dibitatur an scientia et opinion sese compatiantur in eodem subiecto (fols 155ra–157vb).
Dubitatur circa litteram Aristotelis in quam dicit (fols 157vb–159vb).
Finaliter hoc dubitatur an noticia intuitiva potest sine obiecti presentia esse (fols 159vb–160ra).

Notes

1 See Lagerlund (2010), particularly the introduction, for an account of the history of scepticism in the Middle Ages, and Bolyard (2017).
2 In the Middle Ages, these were the two sceptical positions known from Ancient times – although they did not, of course, call either of these views 'sceptical'. They had no knowledge of Pyrrhonism or scepticism. There is a late-thirteenth-century translation of Sextus' *Outlines of Pyrrhonism*, but, as far as is known, it had little or no influence. See Floridi (2002) for further discussion.
3 It is an odd feature of commentaries on Peter of Spain's *Summaries of Logic* that they include a section on demonstrations at all, since the original, and incredibly influential, work (see Peter of Spain 2015; Lagerlund 2017) does not actually contain a chapter on demonstrations. It was Buridan in his commentary who added this chapter. He made it up himself and then commented on it. After his commentary, all other commentaries included a section on demonstrations.

4 See also Fitzgerald (2002: 345).

5 For a general description of the notion of divine deception, see Lagerlund (2017).

6 See Lagerlund (2010). Albert would, I think, adhere to the view that Descartes made famous, that is, the view that God creates the necessary truths. This view had also been defended before him by Thomas Bradwardine. See Normore (1991).

7 See also Fitzgerald (2002: 347).

8 After William Ockham, it became standard in the tradition, to which both Buridan and Albert belong, to explain thinking in terms of language. They accept a kind of language-of-thought hypothesis. For them, all thought is in a language, a mental language, that underlies our spoken and written languages. The content of this language is derived from sensation. Our interaction with objects in the world gives rise to notions (concepts) that are about or represent these objects. These basic notions can then be combined to form complex notions, and propositions with a subject-predicate structure. It is such a proposition, or a complex notion, that is the object of knowledge. See Normore (1985) and Panaccio (2004) for more on this.

9 Like Buridan before him, and Autrecourt before him, he is not using 'evidentia' in sense of the police or a lawyer in court would use 'evidence', but instead it has to do with the nature of the assent. Hence, it is a mental act or an attitude towards a mental sentence. Assent to a true mental sentence is, for Albert, a belief; but knowledge has the additional property of being assented to with an additional evidentness. It comes close to a notion of justification – that is, in the sense that, in addition to believing this mental sentence, I have some added reason for believing it, hence the evidentness that comes on top of the assent. The problem with divine deception is that nothing seems to rise to the level of necessary evidentness – everything can be doubted. See Zupko (1993) for a discussion of 'evidentness' in Buridan; see Grellard (2010) for the same in Autrecourt.

10 Note here that he says 'about its nature' (*de eius natura*), since he assumes that God could have created us with a different nature, and then that what is a necessary truth now might not have been a necessary truth. See Normore (1991) for a discussion of others with this view in the Middle Ages as well as about Descartes' more famous view.

11 An expository syllogism has a singular term as subject term, like the following:
Socrates is a human
<u>Socrates is an animal</u>
Some human is an animal
   These kinds of syllogism were considered evident.

12 In his continued discussion of this question, Albert goes on to question our mathematical and necessary truths as well. He also, unlike Buridan and many others in the same tradition, introduces innate notions to account for the necessity of conceptual truths. The reason why he doubts whether such truths have maximal evidentness is that they ultimately need to be based on notions derived from the

senses, and anything based on the senses would only achieve a level of natural evidentness. See Lagerlund (2010) for more on this.

13 In Broadie (1989: ch. 6), the approach to evident cognition (or notions) in the circle of philosophers and students around John Mair is studied. Mair was an incredibly influential thinker and teacher in Paris at the beginning of the sixteenth century. The view defended by this group of thinkers is very close to the view of Buridan and Albert. There are some very interesting developments added, however, by Antonio Coronel, a later thinker in this group. He edited and published a few of Mair's main works. In his commentary on the *Posterior Analytics*, Coronel attacks the notion of natural evidentness ascribed to *scientia*. He argues that, even putting aside divine deception, such knowledge is defeatable. It amounts to a sceptical attack on Buridan's and Mair's notion of knowledge. See Karger (2010) for a treatment of Coronel's arguments.

14 See Lagerlund (2017) for a general account of the relation between Mair and Buridan, as well as the place of Mair in sixteenth-century logic. Mair's views of cognition has been studied in Broadie (1989) and Lagerlund (2009).

15 See Lagerlund (2009) for more on Mair's view of cognition.

16 There is an interesting discussion of the role of God in cognition, and of whether we can have intuitive cognitions without an object (Mair 1505: 159vb).

17 See Panaccio and Piché (2010) for a discussion of this and Ockham's original solution.

18 See Grellard (2010) on the debate between Bernard of Arezzo and Nicholas of Autrecourt.

References

Albert of Saxony (1497), *Quaestiones subtilissime super libros Posteriorum Analyticorum Aristotelis*, Venice.

Bolyard, C. (2017), 'Medieval Skepticism', in E. N. Zalta (ed.), *The Stanford Encyclopedia of Philosophy* (Spring 2017 Edition): https://plato.stanford.edu/archives/spr2017/entries/skepticism-medieval/.

Broadie, A. (1989), *Notion and Object: Aspects of Late Medieval Epistemology*, Oxford: Clarendon Press.

Buridan, J. (2001), *Summulae de dialectica*, trans. and intro. G. Klima, New Haven: Yale University Press.

Burley, W. (2000), *Quaestiones super librum Posteriorum*, ed. M. C. Sommers, Toronto: Pontifical Institute of Medieval Studies.

Fitzgerald, M. (2002), *Albert of Saxony's Twenty-Five Disputed Questions of Logic*, Leiden: Brill.

Floridi, L. (2002), *Sextus Empiricus: The Transmission and Recovery of Pyrrhonism*, New York: Oxford University Press.

Grellard, C. (2010), 'Nicholas of Autrecourt's Skepticism: The Ambivalence of Medieval Epistemology', in H. Lagerlund (ed.), *Rethinking the History of Skepticism: The Missing Medieval Background*, Leiden: Brill, 119–44.

Karger, E. (2010), 'A Buridanian Response to a 14th Century Skeptical Argument and Its Rebuttal by a New Argument in the Early 16th Century', in H. Lagerlund (ed.), *Rethinking the History of Skepticism: The Missing Medieval Background*, Leiden: Brill.

Lagerlund, H. (2004), 'John Buridan and the Problem of Dualism in Early Fourteenth Century Philosophy', *Journal of the History of Philosophy* 42: 369-388.

Lagerlund, H. (2009), 'John Mair on Concepts', in J. Biard (ed.) *Le langage mental du Moyen Âge à l'âge classique*, Lovain: Peeters.

Lagerlund, H. (2010), 'Skeptical Issues in *Posterior Analytics* Commentaries', in H. Lagerlund (ed.), *Rethinking the History of Skepticism: The Missing Medieval Background*, Leiden: Brill.

Lagerlund, H. (2017), 'Trends in Logic and Logical Theory', in H. Lagerlund and B. Hill (eds), *The Routledge Companion to Sixteenth Century Philosophy*, New York: Routledge.

Mair, John (1505), *Ioannis Maioris in Petri Hyspani Summulas commentaria*, Paris.

Normore, C. (1985), 'Buridan's Ontology', in J. Bogen and J. E. McGuire (eds), *How Things Are: Studies in Predication and the History of Philosophy and Science*, Dordrecht: D. Reidel.

Normore, C. (1991), 'Descartes's Possibilities', in G. J. D. Moyal (ed.), *René Descartes: Critical Assessments*, Vol. II, London: Routledge.

Panaccio, C. (2004), *Ockham on Concepts*, Aldershot: Ashgate.

Panaccio, C. and Piché, D. (2010), 'Ockham's Reliabilism and the Intuition of Non-Existents', in H. Lagerlund (ed.), *Rethinking the History of Skepticism: The Missing Medieval Background*, Leiden: Brill, 97–118.

Peter of Spain (2014), *Summaries of Logic: Text, Translation, Introduction, and Notes*, B. P. Copenhaver, with C. G. Normore and T. Parsons, Oxford: Oxford University Press.

Zupko, J. (1993), 'Buridan and Skepticism', *Journal of the History of Philosophy*, 31: 191–221.

11

Sixteenth-Century Virtue Epistemology

Benjamin Hill

1. Introduction

Conventional thinking about epistemology in the sixteenth century is pretty bleak – there really wasn't much, or at least much that was serious, significant, and now worth remembering it says. The humanists did 'rediscover' the ancient sceptical texts of Cicero and Sextus Empiricus (it is conceded), but they never made good philosophical use of them. But at best their rediscovery set the stage for the great 'epistemological turn' that Descartes (and the other usual suspects) made in the seventeenth century. As far as sixteenth-century philosophy itself is concerned, it contributed little to nothing to our philosophical understanding of human knowledge and to the development of the field of epistemology. Such is the conventional scholarly wisdom.[1]

I hesitate to begin this chapter with a critique of the seventeenth century's great epistemic turn, but I feel that I must. I hesitate because it has already been so ably attacked as a grand historical narrative by others.[2] And yet there is still something about that grand narrative, something underlying its plausibility that persists and, I think, that bears directly and negatively on how we continue to approach sixteenth-century epistemology. That something needs to be addressed at the outset of this chapter because I would like to change the narrative we tell about sixteenth-century epistemology. This something is centred on the notion of what constitutes epistemology, properly speaking. We don't think that sixteenth-century philosophers did anything interesting or important, epistemologically speaking, because we now have a narrow conception of what epistemology does, or should, consist in. Let me start, then, with raising that question: what does, what must, epistemology's subject-matter consist in to be epistemology, in a proper sense? The short answer, of course, is 'knowledge'.

But in what does knowledge, properly speaking, consist? That is another way to formulate the questions with which I would like to start.

To be sure, thinking in the sixteenth century about knowledge was nothing like contemporary epistemology with its Gettier-style counterexamples, its external world scepticism, its disagreements about justification and foundations, and its defeaters for every possible source of knowledge claims. Sixteenth-century philosophers were not interested in conceptually analyzing the term 'knowledge' or debating the necessary and sufficient conditions for knowledge-possession.[3] Nor did they ever seem to think in terms of 'justified true belief'.[4] Truth be told, they even seemed relatively uninterested in enshrining truth as the epistemic value.[5] Finally, they did not create an industry out of devising clever counterexamples to all sorts of knowledge claims, counterexamples meant to function as epistemic *sophismata* for them and their students to endlessly fret over.[6] Simply put, sixteenth-century philosophers simply did not share the same concerns, the same conceptual framework for, or the same approach to knowledge that contemporary epistemologists have. That much is clear.

I suggest that this perception is central to what underlies the negative judgement suffused through the conventional wisdom about sixteenth-century epistemology and the many traditional caricatures of late medieval philosophy as containing nothing but theological metaphysics.[7] From the character of sixteenth-century epistemology, described above, it does not follow that sixteenth-century philosophers were unconcerned with knowledge, that they did not reflect philosophically on it, or that they failed to advance epistemology. At the most, it means only that they did not approach or think about knowledge in the same way that we now do. It might certainly be, in other words, that epistemology in the sixteenth century was a different sort of endeavour than it is now, or even than epistemology was in the seventeenth century.[8] Epistemology, properly called, in other words, very well might contain more than just reflections on justified true belief and clever defeaters of knowledge claims. In this chapter, I want to suggest that this is the case, that epistemology then was quite different from epistemology now, but that it still was, nevertheless, epistemology.

What I wish to offer in this chapter is the idea of using virtue epistemology as an interesting lens for approaching and conceptualizing sixteenth-century thinking about knowledge. I seek to tentatively sketch virtue epistemology as the alternative form of epistemology that animated sixteenth-century thinking about knowledge, in other words. Virtue epistemology has emerged in recent years as an alternative conceptual framework for doing epistemology. Proponents emphasize its utility in resolving the contemporary puzzles about justified true belief, defeaters, and so forth that plague conventional epistemology. That's fine, but it is not what I would like to suggest is relevant for approaching sixteenth-century epistemology. Instead, what I would like to present as relevant about virtue epistemology is its alternative conceptual structure and the ways that its alternative structure changes the questions that epistemologists must face and the means for resolving these. What follows is admittedly impressionistic and not fully developed and justified. I think it prima facie suggestive, interesting to consider, and hope that this will stimulate more detailed investigations into sixteenth-century epistemology and, ultimately, a substantial reconsideration of the material and its status within our historical narrative(s). But this brief chapter will not attempt any such reconsideration, and is intended to be nothing more than a single step towards such a reconsideration.

I will begin with an explanation of virtue epistemology and what it looks like as an interpretive lens. Then I will consider three examples of sixteenth-century phenomena that become interestingly epistemological, or interestingly altered, when viewed through that lens. The first example will be *regressus* theory, which has been thought to be related to scientific methodology rather than knowledge as such. The second example will be various educational reforms. As a topic, educational reforms have been thought to be of little philosophical interest, or of interest only to philosophers of education. I hope to suggest otherwise in this chapter. The third example will be the rediscovery of philosophical scepticism, which, as mentioned above, has been thought to be significant only insofar as it contributed to the rise and development of epistemology as a subject of concern in the seventeenth century. In all three cases, it will be suggested that the philosophers writing on those topics were directly struggling with significant, genuinely epistemological, problems or were exploring something interesting about the natures and connections of various epistemic values. It will be suggested, in other words, that in all three cases they were doing epistemology, properly considered.

2. Virtue epistemology as an interpretive lens

In this chapter, I am arguing that the approach towards knowledge that sixteenth-century philosophy followed was much closer to that of contemporary virtue epistemologists than to that of conventional contemporary epistemologists. Let's begin with what is meant by 'virtue epistemology'. If I were to name a contemporary version of virtue epistemology that seems to parallel most closely the overall trends of the sixteenth-century discussions, I would name Linda Zagzebski's (1996) *Virtues of the Mind*. Perhaps it is unsurprising to see that a contemporary neo-Aristotelian (so-called) epistemology is the best parallel for epistemological thinking at the end of the (so-called) Scholastic era. That's not my reasoning here, however. As we'll see, many of the humanists and Platonists were also virtue epistemologists in Zagzebski's sense. What's really at stake regarding knowledge for all of these thinkers is the concept of intellectual flourishing. In sixteenth-century epistemology and contemporary neo-Aristotelian virtue epistemology, knowledge is approached as a form of intellectual flourishing, and it is this shared basic approach that, in each case, structures their thinking about knowledge. That is my reasoning for explaining sixteenth-century epistemology, using terms from, and parallels with, contemporary virtue epistemology.[9] There was something that they were doing that was like what virtue epistemologists are now doing, in other words. That is the central thesis of this chapter. I would like to be clear that I am not simply trying to read a contemporary trend into the historical material, but am saying instead that their historical concerns map nicely onto what we now label as 'neo-Aristotelian virtue epistemology'. That the aims and methods of epistemology were different for sixteenth-century thinkers, different even than those of contemporary virtue epistemologists, is part of the story of sixteenth-century epistemology, but not a part of the story that I am able to go into here. So, too, were the central problems of epistemology for them, as opposed to even many contemporary virtue epistemologists, and this is perhaps the most interesting and difficult feature of approaching sixteenth-century thinking about knowledge. This latter difference is more pronounced in this short chapter.

What is contemporary neo-Aristotelian virtue epistemology, then? It is a family of approaches to the study of knowledge that are related by two underlying connected commitments. The first is that epistemic agents, hence epistemic agency, is the locus of epistemic value and ought to be the focus for the philosophical study of knowledge. This is meant to contrast with conventional approaches that focus on propositional attitudes as the locus for epistemic value and as the proper focus for epistemologists. The contrast is very similar to that found in two common approaches to the philosophy of language, between a 'language as formal system' approach and a 'language as a human activity' (or 'usage') approach.[10] Conventional epistemology and formalistic philosophy of language abstract away from the distinctively human element to draw out fundamentally logical and structural features of language and knowledge, respectively. In conventional epistemology, that puts the spotlight squarely on evidentiary bases for beliefs and pushes the issues of justification and foundations to the forefront of the problem-space. This focus also magnifies the challenges that exceptions and counterexamples pose, because the relationship and principles being discussed are supposed to be necessary, formal ones.

An alternative approach that locates epistemic value in agents and agency, rather than propositional attitudes, makes the human element of the phenomena central to the project of epistemology by putting the spotlight on the practice of knowing. This pushes forward a different set of issues, such as the proper methods and best practices to follow in the pursuit of knowledge, the proper training and education of knowers, and how to deal with the limitations of knowledge and our epistemic capabilities. Thus, for thinkers who focus on knowledge as a human activity, epistemology was not automatically an autonomous subfield of philosophy abstracted away from the concerns of the world (or from other branches of philosophical study). Rather, for them, epistemology was an aspect of logic and rhetoric combined, and something that directly affected an individual's epistemic practices and agency. Such an approach to knowledge magnifies the importance of exemplars and role models for knowers, as opposed to magnifying counterexamples and defeaters. This is an important point for uncovering less obvious epistemological doctrines and discussion in the sixteenth-century texts.

The second, related, underlying commitment is the identification of epistemology as essentially directed at intellectual flourishing. The idea behind this commitment is that being 'rational' or 'intellectual' is more than just possessing true representations of the world. Much more, in fact; it also includes the possession of certain dispositions or intentions, towards the development of understanding, that orient one's self and one's intellectual agency within the world.[11] Another way to put the point I'm trying to make here is perhaps to say that knowledge is not merely a state of believing certain things but one of being a certain kind of believer and that this latter state involves subjectively adopting a certain set of attitudes beyond simply the love of the true and/or the hatred of the false. This latter state also necessarily involves recognizing additional *epistemic* values – values other than just truth (and/or justification) – and it involves a continued motivation or intention to pursue those additional values, even sometimes over and above the possession of true beliefs. Indeed, given this recognition, it is conceivable that there may even be circumstances in which these other values are pursued not only in addition to true beliefs, but even instead of true beliefs. From a neo-Aristotelian virtue epistemology viewpoint, there need not be any problem with this because the various epistemic values are sui generis and incommensurable and might not be jointly achievable. This conception of epistemology as being about intellectual flourishing, rather than 'knowledge' in the narrowest of senses, expands the field beyond the conventional foci on justified true belief and truth as the epistemic value. Indeed, the commitment points to various attitudes like the love of truth, the drive towards unified or systematized understanding, the desire for new questions or concerns, and a resistance to novelty and change as the real domain of fundamental epistemic values, and perhaps not even truth itself, which might even be conceptualized as a merely regular by-product of the right sorts of epistemic attitudes.

When knowledge is approached in this way, the pressing problems animating the field are vastly different. The focus on intellectual flourishing, for example, draws to the forefront practical problems – problems affecting the epistemic practices and methodology of thinkers embedded in the actual world – rather than counterexamples, defeaters, and fantastical scenarios affecting belief states. Counterexamples, defeaters, and fantastical scenarios sketching out possibilities are great for probing conceptual limits, and for isolating and determining such boundaries in the effort to identify necessary and sufficient conceptual conditions. This seems to have been how the possibility of a deceiving God was used prior to Descartes, for example. But they are of little use in overcoming typical limitations and real obstacles, in providing guidance, or in showing anyone how to achieve intellectual well-being. Indeed, when your conceptualization of epistemology is in terms of the habituation of virtues and their proper integration to constitute wisdom, resolving puzzles about fake barns and the number of coins in a job applicant's pocket seem to be mere distractions not worthy of extended philosophical reflection. (That might be one reason why Gettier-style problems and clever defeaters are not prominent parts of the sixteenth-century epistemological landscape.) Or, if there is any philosophical value in such minor concerns, they are best left until we have satisfactorily resolved the more important issues directly afflicting people's intellectual lives and communities. It is easy to see how such an attitude would arise in one committed to a virtue-epistemological approach to knowledge, a fortiori for a sixteenth-century philosopher whose career prospects don't require him to take such intellectual puzzles seriously and to write journal articles resolving them. There aren't any Gettier-style counterexamples in sixteenth-century epistemology, in other words, because there shouldn't be any (or so one might think) and not because those epistemologists failed to dream up any such counterexamples.

Another fundamental difference between virtue epistemology and (contemporary) conventional epistemology is the way in which the logical space for answers to those problems is more expansive than we customarily recognize.

This is due to the former's commitment to a more extensive set of values as epistemic values. Wonkishness, for example, may be valuable and useful to an intellectual community, and each member should probably possess some degree of it. No one would really want a civic leader who had so little aptitude for or interest in wonkishness as to be completely ignorant of the basic details of the policy decisions and legislative agendas that he was in charge of developing and promoting, for example. But there are other epistemic virtues that contribute to intellectual agency and their value for an intellectual community, and we might embrace someone from the lower-end range of wonkishness because she rates highly with respect to some of these other intellectual virtues. Creativity, for example, is also valuable, as are authenticity and a certain degree of intellectual conservativism, no doubt. Not all of these are truth- or knowledge-directed (authenticity and conservativism, e.g., seem not to be directed at truth or at securing the epistemic value of truth), and some, like creativity, might be valuable even when they do not produce new truths. Changing the questions being asked, which is one dimension of creativity, is often as important as deftly answering the questions traditionally asked, if not more so in many cases, for example. Wisdom is some balance of these intellectual virtues, along with others, of course, and the wisest persons are not always the ones with the most justified true beliefs or the least false beliefs. In summary, I am suggesting that being justified or believing truly might not exhaust the possible ways of reading and understanding the resolution of a sixteenth-century epistemological problem, and as historians of philosophy that is something of which we have to be willing to face when exploring epistemology in the sixteenth century.

For historians, these differences not only explain the lack of focus on many conventional issues; they also suggest that, when such topics do arise among sixteenth-century philosophers, the scope, significance, and approach towards these topics might not be the same as ours. At the very least, we have to be prepared to recognize the possibility that they are not. Moreover, it suggests that they need not be the same as ours *to be properly epistemological problems and solutions.* One way of putting it would be to say that their problem of philosophical scepticism, for example, was not the same as ours (despite shared texts and roots), and that they need not approach it or resolve it as we would, even in ways compatible or commensurable with our resolutions of scepticism, for it to be a properly philosophical and epistemological issue. As historians, we ought to consider that, or perhaps even expect it, when we are going back to consider sixteenth-century texts. (Below, I will suggest that such is indeed the case with regard to the issue of philosophical skepticism.) In short, I am arguing that their forms of, and terms for, doing epistemology were not the same as ours and that we have no real reason to require, demand, or expect them to be. With that overview of virtue epistemology and of how it changes the orientation of the field of epistemology in mind, let's take a look at some of the sixteenth-century epistemological themes and consider them through this virtue-epistemological lens.

3. *Regressus* theory

Aside from philosophical scepticism (to be discussed below), the epistemic issue from the sixteenth century that might be most familiar to readers might be the *regressus*. But most readers might not initially, or naturally, see it as a fundamentally epistemic issue. *Regressus* had a moment in the 1960s and 1970s when it was considered an important precursor to the modern scientific method. John Randall (1961) was the chief Anglophone proponent of this trend, and it was a natural fit with the concerns then current among historians and philosophers of science, concerns that focused on what constituted science and the importance of scientific (and philosophical) methodology. But these issues have largely faded from philosophical discussions, and Randall's historical work was subjected to intense criticism. As a result, *regressus* has dropped out of philosophical consideration. Let us, however, return to *regressus* theory to consider what it looks like through the lens of virtue epistemology, what it looks like as an epistemic issue rather than one about scientific method.

What was sixteenth-century *regressus* theory? It looks a lot like a kind of resolution to a bootstrapping problem that lay at the heart of the Aristotelian account of scientific demonstration. This bootstrapping problem itself is well-known, and Aristotle himself laid it out in *Posterior Analytics* II.19 as a problem with knowing the primitive principles used in scientific demonstrations.[12] In formulating a scientific demonstration, certain primitive principles must be relied upon. To be so used, they must themselves be known prior to, and better than, the scientific principles derived from them in the demonstration. As Aristotle (*Posterior Analytics* II.19, 99b22-5, 1:63) originally put it:

> [Of] knowledge of the immediates, one might puzzle both whether it is the same or not the same – whether there is understanding of each, or rather understanding of the one and some other kind of thing of the other – and also

whether the states are not present in us but come about in us, or whether they are present in us but escape notice.

Aristotle thus suggested that the primitive principles must be known in a different way than the derived principle: so far, so good. The challenge, then, was to outline a different way of knowing the principles that satisfies the condition of being better known than, and known prior to, the scientifically derived theses. Aristotle laid down a form of perception-based induction (intuitive induction) to meet this challenge: sense perception (sometimes) gives rise to memory, and repeated memories give rise to experience; and from experience a primitive principle is derived (99b35-100b5, 1:63–4). The key move was the derivation of the primitive principle from experience – and it was never properly explained by Aristotle. Sixteenth-century thinkers were sensitive to this, and, from this failure in Aristotle, *regressus* theory emerged.[13]

Although Aristotle failed to properly explain the intuitive induction, he left clues as to what he was thinking. He presented a militaristic metaphor to explain what he needed intuitive induction to accomplish:

> [A]s in a battle when a rout occurs, if one man makes a stand another does and then another, until a position of strength is reached. And the soul is such as to be capable of undergoing this. What we have just said but not said clearly, let us say again: when one of the undifferentiated things makes a stand, there is a primitive universal in the mind (for though one perceives the particular, perception is of the universal – e.g. of man but not of Callias the man – e.g. *such and such* an animal stands, until animal does), and in this a stand is made in the same way. Thus it is clear that it is necessary for us to become familiar with the primitives by induction; for perception too instils the universal in this way. (II.19 100a11–100b5; emphasis in the original)

Regressus was offered by sixteenth-century epistemologists as an account of the process of marshalling experiences to 'take a stand', and the resulting 'position of strength' regarding our knowledge of the causal principles to be relied upon in formulating a scientific demonstration. Let's consider Agostino Nifo's and Giacomo Zabarella's versions of *regressus*.

Early in the century (1506), Nifo (1552) described a fourfold process for marshalling such principles into a position of strength. He presented his conception of *regressus* as follows:

> The first [step] is awareness of the effect through sensation or observation. The second is the discovery of the cause through the effect, which occurs by

means of a demonstration of signs. The third is the *negotiatio* of that cause
by the intellect, by which our knowledge of the cause is increased so much
that it could be made the middle term in a demonstration simpliciter. The last
is knowledge of the effect through such a cause in the proper sense, so as to
achieve certainty, and in this way it could be a middle term. (f.8r; quoted in
N. Jardine 1988)

Later in the century (1578), Zabarella presented *regressus* as involving only
three stages, but the main idea behind his *regressus* was the same as Nifo's – the
negotiatio where the principles take a stand as a position of strength in the mind.
For Zabarella, the first stage involves the apprehension of a causal principle on
the basis of sense experience (*demonstratio quod*). The second involves a 'mental
examination' of the cause (Nifo's *negotiatio* or 'the business of the intellect'), and
is where we come to have knowledge, properly speaking, of the causal principle.
The third stage is the reformulation of the principle, so as to serve as a premise
in a scientific demonstration.

It is clear that, for both Nifo and Zabarella, the central move that resolves
Aristotle's puzzle is the *negotiatio* – the negotiation of or 'the intellectual business'
with the cause that generates knowledge of it, properly speaking. In neither case
is the process or method of *negotiatio* clearly specified, so there is not much
to say about it as a mental process: is the process historical, is it empirical, is it
conceptual, is it autopsical, is it philosophical? Yes, it is all of those and perhaps
more, it seems: it is whatever it needs to be. Other than that, there does not seem
to be much to say. It seems like that old 'helpful' advice for writing a book: 'Start
at the beginning, say what you need to say, and the finish with "the end".' Such
advice is appropriate, correct, and apt, but it does not really tell us how to go
about doing that. The situation with *regressus* is not quite that bad; we can say
something more about it. But the parallels with advice about writing a book are
real and appropriate.

What we can say about the process of *negotiatio*, though, is that it is a
critical and investigative one, designed to test the strength of the principle as
a causal principle. And once we are satisfied with its prospects for standing
strong as a causal principle, which results from our being satisfied with our
critical philosophical reflection on it, we complete the second stage, according
to Zabarella. So, to continue with Aristotle's martial analogy, we can see this
intellectual business as like an 'officer' shoring up the organization of the newly
forming phalanx, encouraging others members to join in, and encouraging the
soldiers joined in it to perform as they were trained.[14] There is really no single
way of binding a new phalanx together in the midst of a rout, and one does the

best that one can, using the resources and time that happen to be available until one is ready to fight (or has no choice but to fight). So too, it would seem, with this process of mental examination: how well does the principle fit with our prior instruction, the works of previous scholars and thinkers, our own previous experiences, our informed judgements and expectations about what the causal principle should be, experimentation, and so on? Any and all may be part of the process, and each contributes to the strength of the formation and our epistemic trust in it as they are collected or needed.

Suffice it to say that scholars have not been too impressed with this sixteenth-century process of *regressus* – Zabarella's or anyone else's – and, more importantly, with the prospects that *regressus* has for providing a true resolution of Aristotle's bootstrapping problem with intuitive induction. Jardine (1976: 302) calls it 'illogical' and Palmieri (2017: 337) is, more recently, not inclined to disagree, it seems. That's the right judgement, I think, when we think of *regressus* as needing to resolve a bootstrapping problem by means of cleaning up a circularity of justification or knowledge. But I don't think that same judgement holds up when *regressus* is viewed from the standpoint of virtue epistemology. If we approach the solutions offered from that perspective, we can see Nifo's and Zabarella's problem as different than a bootstrapping problem, I think, and their *regressus* solution as maybe not so bad, or at least not as bad as we thought when it was considered as a solution to a different problem.

Let's consider Aristotle's problem with primitive principles, then, from the standpoint of epistemic practice rather than justification. In practice, intellectual agents want to use the primitive principles while avoiding a number of potential pitfalls. They don't want to be gullible and credulous in accepting just any old principle, and yet they don't want to be so resistant and recalcitrant as to reject every principle that comes along in the hope that a better or stronger one will eventually appear. Think back to Aristotle's metaphor and to how that would play out when we think about epistemic practice. No commander would want a phalanx largely composed of (or even containing) wounded, enfeebled, or hysterical hoplites who are weakly organized and bound together. But no responsible commander would refuse to field a phalanx because it does not consist only of heroes like Achilles or Odysseus, bound to one another like brothers, even if we would all recognize that, other things being equal, such a unit is the absolute ideal; a fortiori, if the circumstances are such (e.g. in the midst of a rout) in which inaction is worse than uncertain or unsteady action. What real practitioners need is to exert some judgement or judiciousness in selecting the principles upon which to rely. Such judiciousness admits of a range of acceptable actual judgements. Context might allow (or require) daring to use a weaker principle than one wishes, as against other times when it allows (or requires) more reserve in deploying and using one in expectation that a better or stronger one will arise. Context might even allow (or require) that one adopt a riskier principle of pursuing greater novelty and relying on less well-known anchors, as against a more conservative one of requiring greater scrutiny in certain situations. This is what epistemic wisdom should help us to confront, in fact. The important thing in both examples is avoiding being uncritical in one's acceptance, without being hypercritical in one's rejection of candidates for a primitive causal principle – much as an officer who requires cajoling the right hoplites to form up with the phalanx cannot enlist everyone running past in the middle of the rout, and yet she cannot wait for the ideal candidates to stumble along. She has to make the best use of the hoplites she has, even while trying to constantly improve the calibre of the line.

How do we go about being critical without being hypercritical? When viewed from the perspective of virtue epistemology, this is the question at which we can see *regressus* as ultimately aiming. Zabarella's second step (and Nifo's third), the *negatiatio*, is the crucial move here because it is what emphasizes the balancing of critical acceptance and rejection. The vagueness of Zabarella's (or Nifo's) *negatiatio* might be a cause of concern for some people, but it ought not to be; it is a clue for the kind of problem for which *regressus* is a solution. It is precisely what is needed when explaining virtuous activity that admits of a wide range of applications and instantiations. It is not a specific procedure; it is a commitment to a certain type of approach indicative of the best practices of other intellectual agents – namely, be critically reflective. Like all habituations designed to produce a virtue, there is no single path to achieving it, and indeed there is no determinate procedure for acquiring it. And that's part of the whole point. Developing virtues, epistemic or moral, is not only complex; it is essentially indeterminate and different for each practitioner. That seems to be part of the nature of a virtue and wisdom itself – there is no procedure or algorithm for performing such an activity. At best, it is a habit to activate within us when the relevant situations arise. That is why nothing determinate can ultimately be said about it. Zabarella says as much as one could – namely, that we ought to carefully explore and consider the suggested principle as part of the process for its acceptance and adoption. That indeed seems to be all that Zabarella is saying here, but that is precisely what ought to be said in this situation, if he is addressing the alternative question about the best practices to inculcate and adopt.

As should be expected from a virtue epistemologist with these concerns, Zabarella walks us through an example of his *regressus* method – the principle that prime matter is a cause of generation.[15] According to Zabarella, this *negatiatio* centres around uncovering the nature of matter, which is implicated in our experience of generation, as potentiality. Whatever we might think of the actual content of his *negatiatio* is irrelevant when we consider its role as a general procedure in the process of knowing; what is important here is the requirement that an investigation into the nature of the alleged cause, such that an understanding of what it is, develops in the knower. In this case, Zabarella offers a metaphysical analysis from within the Aristotelian-Thomistic metaphysics of natural philosophy (contrasting matter with privations and being, and uncovering its unique metaphysical function). It is possible for other virtuous intellectual agents to disagree about the content of this *negatiatio* without failing to be virtuous. Perhaps they would subject the identification of the unique functions of matter to further scrutiny; that's fine, but what is not possible in this context is to simply accept prime matter as a cause of generation without any such investigation, or to reject it without finding it to be incomprehensible within the context of such an investigation. 'Ditto' for uncritically accepting any alternative account of generation, such as that offered by Paracelsus and other chymists and alchymists.

The result, then, of promotion of *regressus* theory was to instil certain kinds of intellectual virtue within natural philosophers and their practice of natural philosophy. It would be unsurprising if we were to discover that Zabarella's main target was the novelties of the chymists and natural magicians, but the very same theory presented in the same way should apply to the sceptics and many of the anti-Aristotelians of the coming seventeenth century. *Regressus* is less a scientific method or logical theory, then, when viewed in this way, than a way of encouraging and promulgating a certain view of good, that is, virtuous, intellectual practice. It is, in other words, a way of advising us to tend towards conservativism in our beliefs and towards respectful acceptance of our community's theoretic frameworks, although without being blindly subservient and uncritically closed towards these.

4. Educational reforms

The second epistemological topic that I would like to showcase from the standpoint of virtue epistemology is educational reform. The sixteenth century experienced considerable changes – upheaval even – in their educational systems, from universities all the way down to local grammar and preparatory schools. Much of the changes and the debates about them concerned the aims and methods of education, as well as the best means for educating youth. Philosophers have traditionally paid little attention to the history of these changes, and, even when they have, they have not usually considered them of epistemological significance. For the most part, this topic has been shunted off to the historians of education. Yet perhaps we are missing something here. From a virtue epistemology standpoint, Jonathan Kvanvig (1992) has argued that education and educational systems ought to be an important part of epistemological reflection, and he seems to be onto something here.[16] If we are to think of epistemology in terms of intellectual flourishing and wisdom (as opposed to just knowledge in the narrow propositional sense), sixteenth-century attempts at educational reform, and their rethinking what is needed to development wisdom in their students, would seem to be suitably epistemological, since focusing on the obstacles to wisdom and on what we can do to remove or overcome them is obviously directly related to thinking about the nature of wisdom and intellectual flourishing.

One thing that we can see, once we begin to think of sixteenth-century educational reforms in this way, is that there were a few different 'movements' throughout the century that focused on different types of wisdom. The humanists, beginning in Italy but quickly moving out to northern Europe by mid-century, tended to be focused on what we might label 'practical wisdom'. Whereas the Jesuits, emerging in the latter half of the century, could be described as focusing more on what we might call 'theoretical wisdom'. The differences might be rooted in the different social contexts that their schools tended to face, but they seem to share an interesting and underlying commonality with regard to the types of intellectual virtues to be developed, and how they could, or ought to, be developed in students. Let's begin with the humanists 'movement' of educational reform and their focus on practical wisdom.

The sixteenth-century humanist educational reform movement never really was a movement in the sense of a unified group seeking institutional social change, and it really began in the fifteenth century rather than the sixteenth. But now we would be inclined to call it a 'grassroots movement', meaning that these were a group of people who shared a coherently overlapping vision and who sought to change their local practices in accordance with that shared vision. The humanist educational reformers, then, largely focused on local pre-university institutions, and sought change by establishing themselves, or their followers, as instructors within these local classrooms to educate students as they saw fit.

The broad contours of what they advocated are fairly well-known, even among philosophers.[17] The humanists wanted education to be principally moral, and to be focused on a type of moral training rather than vocational training. To this end, they sought to change two traditional ways or methods of education. First, they sought to replace the textual tradition of philosophical commentaries with the *belles lettres*. They wanted classical poetry, history, and the philosophical epistle to replace the *quaestio*, the *commentaria*, and the *summa* as the primary texts of study and instruction. They also wanted to return students to the original texts, ideally in their original languages, and not to Latin discussions about the texts. Second, they wanted to replace Aristotle and the Church Fathers as exemplars of wisdom with classical poets and philosophers. Cicero, Ovid, and Plato were their most commonly cited exemplars and authorities, but they were expansive in the classical authors they respected and sought to introduce into their curricula. So much is well-known about the humanist reform movement, as mentioned above. What does this all mean, especially from the standpoint of virtue epistemology?

I think that the best way to approach this is to begin thinking about why they were advocating such educational reforms as these: there was something inadequate about the denominationally dominated educational systems, in their eyes; what might that have been? They were reacting, I suspect, at least in part, to the evolving needs of fifteenth- and sixteenth-century society. Government structures and civic institutions, in particular, were finding it advantageous to have their councilors, community leaders, and citizenry, more generally, be more broadly educated. Prudence and practical wisdom among the civic decision-makers within the community was becoming more and more valued, as the governmental and institutional landscapes become more entangled, more complex, and more bureaucratic. Even smaller provincial towns were caught up in the developments trending towards the rise of modern nation-states and institutionally dominated political and legal interactions. That civic need put pressure on cities to develop and expand their schools and the educational opportunities for families within their realms, and, more importantly, it put pressure on a certain kind of education. It is this environment in which the humanist reform movement needs to be philosophically examined and assessed.

This environment strongly suggests that, when the humanists spoke of education being principally moral, they weren't especially interested in personal (or public) behaviours or conditioning any especially thick conception of rightness (cf. Grafton and Jardine 1986). The Church took care of that training (such as it was), for the most part. It suggests instead that they were interested in practical wisdom, which in truth is more about a way of thinking and reasoning about values (although not disconnected from behaviours, of course) than about instilling or conditioning certain behaviours in people. Practical wisdom or prudence is the way that we discover the 'golden mean', and navigate the complex and fluid contexts in which virtuous behavior takes place. It goes without saying, I hope, that, according to moral virtue theorists, knowledge about what action or behaviour is right or wrong in a virtue-ethical framework is not humanly possible; even the range of virtuous actions is itself contextually determined. What is needed, if you think that you are looking for civic leaders who display prudent judgement, is a leader who can read a situation, identify and assess a list of possible actions, and pursue one of these that will be appropriate to that context, appropriate and ideally advantageous at the same time. Civic prudence and practical wisdom will be more or less the same thing as personal prudence and practical wisdom, albeit directed at a slight different set of concerns and exhibiting a slightly different set of character traits. Thus, within the sixteenth-century context, and with that being the ultimate goal of the educational system, educating students so as to develop practical wisdom meant providing them with the means for exhibiting the type of prudent judgement just described.

Prudent judgement in this sense requires a number of intellectual capabilities. For a start, we want to emulate and follow the wise and virtuous among our elders and predecessors. This requires, among other things, that we be able to recognize who were the wise among our elders and predecessors (and who were the rash or the unwise), what issues and circumstances they faced, what they decided on as a course of action, and finally what were the consequences of their course of action and how it was actually assessed by wise people (and even 'the judgement of history'). And what might be a better way to present and promote awareness of this kind of material than the move to *belle lettres* and the elevation of classical authors and philosophers, and the people they describe and assess, as exemplars for prudent judges? If wonkishness is an epistemic characteristic of Aristotle, the Church Fathers, and the many commentators on their works, for example, civic leaders needed only a smidgen of that, and are better produced by looking at more balanced examples of epistemically virtuous exemplars, those who could use philosophy and theology for a community's good and well-being, but who are not necessarily trying to add to philosophical or theological knowledge. It seems not only appropriate but exactly right, then, for the humanists to argue that a good way to promote the development of prudent judgement in citizens and civic leaders is the study of classical literature and philosophy, especially Cicero and the Socratic dialogues. It seems exactly right, because classical authors and figures wrestled with complex situations and acted more or less virtuously within them, as well as reflecting and commenting on these situations and actions just as, we hope, our students someday will do. Indeed, classic literature can expose agents to situations they have not encountered before, as well as helping to develop the agent's skill in reading the situation. Classical literature provides exemplars to emulate, as well as examples of unwise people to avoid emulating. It can show us what they determined the appropriate course of action to be in their situations, as well as often illuminating their deliberations and reasons. And classical literature can show us what happened to those people in those situations, as well as providing discussion and assessment (both classical and contemporary) of the character and decisions of these people. The study of all these things will help to make almost anyone more prudent and wiser. It is a big part of why much of this literature remains popular and significant today. If we conceive of the epistemic problem confronting the humanist reformers as the problem of developing practical wisdom within a commonwealth, we can see why, I suggest, they advocated these reforms, and that their ideas were not bad ones.

But we can see a bit more, too – namely, what went into the concept of wisdom in the minds of the sixteenth-century philosophers. One of the more notable features in this regard is the importance that analogical reasoning played within their conception of wisdom. To make proper use of the classical literature within sixteenth-century social situations, thinkers had to recognize what was relevant, and what was not, about the classical stories; they had to recognize the times when, and ways in which, their lives and decisions were analogous to those of classical figures. If one were to use the rage of Achilles, for example, one would need to focus less on the specifics of what Agamemnon took from Achilles (an enslaved concubine), and more on what this did to Achilles (wounded his pride). Though the former may not have been much of a danger in most sixteenth-century circles, the latter was all-too frequent and dangerous, and the first step in recognizing the applicability of Homer to one's own situation would be the ability to see not only Achilles' rage for what it was but also whatever one feels within oneself when a patron or higher power withdraws a favour. But the use of analogical reasoning by a prudent humanist judge does not end there. It continues with assessing the ways in which one's own character is like, and ways in which it is unlike, potential exemplars, the ways that the classical figures' options may or may not be available to one's own character, and finally the ways in which one's situation is likely to lead to consequences similar or dissimilar to the classical ones. Practical wisdom in the sixteenth century was quite dependent, then, on a robust form of analogical reasoning, and this dependence opens the door to finer-grained analyses of sixteenth-century practical wisdom that might determine analogical reasons and recognition of the analogical relationships between situations that are constitutive, or at least even strongly indicative, of the essence of wisdom. Furthermore, the importance of analogical thinking as an epistemic value standing alongside straightforwardly alethic thinking would be an even more interesting, fine-grained, conclusion of investigations into humanist educational reforms from a virtue-epistemological framework. I wish that I could pursue it in more detail here, but hopefully the prima facie appearance is clear enough for our purposes.

The Jesuits' educational reformers can be seen as adding a concern with 'theoretical wisdom' to the humanists' focus on practical wisdom, as mentioned above.[18] What I have in mind by 'theoretical wisdom' is different from simply knowing the truth and being able to explain it. It also involves being able to read a context in which theoretical truths are discussed or examined, being able to see lines of questioning or attacks on the truth, and being able to avoid or defuse those lines of questioning or attack in defense of the truth. It is, in other words, a set of skills related to spreading, distributing, and defending knowledge, rather than skills related to the acquisition of knowledge. This focus on the distribution of knowledge rather than just its acquisition is what differentiates theoretical wisdom from the sorts of intellectual skills usually recognized by today's practitioners of conventional epistemology. It is also why the Jesuit reform movement could be seen as utilizing non-alethic epistemic values within a broadly virtue-epistemology framework. For the Jesuits during the sixteenth century, an important part of intellectual flourishing and being intellectually virtuous, in addition to being knowledgeable and acquiring knowledge, was distributing knowledge within their communities. Their educational reforms were designed to promote the development of these intellectual skills in their students (among other things, of course). And those skills go beyond the skills directed at true belief. This is what I would like to emphasize in the next few pages. Let's begin with some aspects related to the ultimate goals of education, according to the Jesuits.

What led the Jesuits to this conception of theoretical wisdom and its importance were aspects of its development as a religious order. The Jesuits were originally conceived to be an apostolic order, which meant that they would be sent out to do missionary work. They soon established education as their primary mission, education ranging from grammar and preparatory academies through university and graduate education. There were bumps along the way in pursing this, none the least of which was a shortage of good teachers at all levels within the order. This was an important challenge for the Jesuits throughout the 1560s and 1570s, and a significant factor underlying their educational reforms that culminated in the 1599 release of the revised *Ratio studiorum*.

Theoretical wisdom, in the sense described above, requires a kind of moderate conservativism with regard to knowledge. This is very similar to the kind of moderate conservativism that we previously saw being associated with *regressus* theory. For the Jesuits, this conservativism is rooted in the aim to ultimately produce teachers rather than the researcher-teachers with which we at the university level are most familiar today. Most of the Jesuits' students, and virtually all of the lay students, were not destined to be scholars and innovators. Thus, they need not acquire innovative methods or new perspectives on ideas. They needed to know the truth, how to explain it, and how to best defend it when it was threatened. I would liken the moderate conservativism being scrutinized here to the conservativism that continues to persist to this day within secondary education and most lower-level introductory university courses: those courses are not designed to present cutting-edge research, but instead are designed to equip the students to enter into the ensuing discussions about the material, and the people instructing such students need to know about those ensuing discussions but need not themselves be contributing to those discussions or to be creators of new knowledge regarding them. For the sixteenth-century philosophers, the difference was that this conservativism extended into upper-level university and graduate education as well as lower-level introductory courses (and, truth be told, seems not all that different than the moderate conservativism that seems to operate within Zabarella's example of a *regressus*). Nevertheless, this conservativism was moderated by the need to introduce students to alternatives and to criticisms of the truth, at the very least as a means for forearming them against possible lines of hostile attack. In addition to this desideratum, moderate conservativism needed to instil in the students a robust sense of intellectual curiosity (so that they could stay abreast of, if not ahead of, new lines of attack). It also needed to instil this in them without lessening or compromising their healthy respect for, and allegiance to, the received view regarding what the truth is. The Jesuits' need for theoretical wisdom, then, required a delicate balance of desiderata that could potentially pull in opposite directions – curiosity about the new, and allegiance to the status quo.

Although there is a common perception of the Jesuits in the early modern period as reactionary and hidebound anti-scientists, this is not quite accurate, at least for the period we are considering, the late sixteenth century. The text of the *Ratio studiorum* supports a more moderated conception of their conservativism

towards knowledge, rather than that suggested by the common perception of
them as extreme reactionaries. Consider the famous strictures against deviating
from the teachings of Aristotle and Aquinas:

> He shall not depart from Aristotle in matters of importance, unless he find [*sic*]
> some doctrine contrary to the common teaching of the schools ... He shall be
> very careful in what he reads or quotes in class from commentators on Aristotle
> who are objectionable from the standpoint of faith, and he must be cautious lest
> his pupils come under their influence. For this reason he shall not give separate
> treatment to the digressions of Averroes (and this holds for others like him).
> But if he quotes something of value from his writings, he should do so without
> praising him.... He shall not attach himself or his students to any philosophical
> sect, such as the Averroists, the Alexandrists, and the like and he should not
> cloak over their errors or those of similar sects.
>
> Members of our Society shall expressly follow the teaching of St. Thomas in
> scholastic theology. They should consider him their own teacher and should
> make every effort to have their students hold him in the highest possible esteem.
> Still, they are not to consider themselves so restricted to his teaching that they
> may not depart from him in any single point.... The members of the Society
> therefore should not be more strictly bound to him than the Thomists [the
> Dominicans] themselves. (Farrell 1970: 40, 34)

Each expresses limitations and qualifications to the strictures against deviating
from the teachings of Aristotle and Aquinas. This is clearest in the case of
following Aquinas in scholastic theology. But it is also evident with regard to
Aristotle's teachings: 'in matters of importance, unless'. We need to recognize the
moderating influence of that, first of all, but that does not exhaust the reasons
for reading them as moderated strictures. Remember also the context within
which the *Ratio* appeared, and through which we must read and understand
it: the *Ratio* was a political and quasi-judicial document, which means that its
final language was arrived at via compromise, and outlines the most extreme
position of the order as a whole. It is the most extreme position because it acts as
a boundary that teachers ought not to cross, lest disciplinary measures be applied
to them. The explicit statements within the *Ratio*, then, were the expression of
the most restrictive set of values under which they were to operate. And, at
its most restrictive, Aquinas needed to be held in esteem by the students, and
teachers had to be careful in how they presented Averroes. Some restrictions,
like that against teaching Averroism, were clearly the result of larger and deeper
political battles within the Catholic Church.[19] But, even then, the permissibility
of engaging with Averroes or Alexander is explicitly granted, as a teacher deems

necessary, provided that it is handled in the right sort of way, that is, not in a way that pushes the students' allegiance towards Averroes or Alexander. This seems like a fairly permissive concession, given the context of the popularity and political and doctrinal dangers of Averroism during the Counter-Reformation Church. And that's just the formulations of the strictures. As will be emphasized below, actual practices and the enforcement of them seemed to be more tolerant and permissive of such teachings. This seems to me to be noteworthy and illuminative, regarding their conceptions of the value of critical interpretations and perspectives towards their conception of the truth. The value of critical engagement with difficult and contrary material outweighs the potential dangers of creating sympathetic followers of false ideas.

Perhaps even more illuminative than the text are the actual practices that the Jesuits allowed in the classroom and across their written works. Again, the picture that emerges here is pitched towards permitting critical interpretations and perspectives. It is well known, for example, that Francisco Suárez was fair-minded and inclusive in presenting and engaging with material contrary to Aquinas' and Aristotle's positions, or even his own published positions. He was so famous for this that he was brought to the *Collegio Romano* in part to showcase his classroom style and to assist in the development of the *Ratio*. Suárez's pedagogic approach had considerable influence while the document was being drafted and discussed. Furthermore, his extensive use of modern materials and resources in his writings also attest to his and the Jesuit commitment to open engagement with critical perspectives, and emphasizes their commitments to theoretical wisdom, in the sense presented above. Jesuit scientific practice during that late sixteenth century is yet another factor that points towards a genuine valuing of intellectual curiosity, and a willingness to explore and engage with new ideas and material running contrary to the received truth. Much of the negative reputation that the early modern Jesuits now have is rooted in the rejection and persecution of Galileo, and in General Claudio Aquaviva's 1611 crackdown on the teaching novelties (*De soliditate et uniformitate doctrinae*), which seemed to function as a ruling that fixed a more rigid and conservative interpretation onto the strictures expressed in the 1599 *Ratio* than it was previously understood to be.[20] But both of these events are later than the period and attitudes about which I am talking. They date from the 1610s and 1620s, whereas I am concerned with the 1580s–1600s. And both events mark a real turning point in the Jesuit educational reform movement, as well as in the order as a whole, scholars seem to agree. Before Aquaviva's crackdown and the Jesuits' battle with Galileo, they were much more open in their classrooms, as well as in their own thinking about and engagement with new and potentially subversive material. This, I would say, attests to the real ways that their epistemic values were moderated by their respect for engagement and teaching during this earlier period.

I would like to mention briefly another educational reform movement that might benefit from being viewed through the lens of virtue epistemology: namely, the Ramists' attempt to reform the logic curricula. The Ramists attempted to replace logic, especially formal logic, with dialectics and rhetoric, and sought a universal method for discovering and inventing new arguments.[21] It was extremely contentious and controversial. But what is really intriguing is just how violent the debates about it became. Quite literally, riots were started and people were killed, all over the structure of the logic curricula. Approaching the debates over Ramism as a disagreement about fundamental epistemic values may help to explain why they were so contentious and violent, as well as to illuminate more about the context of the debate and what was at stake in it. If it were over the kinds of epistemic values to be pursued within a university education, it would in fact have not really been about the logic curriculum but about something deeper and more fundamental to their projects as intellectuals and educators (and themselves as thinkers). It can be seen, then, as follows – as traditional Aristotelians and scholastics clinging to the value of truth for intellectual flourishing, and emphasizing the importance of learning how to assess schematized arguments for formal validity as a natural reasoning capacity, with Ramists, however, rejecting the utility of such a skill, and advocating persuasion and facility in convincing others through natural reason as the more important intellectual capacity to develop and teach. Students, especially, would be much better served by being taught such a useful skill, Ramists typically argued, since they were to be priests and preachers, citizens and civic servants, and councilors and community leaders.[22] Prima facie, the practical-versus-impractical divide between formal logic and dialectics can be seen as centred on the ultimate aims of logic and logical education, which seem to be directly about divergent epistemic values. Thus I would suggest that, prima facie, Ramism, too, might benefit from being viewed through the lens of virtue epistemology, and that reconsideration from this perspective seems intriguing. Perhaps more could be said about this at a future date.

5. Scepticism

The final epistemological topic that I would like to showcase, as seen through the lens of virtue epistemology, is philosophical scepticism. The basic story behind sixteenth-century scepticism should be familiar to everyone, thanks to the groundbreaking work of Richard Popkin. In his analysis, the significance of sixteenth-century scepticism lay in the seventeenth century – it led to the epistemic turn of Descartes and the other epistemological heroes of the seventeenth century. This happened, however, because the sixteenth-century rediscovery and revival of ancient forms of scepticism led to a *cris pyrrhonienne*. Sceptical arguments were used by sixteenth-century philosophers to attack human knowledge and reason, which, within the context of the religious debates and disagreements roiling the age, resulted in fideism becoming the only acceptable epistemological position. In other words, in rejecting human reason, they argued, we ought to embrace religious faith as the only legitimate alternative basis for belief. This acceptance of faith instead of reason as the basis for belief in turn drove sixteenth-century philosophers to a version of epistemological fallibilism. Any beliefs based on reason and typically called 'knowledge' are really uncertain and held to be merely fallible opinions, according to Popkin. So, we have two core epistemological theses within his analysis: a negative thesis about the use of sceptical arguments to establish an anti-intellectualist fideism, and a positive thesis that knowledge is eliminated and redefined or recharacterized as fallible belief or opinion.

Recently, scholarship has begun questioning Popkin's analysis, especially his negative thesis regarding the fideistic uses of sceptical arguments. Two related lines of questioning are the most common here. The first line concerns a refocus on the significance of Academic scepticism, as opposed to Popkin's focus on Pyrrhonism. Scholars are now noting a much broader and deeper commitment to Academic forms of scepticism among sixteenth-century philosophers (see Paganini and Neto 2008; Neto 2014). The difference is interpretively significant because fideism is supposed to result from the Pyrrhonian's commitment to *epoché* or the suspension of belief, a commitment that is not present in the forms of Academic scepticism recognized in the sixteenth century.[23] Sixteenth-century philosophers saw sceptics as Academics who accepted that actions are to be based on a lower form of knowledge or belief, probable belief, which is engendered by the sceptical arguments themselves. There was, those philosophers thought, no *epoché* but instead a lesser form of knowledge, or a kind of properly rational belief, that was tied to motivations and actions. Indeed, there are lots of ways of looking at Pyrrhonism, but if we look at three major aspects (the manifestation of *epoché*, a focus on evidence and criteria for truth, or a rejection of any epistemic status for the 'appearances' that guide and ground action), all are largely absent from sixteenth-century discussions of scepticism. The second line concerns the recognition that, while sixteenth-century philosophers did indeed push the vanity of human knowledge and used sceptical arguments to attack reason, they almost always did so at the very same time that they were developing or maintaining properly epistemological theses of their own. They were, in other words, pushing forms of knowledge at the very same time that they were attacking it, which seems mysteriously inconsistent if Popkin's analysis were correct. Agrippa (Compagni 2008, 2017) and Sanches were clear examples of this kind of thinking, but even Montaigne (Neto 2017) seems to fall into it. If Popkin were right, they would, in some sense, be philosophic schizophrenics. But there is no reason to think that they weren't consistent and rational; so, the critics reason, it seems more likely that Popkin's analysis is somewhat misdirected, and that something else must have been going on in sixteenth-century scepticism.

Now, here's where the virtue epistemology lens helpfully enters, I suggest. First, a virtue-epistemological reading of the sixteenth-century uses of sceptical arguments makes good sense of the absence of *epoché* and the frequent appearance of Academic forms of skepticism, at the same time that it provides an explanation for how thinkers could have consistently deployed harsh sceptical arguments against knowledge while still committing themselves to the possibility and existence of human knowledge. The key behind this aspect of the reading is to see the attacks on reason, and the appeals to the vanity of knowledge, as importantly limited. Limited – how so? Limited, by being in the service of eliminating the intellectual vices of arrogance, conceit, hubris, and surety, and fostering the intellectual virtues of humility, openness, and self-reflective questioning – though not necessarily any abandoning – of one's beliefs. Instead of reading them as thinking of sceptical arguments as acidifying, as dissolving, knowledge and reason, we can read them as thinking of it as an intellectual salve and corrective that has to be used to regulate and correct human intellectual activity rather than to subvert it.

There are a few reasons that seem to suggest and support such an alternative reading. The first is simply that it resolves the textual contradiction at the heart of the Pyrrhonian, fideistic reading: there is no inconsistency in Henry Cornelius Agrippa, for example, violently declaiming against establishment intellectuals and every knowledge-based profession in his 1530 *On the Vanity and Uncertainty of the Arts and Sciences* while at the same time advocating for, and developing, a defense of natural magic; or in Francisco Sanches devastatingly critiquing human knowledge in *That Nothing Is Known* (1581), while in the same work touting it as the first in a series of epistemological texts, and as a preface to two other books that will present a defence and positive account of human knowledge.[24] No contradiction or tension between their projects arises, because the limited use does not exclude the development of knowledge in general or the development of other forms of knowledge.

It goes farther than this, however – farther than simply resolving the textual contradictions or conflicts. This alternative reading also provides an explanation for those limitations on scepticism's uses, a relatively simple and straightforward explanation, in fact. Ancient scepticism, especially Pyrrhonism, was often conceived of as a purgative for beliefs. The sceptical arguments were vomit-inducing medicines that would rid a patient of particularly noxious, Stoic beliefs. Let's suppose that we're thinking of knowledge in terms of intellectual flourishing, and of intellectual virtues and vices, when we encounter this way of thinking about the sceptical arguments. It is no great feat and requires little genius to extend this purgative metaphor to the intellectual vices and habits and attitudes that afflict many of us. It would be easy, in other words, to see sceptical arguments as an effective and useful purgative to the noxious attitudes and habits that lead directly to the intellectual vices. By its very nature, such an extension of the purgative metaphor is limited: it applies only to the noxious attitudes and habits, not all of them, and it does not apply directly to beliefs, or at least not to all of them or to beliefs as such. Such limitations are even more obvious from within the Galenic, humoral, pathology through which any sixteenth-century thinker would have conceptualized the metaphor: just as, by ridding the body of the noxious fluids, the purgative restores the normal, that is, the proper, balance of humors and disposition, so too the sceptical arguments will restore one to a proper intellectual outlook and attitude, that is, the proper dispositions and virtues, that are necessary for and conductive to a flourishing intellectual life. For sixteenth-century philosophers and thinkers, the natural way to approach sceptical arguments would have been as being powerful, yet limited in scope – which strongly suggests that the general and long-term consequences of the uses of these sceptical arguments, as destroying evidence as such and evidence-based beliefs, and the *cris pyrrhonienne* that this might have engendered, was a seventeenth-century discovery rather than a sixteenth-century one (as Popkin's thesis suggests). All of this also fits very well with Maia Neto's (2017) new analysis of the context of Montaigne's *Apology* and its use as a kind of 'morning after' purgative to avoid the probablistic arguments in favour of Calvinism that was floating around France in the late 1570s. Even if Montaigne were applying it to a particular belief or set of beliefs in this case, it was meant to be limited in the way outlined above. But on the whole, across his entire set of essays, Montaigne's deployment of scepticism seems better understood as applying to intellectual vices and bad intellectual habits rather than even particular beliefs, to say nothing of belief as such.

There is another interesting feature of this virtue-epistemological limitation on the scope of sceptical arguments that is worth mentioning – namely, the way in which this limitation is very different from Popkin's notion of mitigated scepticism as a limited form of scepticism. Although both are kinds of limitations that are placed on scepticism, they limit it at different points and in very different ways. Popkin's notion of mitigated scepticism is supposed to avoid or bracket the negative consequences of the deployment of the sceptical arguments and, especially, the sceptical rejection of knowledge and reason. Mitigated scepticism involves a fundament change to the structures and natures of human cognition, motivation, and agency that accommodate our sceptical affliction. According to mitigated scepticism, instead of being creatures sensitive to reasons and beliefs, we are to be able to adjudicate between mere appearances, and to use mere appearances as motivation and the motive forces for initiating, guiding, and governing our actions and activities. Mere appearances, in other words, are supposed to take on all the usual cognitive functions of beliefs and knowledge, even though they not only lack all of their epistemic features, but they are considered by the agent to be absolutely bereft of any epistemological standing whatsoever. That's a hard road to travel, but it's completely unnecessary for a sceptical virtue epistemologist. With their focus on purging intellectual vices, they are limiting the scope of the sceptical arguments and not their consequences. Indeed, the purgative consequences are the whole point of the sceptical arguments in their conception, and those consequences are salutary. For a sceptical virtue epistemologist, the usual structures and nature of human cognition, motivation, and agency remain just as they always were: humans are sensitive to reasons and belief, and reasons and belief generate principles for action that motivate us to act, principles that guide and govern our actions and activities. Sceptical virtue epistemologists might rid us of some beliefs, but by and large they are aiming to change the process for acquiring and sustaining beliefs, by restructuring our processes for intellectual engagement. To put the difference simply: for the sceptical virtue epistemologist, what scepticism is supposed to change is the believer and her habits and dispositions, especially with regard to the care and sensitivity with which she approaches and handles her beliefs, whereas for the mitigated sceptic what is supposed to change is the system of beliefs and the ways that beliefs interact with the agent's cognitive processes.

A virtue-epistemological reading of sixteenth-century scepticism fits well with the recent trend within scholarship towards questioning Popkin's negative thesis. I think that paying attention to it as an interpretive lens for sixteenth-century scepticism will bolster the status of the critical work and that paying attention to the new critical historical work will bolster the status of virtue epistemology as an interpretive lens. But it is also worth noting that a focus on intellectual virtues and vices is present within even the texts that seem to Popkin to be most fideistic. For example, there is a famous passage from Montaigne's *Apology* that is presented as a statement of the fideistic conclusion:

> Scepticism 'shows us Man naked, empty, aware of his natural weakness, fit to accept outside help from on high: Man, stripped of all human learnings and so all the more able to lodge the divine with him, annihilating his intellect to make room for faith; he is no scoffer, he holds no doctrines contrary to established custom; he is humble, obedient, teachable, keen to learn – and a sworn enemy of heresy he is freed from the vain and irreligious opinions introduced by erroneous sects.'

But notice that Montaigne places at least as much emphasis on the intellectual virtues that follow from being purged by scepticism – humble, obedient, teachable, and keen to learn. The intellectual virtues are there, and are prominently placed. Conventional readings need to address and explain them (and, to my knowledge, they do not yet do this). On a virtue-epistemological reading, they are right where they should be, as the salutary consequences of taking the sceptical medicines. Virtue-epistemological readings have to explain the reference to 'annihilating the intellect', and other such fideistic leaning references, to be properly established. Although I won't go into that here, since I am only laying out an impressionistic case for adopting the reading as a working hypothesis, let me say simply that such comments and hyperbolic appeals do not seem out of place in a work that is designed to change intellectual habits and expunge vices, as opposed to a work talking about the workings of the mind and knowledge. I would argue that, as a linguistic or authorial act, in other words, comments like that are of a piece with the hyperbolic ways of talking to which we naturally subject ourselves (or our charges) when trying to motivate a change in habits and behaviours (e.g. 'get off your lazy backside and get moving, you pathetic sot; you need to get your workout in; you are going to die unless you get up and get active'). I don't think that we need to adopt a virtue-epistemological reading of these texts to recognize that they are not dispassionate descriptions of knowledge and the workings of the human mind, as contemporary philosophical epistemology is supposed to be, but rather are calls to change our ways (Agrippa) or are presentations of one's personal struggles with changing one's own attitudes and outlooks (Montaigne and Sanches). So, I don't see such statements as entailing a fideistic reading of these sceptical texts or as a hindrance towards a virtue-epistemological reading of them; but more needs to be said about them. In any case, we can say, I think, that a virtue-epistemological reading of the sixteenth-century texts fits nicely with recent trends in scholarship questioning Popkin's negative thesis.

I would like to suggest also that a virtue-epistemological reading seems to nicely incorporate Popkin's positive thesis regarding the rise of fallibilism.[25] Remember that he saw fallibilism as resulting from scepticism. A virtue-epistemological approach towards sixteenth-century scepticism also reveals that fallibilism seems to be the result of scepticism. But it differs from Popkin's analysis regarding what fallibilism is or in what it consists. Although fallibilism did not arise as part of a principled and desperate reaction to the absolute failure of knowledge and the rise of fideistic belief, it was caused by the epistemic limitations that follow from the loss of certainty within knowledge. But its difference from Popkin's fallibilism and merely probable opinions is that, within a virtue-epistemological framework, fallible knowledge can and does retain a properly epistemic status. For sixteenth-century philosophers, in other words, fallible knowledge is nevertheless knowledge in a proper sense. A virtue-epistemological framework has room for this because it has room for multiple epistemic values, epistemic values that go beyond truth, certainty, and justification. Making sense of how sixteenth-century concepts such as those of fallible knowledge, practical knowledge, and moral certainty can be properly epistemic has not worked well within Popkin's Pyrrhonian and fideistic framework. Prima facie, a virtue-epistemological one offers hope that detailed analyses and reconsiderations within its terms will shed enough light on these concepts to make sense of them, and to narrow down when (and why) they lose their epistemic status as the seventeenth century unfolds.

6. Conclusion

The message of this impressionistic chapter has been about the nature and promise of a virtue-epistemological interpretive framework for sixteenth-century epistemology, rather than a fuller defence of the thesis that sixteenth-century epistemologists thought of knowledge in virtue-epistemological terms. It is hoped that the current and ongoing projects of scholars like Robert Pasnau, Henrik Lagerlund, José R. Maia Neto, and Vittoria Perrone Compagni will provide fuller defences of this thesis. I see their research as moving in this direction, even if they are not quite presenting it in these terms. It is hoped that this chapter can draw out some important features of both the sixteenth-century epistemological material and the developing trends in scholarship in ways that are helpful and productive, and will at least indirectly contribute to future scholarship. Such are the modest and limited aspirations I have for this wide-ranging romp across sixteenth-century approaches to, and treatments of, knowledge.

Notes

1 Richard Popkin was the driving force behind the idea that the sixteenth century's contribution was the rediscovery of ancient sceptical texts, especially the texts of Sextus Empiricus. The *loco classicus* is his *The History of Scepticism* (2003). The idea of a seventeenth-century 'epistemological turn' is Rorty's (1979). But neither Popkin nor Rorty invented or established the historical narrative, which, as a historical narrative, goes back at least to the nineteenth century. Popkin, Rorty, and many others have contributed to its development and entrenchment.

2 See, for example, Hatfield (2001), Ayers (2004), and Lagerlund (2010).

3 Robert Pasnau (2016) has noted this, and is using it to reconceive what epistemology was, and could look like. See also Pasnau (2013).

4 For a recent discussion of the absence of 'justified true belief' as a central presumption among early modern philosophers, see Antognazza (2015).

5 Many medieval thinkers accepted truth as an epistemic value, and some even recognized it as a condition for knowledge. The point here is that, as a tradition, it does not seem to have fetishized truth as an epistemic value, as conventional contemporary epistemology seems to have done.

6 There is one notable exception – the possibility of a deceiving God. Some see this is a precursor to Descartes' evil demon. This counterexample can be found in writings original to the sixteenth century, but it is not entirely clear that those texts structure their discussions in quite the way that Descartes did or as contemporary talk of defeaters to knowledge-claims do. As Lagerlund emphasizes in this volume, there was a robust medieval tradition surrounding this counterexample that extended into the sixteenth century (and beyond). The claims I am making here are compatible with, and I hope extend, the ideas that Lagerlund has been uncovering for the period leading up to the sixteenth century.

7 The work of Henrik Lagerlund, among others, has done much to dispel this characterization and to focus on important themes related to epistemology that have reverberated throughout the later medieval period. I am indebted to his work, and am building on it in this chapter.

8   Although I would like to rethink seventeenth-century epistemology from this perspective.

9   With that being said, however, an important difference between contemporary virtue epistemology and sixteenth-century epistemology was that, as far as I can see, no sixteenth-century thinker seemed inclined to apply their reflections on knowledge to the problems and puzzles currently animating contemporary philosophy, unlike many contemporary virtue epistemologists. Some of Ernest Sosa's work (e.g. 2017) is a representative example of this.

10 See Stainton (1996) for more about these approaches in the philosophy of language. He identifies three perspectives on language: the system perspective, the knowledge perspective, and the use perspective. I am seeing parallels between the first and third of Stainton's perspectives.

11 A footnote is not the proper place for a substantive criticism; but this is what we have, so here goes. Greco and Turri (2017), by characterizing virtue epistemology as essentially 'normative', misrepresent what is constitutive and distinctive about it, which is that it is about epistemic practices or activities. Their characterization fails to properly distinguish virtue epistemology from traditional epistemology, which is also essentially normative (the truth and/or the justification norm), and, it seems to me, fails to capture the multivalent and intentional nature of intellectual flourishing, which I am trying to briefly articulate. Recognizing this is, I think, important when using virtue epistemology as an interpretive lens for sixteenth-century epistemology.

12 This problem, as well as *regressus* theory itself, is part of the epistemological tradition identified and discussed by Lagerlund in this volume.

13 For more about sixteenth-century *regressus* theory, and for discussion of different versions (Agostino Nifo's, Girolamo Baldunio's, Giacomo Zabarella's, and Alessandro Piccolomini's), see N. Jardine (1988) and Palmieri (2017).

14 Although, strictly speaking, in Greek phalanxes it would have been the hoplites themselves doing this among themselves and not an 'officer' specially charged with commanding them; but perhaps this detail in the analogy can be safely ignored.

15 For more on Zabarella's *regressus* and the example through which he walks us, in addition to Jardine (1976) and Palmieri (2017), see South (2005).

16 See also Baehr (2015).

17 A good collection of fifteenth-century texts that laid the groundwork for the humanist reform movement of the sixteenth century is in Kallendorf (2002). This includes Aeneas Piccolomini's very influential and important *Of the Education of Boys* (1450).

18 It should be recognized that these two categories of 'movements' are not mutually exclusive and contradictory. The Jesuits found room within their thinking for many of the ideas and approaches advocated by the humanist educational reformers.

Furthermore, they never did, and never meant to, exclude practical wisdom as one of the aims of their educational system. Nor did the Jesuits believe that they weren't educating civic leaders and citizens, and they shouldn't have believed that. They knew that they were educating lay students, as well as future members of the order. It is best to recognize the Jesuits as adding a further dimension and desideratum to the humanist educational ideal, that of producing good Jesuits, which means producing future teachers and scholars of the arts as well as of theology.

19   The reference to the Lateran Council in this context makes this clear. For more about Averroism in the sixteenth century, see Richardson (2017).

20   Aquaviva was superior general of the Jesuit order from 1581 to 1615. For discussion of his prohibition and its effects on Jesuit science, see Feingold (2003: 1–46).

21   For more about Ramism, see Knuuttila (2017). It was, by and large, an extension of trends and themes present in humanist critics of scholastic logic, especially Vives and Valla. For more about this humanist background, see L. Jardine (1988).

22   Knuuttila (2017: 255) recounts such practical concerns as being the reasons cited for requiring the Ramism to be taught in Swedish universities and schools.

23   Sixteenth- (and seventeenth-)century conceptions of Academic scepticism were largely based on Cicero, and tended to recognize Philo of Larissa's more epistemologized version rather than Aenesidemus' version. The current scholarly consensus is that a more epistemologized reading of Carneades and Philo of Larissa is a misreading, and that both probably held a version rejecting all knowledge, including probable and fallible knowledge, like Aenesidemus. Such a point is, of course, irrelevant when discussing the sixteenth-century reception of Academic scepticism.

24   Sanches never give us any indication that he inclines towards a fideistic resolution of the sceptical doubts generated in *That Nothing Is Known*. His positive epistemological works were *Inquiry into Things* and an unnamed work on philosophical method. We don't have either work, unfortunately. It is not clear whether the works were lost or were never written in the first place, but neither option detracts from the fact that acquiescing to religious faith and abandoning human reason was never Sanches' intent.

25   This is an epistemological theme that, in this volume, Lagerlund has also identified, and that he suggests antedates Popkin's *cris pyrrhonienne*. The form of fallibilism that I am finding here fits better with Lagerlund's than with Popkin's.

References

Antognazza, M. R. (2015), 'The Benefit to Philosophy of the Study of its History', *British Journal for the History of Philosophy*, 23: 165–72.

Aristotle (1984), *The Complete Works of Aristotle*, ed. J. Barnes, Princeton: Princeton University Press. (All citations of Aristotle are from this source.)

Ayers, M. (2004), 'Popkin's Revised Scepticism', *British Journal for the History of Philosophy*, 12: 319–32.

Baehr, J. (ed.) (2015), *Intellectual Virtues and Education: Essays in Applied Virtue Epistemology*, New York: Routledge.

Compagni, V. P. (2008), 'Tutius ignorare quam scire: Agrippa and Scepticism', in G. Paganini and J. R. M. Neto (eds), *Renaissance Scepticisms*, Dordrecht: Springer.

Compagni, V. P. (2017), 'Heinrich Cornelius Agrippa von Nettesheim', in E. N. Zalta (ed.), *The Stanford Encyclopedia of Philosophy* (Spring 2017 Edition): https://plato. stanford.edu/entries/agrippa-nettesheim/.

Farrell, A. (trans.) (1970), *The Jesuit Ratio studiorum of 1599*, Washington, DC: Conference of Major Superiors of Jesuits.

Feingold, M. (2003), 'Jesuit: Savants', in M. Feingold (ed.), *Jesuit Science and the Republic of Letters*, Cambridge: MIT Press.

Floyd, J. and Shieh, S. (eds) (2001), *Future Pasts: The Analytic Tradition in Twentieth Century Philosophy*, New York: Oxford University Press.

Grafton, A. and Jardine, L. (1986), *From Humanism to the Humanities: Education and the Liberal Arts in Fifteenth- and Sixteenth-Century Europe*, Cambridge, MA: Harvard University Press.

Greco, J. and Turri, J. (2017), 'Virtue Epistemology', in E. N. Zalta (ed.), *The Stanford Encyclopedia of Philosophy* (Spring 2017 Edition): https://plato.stanford.edu/entries/ epistemology-virtue/.

Hatfield, G. (2001), 'Epistemology and Science in the Image of Modern Philosophy: Rorty on Descartes and Locke', in J. Floyd and S. Shieh (eds), *Future Pasts: The Analytic Tradition in Twentieth Century Philosophy*, New York: Oxford University Press.

Hill, B. and Lagerlund, H. (eds) (2017), *The Routledge Companion to Sixteenth-Century Philosophy*, New York: Routledge.

Jardine, N. (1976), 'Galileo's Road to Truth and the Demonstrative Regress', *Studies in History and Philosophy of Science*, 7: 277–318.

Jardine, N. (1988), 'Epistemology of the Sciences', in C. B. Schmitt and Q. Skinner (eds), *The Cambridge History of Renaissance Philosophy*, Cambridge: Cambridge University Press.

Jardine, L. (1988), 'Logic and Language: Humanist Logics', in C. B. Schmitt and Q. Skinner (eds), *The Cambridge History of Renaissance Philosophy*, Cambridge: Cambridge University Press.

Kallendorf, C. W. (ed. and trans.) (2002). *Humanist Educational Treatises*, Cambridge, MA: Harvard University Press.

Knuuttila, S. (2017), 'Logic, Rhetoric, and Method: Rejections of Aristotle and the Ramist Affair(s)', in B. Hill and H. Lagerlund (eds), *The Routledge Companion to Sixteenth-Century Philosophy*, New York: Routledge.

Kvanvig, J. L. (1992) *The Intellectual Virtues and the Life of the Mind*, Savage, MD: Rowman & Littlefield.

Lagerlund, H. (ed.) (2010), *Rethinking the History of Skepticism: The Missing Medieval Background*, Leiden: Brill.

Neto, J. R. M. (2014), *Academic Skepticism in Seventeenth-Century France: The Charronian Legacy 1601–1662*, Dordrecht: Springer.

Neto, J. R. M. (2017), 'Scepticism', in B. Hill and H. Lagerlund (eds), *The Routledge Companion to Sixteenth-Century Philosophy*, New York: Routledge.

Nifo, A. (1552), *Expositio super octo Aristotelis libros De physico auditu*, Venice.

Paganini, G. and Neto, J. R. M. (eds) (2008), *Renaissance Scepticisms*, Dordrecht: Springer.

Palmieri, P. (2017), 'On *Scientia* and *Regressus*', in B. Hill and H. Lagerlund (eds), *The Routledge Companion to Sixteenth-Century Philosophy*, New York: Routledge.

Pasnau, R. (2013), 'Epistemology Idealized', *Mind*, 122: 987–1021.

Pasnau, R. (2016), 'Why Modern Philosophy Turned toward Epistemology', presented to The Society for Medieval and Renaissance Philosophy (Pacific Division Meeting, American Philosophical Association). Audio recording available at http://www.colorado.edu/neh2015/lectures.

Popkin, R. H. (2003), *The History of Scepticism: From Savonarola to Bayle*, rev. edn, New York: Oxford University Press.

Randall, J. (1961), *The School of Padua and the Emergence of Modern Science*, Padua: Editrice Antenore.

Richardson, K. (2017), 'Averroism', in B. Hill and H. Lagerlund (eds), *The Routledge Companion to Sixteenth-Century Philosophy*, New York: Routledge.

Rorty, R. (1979), *Philosophy and the Mirror of Nature*, Princeton: Princeton University Press.

Schmitt, C. B. and Skinner, Q. (eds) (1988), *The Cambridge History of Renaissance Philosophy*, Cambridge: Cambridge University Press.

Sosa, E. (2017), *Epistemology*, Princeton: Princeton University Press.

South, J. (2005), 'Zabarella, Prime Matter, and the Theory of *Regressus*', *Graduate Faculty Philosophy Journal*, 26: 79–98.

Stainton, R. J. (1996), *Philosophical Perspectives on Language*, Peterborough, ON: Broadview Press.

Zagzebski, L. T. (1996), *Virtues of the Mind: An Inquiry into the Nature of Virtue and the Ethical Foundations of Knowledge*, Cambridge: Cambridge University Press.

Index